THE MAJORITARIAN SOLUTION

Re-establishing America's Purpose

James Hufferd

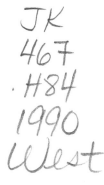

UNIVERSITY
PRESS OF
AMERICA

Lanham • New York • London

Copyright © 1990 by
University Press of America®, Inc.
4720 Boston Way
Lanham, Maryland 20706

3 Henrietta Street
London WC2E 8LU England

Library of Congress Cataloging-in-Publication Data

Hufferd, James.
The majoritarian solution : re-establishing America's purpose / by
James Hufferd.
p.   cm.
Includes bibliographical references.
1. Business and politics—United States.   2. Corporations—United
States—Political activity.   3. Income distribution—United States.
4. Legitimacy of governments—United States.   I. Title.
[JK467.H84   1990]
320.5'13'0973—dc20   89–77286 CIP

ISBN 0–8191–7748–2 (alk. paper)
ISBN 0–8191–7749–0 (pbk. : alk. paper)

To

GW

&

GFW

ACKNOWLEDGMENT

I would like to thank the editors of the Kiplinger Washington Letter for special permission to quote from their May 3, 1985 edition.

JH

THE MAJORITARIAN SOLUTION

James Hufferd

PREFACE

There is a disconcerting movement away from the values of democracy in this country. The meaning of the word itself has shifted dramatically over the past few years as we have begun to accept a vast amount of control over our lives by forces that seem far superior both in power and knowledge to the common citizen. As a result, an open, national debate of over 250 years' standing on the issue of the public's right to actually shape American national policy has lapsed, by the last half of the 1980s, into a strange and ominous silence.

Intense discussion of this, the fundamental issue of public policy, began many years before the American Revolution, reached new peaks of interest in the generations that followed that momentous event, and again claimed the public's attention in the uncertain days of the Vietnam War in the late 1960s. Today, the open, often heated debate that previously led to judgment by the American public and majoritarian decision making at every crucial turn in our history, has all but vanished from the scene.

The pause in this traditional American argument over the public's role seems, at first, to reflect a loss of faith in the public's capacity to judge on the part of life-long proponents of a broad, multi-faceted constituency in American life. Yet the reluctance of many usually-reliable spokesmen to engage the narrowed American power structure that has emerged larger than our national life, might be seen more accurately to reflect an acquiescence to the public's infatuation with what was billed by the Reagan administration as "individualism."

Still, most Americans must eventually come to realize, even without the crystalizing role of debate, the identity of those "rugged individuals" who suddenly seem to have a corner on power and lasting benefits from our system of government and production. Those so favored are not actually individuals at all, but, instead, collective, corporate "citizens" without a social security number or a single vote of their own.

Indeed, such are bound to be the "fittest" in the land in an economic sense. Those favored collective (not individual!) powers are now true giants, in firm control of both the forces of production and finance and, of at least equal importance, communication. Their executive officers are in joint command of the nation's stock of resources, and they can usually sell us anything they wish. And they push their wares with a studied vengeance. We have never learned how to govern them under national law; rather, they have now gained the means to effectively govern us.

Thus, the classic symptoms accompanying one faction's cornering of society's power are now visible all around us: Generation of wealth, being favored, has surged, while the circulation of and access to the benefits of increased wealth have narrowed sharply and indeed dangerously.

This book is basically an account, focusing mostly on recent times, of the historic debate in America over democratic control (meaning, literally, government by or accountably representing *people*, as opposed to willful, collective giants with collective power and wealth). The story as presented will concentrate on two levels. First, on the political action itself that led to the creation of a flexible, workable constitutional framework after our Revolution, and to its subsequent erosion; and second, on the related interpretations of changes and events by a broad array of shrewd, contemporary observers who have endeavored to make sense of this unfolding American national saga.

My objective is to help start a new, more purposeful public debate over the American public's role in the system, along more sharply-drawn lines than are common in public discourse at present. In the process, I hope to help stimulate a necessary new awareness of the issue of political accountability, perhaps the most important issue now being decided in America. It is, however, presently being decided in the managerial fashion of the age: scrupulously out of the public eye, behind the political woodshed with the giants who are able to alternatively arrange to fund and equip and deny funding to contemporary politics.

I have endeavored to add to the discussion a new element of explanation, with the *diastolic/systolic* (wealth generating/benefit circulating) formula that will be introduced. I am urging this new scheme as a formalized, broader, Western way of judging a society's fitness, as opposed to the narrow, one-dimensional laboring-class formula introduced by Marx and at least formally adopted in the countries of the Eastern Bloc, and, equally, to the radical, one-dimensional counter-formula recently once again touted in the West. The imperfect analogy I will employ for the workings of the mainsprings of society is the action of the heart, the organ of both the life blood's critical concentration, and its circulation to the rest of the infinitely multi-functional body. This simple model will, I believe, adequately indicate the need that is now

x

being systematically neglected or denied of maintaining a working balance. On one side, the health of the nation requires production of wealth through a strong private sector (the *diastolic* element). And on the other, it requires very wide circulation and access to the benefits produced, guaranteed by broad-based control of the system (the purpose of the recurrent *systolic* force in society). To put it another way: If the pump is the sole beneficiary of the blood, you're dead; if it's the main beneficiary, you're sick.

The means of organizing leadership codified in the two-centuries-old Constitution of the United States, though increasingly blunted and circumvented over the years, provide a systemic balance of precisely the sort still required. This is because, as I will demonstrate, such a balanced system was deliberately established by the Constitution's framers. Their dual purpose in so doing was to protect and facilitate the two vital aspects of society's permanent basic interest, which I have identified as the *diastolic* and the *systolic*, and which are today referred to, as though they were mutually independent, as private interests and the public interest.

I am, personally, a teacher and writer, a partisan of recreation and cultures domestic and foreign. My basic concerns and interests, like those of most private Americans, are too varied to turn over to anonymous interest group representation, but are legitimate interests nevertheless. Like most human beings, I care and want passionately to meaningfully belong. The analyses I offer are, unless otherwise stated, my own. The only solid and thoroughly American imperative that I am convinced it is necessary to defend until one runs out of paper and pen, is a simple matter of procedure: We must not permit "them" to define and decide the issues of our rapidly-changing society while feeding the American people pronouncements and plebiscites, a routine followed in all closed and dominated political systems on both the left and the right. We must re-establish the value and purpose of citizenship. Then, pro-public policies can -- indeed, *must* -- follow.

Hence, the message of this book is straightforward: We need, and need desperately, to find a late 20th-century way to reinstate the voting public, instead of the self-aggrandizing, mutually-antagonistic surrogate community of "interests," as our government's main constituency.

If fine-tuning the rules to once more favor a decisive public role in a world that has tremendously changed during our collective lifetime should require a timely correction in the Constitution itself, then we must as a society insist on making it. The alternative *will* be increasing domination and an increasingly plundered public. As I will endeavor to show, a correction of sufficient impact to accomplish the end of re-establishing the public in the main role, completely within the present framework with its vital safeguards, is possible.

Almost 200 years ago, founding fathers James Madison and Thomas Jefferson, among others, fought and eventually won a bitter but today little-remembered struggle to establish basic majority government. They did so through effectively extending citizenship, applying the framework of the emerging Constitution, and facilitating full economic participation to help solve society's problems.

Two generations later, President Lincoln with rare foresight dreaded the impending *loss* of the reality of national self-government to new, fast-growing, purposefully ungovernable interests. The continuing legacy of the gradual loss of political authority in the 19th century over the actions of American's powerful, rising collective actors -- then national and now enormous, world-scale financial collectives -- is seriously lessening the actual nation's capacity to act in concert to meet its basic needs in a far more competitive and increasingly unsympathetic world today. The balanced and balancing harmony between the *two* great positive forces of economic growth and democracy that admirably distinguishes our basic system on paper, thus demands a new foundation in fact.

The chapters that follow will, I believe, cite ample reason for both despair and hope regarding the now dangerously neglected priority of establishing American basic domestic and foreign policy objectives in tune with the informed consent of the American public.

JH

Chapter One

INTRODUCTION: THE ARGUMENT RAISED

- A New Social Law -

What does having a democracy require? John Stuart Mill, a prudent 19th-century Englishman, insisted that a distinction be maintained in political discussion between "governing" and "controlling." Only a select few could govern in a mass society, he pointed out, while the permanent public interest might require the people to ultimately control the system by selecting their governors.

Most Americans today would probably grant such a distinction, provided a distinction is really needed. Yet, Abraham Lincoln, perhaps the most prescient of America's presidents, and Mill's contemporary, placed the emphasis altogether differently, on the value rather than the begrudged necessity of popular participation in controlling the society. It is not trite even today to remember that Lincoln feared the impending loss for an all-too-cynical world of the example, and what he took to be the reality, of "government of the people, by the people, and for the people." The purpose of America in the world, he believed, depended upon that reality.[1]

There is much evidence that Americans in his day tended to agree with Lincoln's assessment of the greater role of American democracy. In the meantime, the United States has come to be widely perceived abroad, over the first two centuries of its independent existence, according to two main distinguishing features.

First, the early republic became known, at least to the less-than-rich who are a permanent majority in the Western world as well as elsewhere, as the main source in modern times of a complex of attitudes and ideas widely hailed as "democratic freedom." This complex of distinguishing American attitudes was idealistic, as well as loosely defined, and many in Lincoln's time and before dismissed the habit of combining the two notions as airy and contradictory. But the idea, as well as the imperfect

---

1. Mill, J. S., *Utilitarianism, Liberty, and Representative Government* (1861), New York: Dutton, 1951, p. 305; Lincoln, *Gettysburg Address* (1863).

reality of it that Lincoln was referring to, was productive for much of 19th-century humanity in the sense of offering hope.

Secondly -- and mostly within the past 125 years -- this particular New World country has become known, especially abroad, as the source of fabulous, seemingly limitless wealth, supposedly accessible to all but an unfortunate bottom layer of America's citizens. This kind of wealth has, of course, been accompanied by all of the great national power that such wealth could buy.

The stock of the older of these two visions of America seems to have declined on the world market. That is, the old, radically held belief in American old-style democracy has become, in the past generation, largely passé in countries overseas. In the meantime, the stock of the other, more substantial attribute (great economic abundance) has soared to the skies, fallen low, and started another very cautious rise in world opinion, all within the last forty years.

Long-enduring perceptions are seldom completely unfounded. The governing question, then, must be: just how accurate *is* the widespread general perception of America's sporadic, but still fundamentally solid, economic power, coupled with the waning of its democratic commitment, faced now with tremendous material inducements for an increasingly powerful handful of its citizens?

The relative standing of these two attributes (i.e. wealth and democracy) in the American system today can, ironically, perhaps best be expressed in dollars and cents terms. Specifically: in the U.S., where the wealthiest two percent of the citizens now own fully one-third of all productive assets and control far more by monopolizing the so-called "rights of ownership" in large companies, corporate earnings have recently soared to all-time highs. This new bounty is scarcely shared, though, by the masses of equally essential and systemically dependent wage earners, small business people, and taxpayers at large who, along with the growing number of system failures and dropouts at the bottom, prosper neither as controlling owners nor primary lenders. The reverse has, in fact, occurred.

While the nation's gross disposable income rose by 8% in the three years preceding 1986, and by 12% through 1988, much, if not most, of the gain actually stemmed from a feature of the deferred burden of individual taxation. That is, from the significantly increased institutional profits produced by the federal government's sudden, acute demand for massive loans from the largest corporate institutions to pay its bills -- and

2

not from increased output and correspondingly higher wage levels for most people. Attest our continuing *loss of both* international competitiveness and real wages during the period. The contrived accumulation of society's wealth at the more-visible top of the scale has been elegantly deceptive.

The colossal, necessary rescuing loans to the Treasury that were called forth from private sources both in the U.S. and abroad, in order to meet the suddenly and deliberately revenue-deficient government's obligations, were attracted quietly and overnight in the early 1980s by a precipitous, demand-induced rise in interest rates on government securities. Now that the colossal interest and principal on these artificially necessitated loans are annually coming due, they are repayable to the overwhelmingly large-corporate creditors principally out of individual income taxes.

A new obligation of such magnitude (an additional $200 billion per year more or less, depending on whether internal government fund borrowing is counted, added to the principal of the national debt for several years running) obviously must render our version of "government for the people" *unable* to perform adequately many of the useful and vital functions (not to even mention frivolous ones) that it could formerly find means to perform on roughly the same overall income. Still, the massive, direct redistribution of the nation's income upward, mainly into collective and managerial hands, must continue to mount, if at a slower rate, in order to service a staggering new level of obligation that was sold to a grateful public at the outset as a "tax cut."

Let me document these unsettling claims. During the early 1980s, the fluctuating rates of interest on government securities suddenly swelled beyond 12 percent. Such rates contrasted with the 4 to 5 percent rates of the mid-1960s and the 6 to 7 percent range that held through the end of the 1970s.

The dramatic increase in government borrowing that had suddenly become necessary at the new, very much higher rates, led to a huge but not unpredictable 75% expansion in the government's annual interest liability to domestic holders of bonds, T-bills, and T-notes, in just the three years ending with 1985. Consequently, by the mid-1980s, well over $100 billion of earnings per year were removed from individuals' private incomes and diverted -- not into human development and public infrastructure as before -- but directly into the remote, unregulated, unsharing alter-American realm of institutional finance and profit taking.

In individual terms, this unannounced, non-owner public plan of corporate finance had already quietly produced a government-sponsored annual redistribution of earnings from private taxpayers' accounts

3

primarily into corporate coffers, of over $500 per capita for every living American adult and child by tax year 1984 -- up by $233 over the 1981 level. Or, to express it in terms of the hallowed American family, over $1,500 per household was and is currently being removed and directly redistributed upward to corporate lenders each year, pointedly without the public's suspicion or approval. The cumulative nature of interest on a growing debt virtually insures that this particular toll on the public will continue to rise, almost regardless of current budget levels, and that the role of government will continue not to decline in cost, as one advertised, but instead, to shift away from public service and into perpetual corporate finance at taxpayers' expense.[2]

Questions raised by this stupendous, though somehow still largely secret, plan of income redistribution and restructuring must be many. Perhaps chief among them: *Why* was the public never informed of, and asked to lend its support to, such a plan? And, if we are in some sense still a democracy, what has the word now come to mean?

But the most pertinent question of our time for Americans must surely be: How can an open, democratic system, all but overwhelmed by nearly-continuous national elections, produce such a grandiose, unpalatable, and oppressive result for its citizens? The answer to this question is no doubt suspected by many millions of Americans, who may not, however, suspect the literal price being exacted from them personally.

There is a well-known and widely-held view, both in this country and among informed people abroad, that the top-most level of American democracy, even with some public-spirited candidates participating, has already become much more a matter of charade than reality. Assuming for the moment that this view is correct, does it follow that such a poignant and cynical outcome to the world-renowned, carefully crafted American experiment in individual worth and participation is inevitable, and that the condition itself is irreversible? Such questions demand serious answers, because the right to literally everything in America is at stake, and the loss of democratic control implied obviously outweighs even the size of our celebrated government deficit in urgency and importance.

---

2. U.S. Dept. of Commerce, *Survey of Current Business*, 64:11 (Nov. 1984), p. 7; 63:11 (Nov. 1983), p. 12; U.S. Dept. of the Treasury, *Treasury Bulletin*, 4th Quarter, Fiscal 1984, p. 17, 33; *Federal Reserve Bulletin*, 71:1 (Jan. 1985), p. A26; *USA Today*, Feb. 11, 1985, p. 5A.

There has, in fact, been a dramatic change in the direction of national policy and an erosion of public accountability under the past several American administrations, and, not surprisingly, upon reflection, most especially since 1981. As I will explain in some detail in Chapters 2 and 3, this shift is mainly the direct result of increasing, unchecked concentration of political power into the hands of one single sector of society. Such concentration of power, in opposition to the undeniably intended role of broadly-controlled democratic institutions, is being exercised by a new kind of effective majority. Not a majority of voters, such as some of the framers of the U.S. Constitution openly feared. To the contrary, by an effective, anti-public *power* majority on the vast majority of important national issues, constituted through tremendously superior organization and the ability to pay directly for political influence and favors from sympathetic, supported officeholders. It is, of course, not in its essence a new phenomenon; yet, increasingly now, a single, narrowed, super-organized and super-wealthy small segment of the American public has become the *sole* beneficiary of significant programs and approved legislation.

The basic reality of this changing situation has not gone unnoticed. Many Americans have long realized, judging from the conversation heard on virtually every corner in America during recent election years, that common citizens are no longer the primary constituency being wooed by candidates in presidential and congressional elections. That distinction, instead, has increasingly come to belong to the clusters of major interest groups that can (regardless of how or by guise of what issues it is collected from public contributors) produce the needed financial support to wage a candidate's successful campaign. And these new sovereigns can, to a growing extent, also insure the congressional and bureaucratic support a successful presidential candidate will need in order to govern. Such is so widely assumed that literally scores of millions of potential voters, quite unlike voters in supposedly world-wise Western Europe, now find it not worth their while to participate. The difference now is that one of those vying interest groups has, through an unexpected turn of economic events, all but vanquished the rest and inherited a *majority* of effective power.

One striking result of the deepening, decades-long feeling of political inconsequence on the part of much of the American public is that scarcely half of the electorate went to the polls in 1980. A proportion certainly no larger than that voted in 1984, when the winner, Ronald Reagan, was elected with well under 30 percent of the potential, eligible vote. Nor was the public's most telling verdict to improve one iota in the 1988 national election.

5

Such numbers compare badly to the average turnout of 62 percent nationwide for the 1952 through 1968 presidential elections, even while the impact of civil rights on voting strength had not as yet occurred inside or outside the South. And they compare even worse to the routine, non-compulsory turnouts of 80 to 90 percent in nationwide elections in West Germany, Sweden, and other Western countries within the last ten years.[3]

But the main, outward results of the narrowed alignment within the system that was slowly and painstakingly constructed under the eye of an emerging one-sector power majority, only began to show up visibly in the 1980s. This is true even though President Eisenhower clearly warned Americans in his televised Farewell Address to the nation back in 1961, of the danger to democracy that the already powerful, rising large corporate interest bloc was then beginning to pose.[4] The carefully crafted current upward redistribution of wealth by government action that I described is but one, though a very telling, manifestation of the emerging power majority's newly-realized realignment of muscle and resulting benefits.

Earlier in this century, the interest of the public, recognized by elected politicians as still sovereign, was reflected in public policy and law. The interest of the public then was, and indeed had to be, recognized and defended by public-spirited and self-serving lawmakers alike. Political incursions by special interests beyond certain strictly defined limits were, in that not-remote period, treated as intolerable scandals.[5]

Today, the system of sovereignty has been restructured by the simultaneous decline of the labor movement, agriculture, and small business. As a result, the once-touted equilibrium between the two facets of America's dual achievement -- economic strength and democratic control of public policy -- has been unceremoniously jettisoned, as I will

---

3. Burnham, Walter Dean, *The Current Crisis in American Politics,* Oxford Univ. Press. 1982, pp. 134-5, 184, 290.

4. President Eisenhower, televised "Farewell Address to the American People," Jan. 19, 1961. He spoke in particular of the new and unprecedented "conjunction of an immense military establishment and a large arms industry," and warned the nation to "guard against the acquisition of unwarranted influence, whether sought or unsought, by the military industrial complex." He concluded that "the potential for the disastrous rise of misplaced power exists and will persist."

5. See Berle, Adolf A., *The American Economic Republic,* New York: Harcourt, 1963, pp. 14-15.

describe. The politically successful new power majority tends to view the idea of broadly-shared public approval of and benefits from real policy as a totally unnecessary hindrance. The growing pressure of international business competition has, in effect, blown the remains of our fragile, bilateral sense of national values to the winds. Ruinous, short-run corporate profitability has already practically become, as I will detail in Chapter 3, the sole criterion governing political as well as individual economic behavior in American society.

Seeking to explain why just such a situation seemed likely to follow, John K. Galbraith pointed out some years ago that, at the start of the 20th century, business corporations were still largely confined to a few industries where large-scale activity was a necessity. These included "railroading, steam navigation, steel-making, petroleum recovery and refining, some mining." Most other operations, such as news publishing, grocery selling, and commercial entertainment, were still predominantly in the hands of individuals and partnerships. But by the 1970s, even before the new age of high-tech industry, "the largest 200 manufacturing firms in the United States -- one-tenth of one percent of all manufacturing firms -- had two-thirds of all assets used in manufacturing and more than three-fifths of all sales, employment, and net income."[6]

The necessary cooperation by the great majority of differing interests originally represented in the system, an expedient urged by the most influential of the founding fathers as a public safeguard, has thus given way. In its place is a single, enormously powerful interest group (divided in some respects, united on the most vital matters of shared viewpoint) that is more powerful than all other, competing interests combined. The rivals of large business and large finance for political influence have included environmental groups, organized labor, farm organizations, municipalities, consumer lobbies, organized minorities, small business, education, and the perennially poor, *all* of which have of late fallen on very hard times. Meanwhile, large corporate business has, uniquely, surged.

The Constitution and many of our laws still reflect the sort of political balance that motivated the system's originators, and many of our legislators and administrators are, and will no doubt continue to be, responsible to the public. Yet, what is, in effect, the sort of tyranny of

---

6. Galbraith, John Kenneth, *The New Industrial State*, 3d edition, New York: New American Library, 1978, p. 1.

the majority that Madison first discussed in *Federalist 10*, is issuing from a concentrated source and exercised in ways he could scarcely have foreseen. The new power majority comprised of one interest group is bringing rapid, sweeping change -- directly favoring only large corporate business -- to the entire social and economic fabric of our society. The power majority might possibly still somehow lose a national election sometime along the way. But, unless checked by some national diaster or deliberately by a re-assertive public, it will only return prepared to dominate more firmly, because its self-serving power is now simply too great.

Thus, there exists a clear common denominator behind the simultaneous, rapid increase of inequality in income and opportunity in the United States on one hand, and the steady decline in respect for the practice of American democracy both at home and overseas on the other. The problem is, simply stated, the unequal emphasis now accorded within the system to one of the two main positive aspects of our national character (i.e., presently, the advanced, corporatized technostructural system, leading by itself only to gross maximization by the most resourceful of businesses). The other vital aspect (i.e., community-based authority, leading to a broadening of benefits and participation) is, correspondingly, being both simply disregarded and angrily eroded.

One of these two main aspects of our national tradition, involving economic and technical advances, I will hereafter refer to as the *diastolic* phase of our shared life. The other phase of our national life, which I will refer to as the *systolic*, involves the subsequent effort on the part of the whole society to share as fully as possible in the benefits produced by *diastolic* activity.

Obviously, the many-faceted public can best gain access to a rewarding and incentive-giving share of benefits through the exercise of a just and full share of control over the process of decision-making. In the natural course of events, in ours or any other non-totalitarian society, for every *diastolic* stroke, or new major advance in the production of wealth, a *systolic* stroke, or a pronounced, broadly based effort to gain full access, will directly and inevitably follow. Indeed, this *systolic* reaction is bound to occur whether the system's constitutional machinery is adjusted to ease and productively accommodate the second phase of a normal socioeconomic cycle or not. And the longer, in general, the second phase is deferred by the initial beneficiaries, the greater the

8

underlying dissatisfaction that will build, and the greater and less-manageable the internal pressure that must inevitably result. This pattern appears to be so reliable, at least in modern Western-style societies, that it could well be regarded as a social law.

- What is Revolution? -

One of our murkiest, most overused words is "revolution." It is a fair question to ask whether there really is *any* commonality of meaning among the different ways in which the word is used. There was, we Americans are assured from earliest youth, a great revolution in America once, but meaning what we are not so sure. There have been Marxist revolutions, presumably implying something very different. And then there was the "Industrial Revolution," as well as the so called "High-Tech Revolution" being bandied about now.

So, then, is one word appropriate for all of this range of apparent meanings? Could the connecting links between such seemingly disparate events be strong enough to somehow qualify as a single concept? My small investigation of this matter led me to an unexpected discovery. It is this: Depending on their ideological bent, modern writers on the theme of revolution seem to have not one, but either of two basic meanings in mind. Some refer to revolution (literally meaning rapid change, or a sudden turn-about in conditions) in the sense of a political struggle against repression by an elite. Others, meanwhile, have in mind rapid economic or technological change, implicitly favoring the innovators, and especially the major financial backers who sponsored it. So much is clear.

But, curiously, I found that authors who expounded at great length on activities conforming to either one of these meanings rarely wrote as much as a single paragraph regarding the other. And this, once I had discovered it, had the curious effect of leaving their subjects dangling, lacking the appropriate explanatory context, regardless which half of the revolutionary phenomenon they chose to pursue. Consequently, the dozens of books I found whose subject was "revolution," could be neatly divided into two conceptually separate stacks.

This radical interpretive schism struck me as particularly odd. Especially in light of the undeniable fact that the realities underlying the artificial "pair" of like-named concepts, so scrupulously segregated (one might refer to them as the "*diastolic* revolution" and the "*systolic*

9

revolution"), are naturally-linked parts of any discrete unit of socioeconomic change. (Two strokes = one revolution).

A bit more investigation revealed that these two "separate" concepts of revolution have actually evolved separately (and, as it turns out, dangerously, in view of the hostile energy they involve and their determined lack of mutual understanding), over at least the past 200 years. Yet, to repeat, the two involve respectively the two mainsprings of human activity: economic and technical advancement, spurred by uncommonly-large profit on one side, and on the other, the strong urge of all the rest of society to share in newly-available material and social benefits.

Prominent examples of "revolutions" that exclusively involve the first (*diastolic*) phase of human activity include the mercantile, industrial, and high-tech revolutions of the last three or four centuries. Examples of the subsequent (*systolic*) phase of incremental change include the French and American revolutions, as well as the 19th-century gradual democratization of politics throughout the West. Marxist revolutions, meanwhile, have seemed to involve an attempt to seize and pragmatically manipulate *both* of society's vital mainsprings.

Distinctive sets of characters tend to be involved in the two carefully-segregated phases of activity in Western countries, usually in accordance with their social stations and functions. These sets of characters are also, however, vitally interdependent, as much as they customarily disdain each other. The result is that neither group can actually gain much of anything in the long run by subduing the other's interests, although such is not infrequently claimed on both sides. Self-interested hostility between proponents of the two "separate" phases of one in the same social system instead would seem to be short-sighted, anti-social, wasteful of resources, and destructive of the dually-constituted community. In fact, *diastolic* incentives are as necessary to ongoing community life as are effective and regular means of satisfying *systolic* demands. Neither side's interests can be long suppressed or slighted within the system without producing serious adverse consequences for both. America's spectacular success was the primary result of insistently balancing, despite powerful opposition, the initial equation.

10

- For Lack of a Proper Model -

Unfortunately, at least for purposes of this discussion, descriptions of the sort of bilateral social dynamic suggested here have been anything but common in social and historical literature.

One of the only two examples I am aware of, but almost certainly typical of the whole minute genre, is a quite-specific description of a past society. A sociologist, Robert Carneiro, has argued convincingly that the pattern of cultural expansion in Anglo-Saxon England follows a pair of sequential curves, one following the other in time.

As fellow-sociologist Richard Newbold Adams explains in his interpretation of Carneiro's finding, "the first [curve], running from 450 A.D. or before until 650 A.D., had a steep slant, the second, from 650 A.D. until the Norman Conquest, had a much flatter slant. ... The first period was one of cultural development, in which ... new devices for controlling the environment were being invented, discovered, or borrowed from beyond the borders of the political unit. The second period was one of cultural growth, during which the new available traits diffused over the geographical extent of Anglo-Saxon England. ... For example, the first water-driven grain mill was reported in 762 A.D. and by 1086 A.D. the number had risen to 5600." Thus, a "qualitative" development is seen to be followed by an equally significant "quantitative" change.[7] And so it goes! The second proponent I know of, of the binary, or two-stroke persuasion, is much broader in applying the concept to the world, but comes from a totally unexpected quarter. I shall introduce this second proponent a bit farther on.

Until recently, the slow-moving drift of orthodox social theory (necessarily an amalgamous, over-conservative view of reality, trailing it badly at times) occupied a rather simplistic position regarding the nature of modern America that came to be known as the "theory of industrial society." This general explanation held that a virtual stalemate had been reached in the fight for control between the contending owners of industry and finance in the United States, and the nation's wage-earning majority. Each side had concluded it could no longer advance very much farther against the other, the theory stated, leaving a dull but fortunate

7. Carneiro, Robert L., "The Measurement of Cultural Development in the Ancient Near East and in Anglo Saxon England," *Transactions of the New York Academy of Sciences*, 2d Series (1969), 31(8), pp. 1018-22; Adams, Richard Newbold, *Energy & Structure*, Austin: Univ. of Texas Press, 1975, p. 285.

balance between the two vital but potentially hazardous and antagonistic great interests, so far as the broad interest of the public was concerned.

That is, assuming the public still *was* concerned. Perhaps tellingly, many of the "industrial society" theorists who were at work describing America's fortunate balance of active interests, were also constrained to report that a fair proportion of the public was perpetually "stoned" throughout the later 1960s and 1970s on TV and prescription drugs, when the "age of entertainment" was yet in its infancy.

Whether the vague "industrial society theory" was ever, in fact, actually useful as an explanation is an open question. Assuming that it was, our abrupt entry into the "Post-Industrial Age," with its accompanying sharp drop in the number of blue-collar workers and growing dissatisfaction with government's expensive attempts to ease the results of malaise and displacement, has rung its death knell.

The broad political result of the sudden profound lessening of institutional blue-collar and social activist power has been, not unpredictably, a one-sided one. The surviving single-interest side, possessing the *majority* of the effective power to organize and finance politics after the shift, was then able to frame the next agenda. That triumphant side was, of course, the powerfully organized international-scale business and financial sector.

Hence, the positive forces hailed by the "industrial society" descriptive model proved too fleeting and fragile, when the all-important balance being heralded quite suddenly tipped. For a general model, it was too short-sighted.[8]

Meanwhile, throughout the '60s and early '70s, a number of dissenters from this standard view expressed a far more unsettling opinion. They held that the long-ascendant Western nation state itself was steadily being relegated from within by a new unit of sovereign power, a type of functional unit whose growing might was permitting it to become an authority in its own right, unbeholden to the state or to anyone else. This modern super-unit was the multinational corporation.

About two thirds of all such giant stock companies, it was pointed out, were headquartered in the United States. Not surprisingly, their actions already represented the reality of America in the eyes of many residents of countries overseas. And, being as single-minded as frequently advertised (i.e., out for fast, sustaining profits), these new

---

8. Giddens, Anthony, *Sociology, A Brief But Critical Introduction*, New York: Harcourt, 1982, pp. 60-62.

American-bred and -nurtured multinationals were far more aggressive in their activities than was the U.S. government itself. The government, beyond and apart from its jurisdictional incapacity, proved reluctant to restrain or limit these rambunctious spawn in any way, for fear of restraining vital American commerce, if not of actually losing election-year funding.

Business economist George Ball, among a fair number of others, predicted the coming global dominance of the multinationals over two decades ago. He based his prediction on their dramatic growth in typical unit size and ability to operate independently. He also noted the corresponding decline in the number of actual units involved as takeovers and all-out price wars abounded, much abetted by the true chaos of international jurisdiction.

The days of the nation-state as a first-line economic actor in the West were, according to Ball and like-minded others, very strictly numbered. They predicted that the very survival of countless millions, even billions, of individuals worldwide would soon be at the beck of the resource-crunching behemoths, the minds of whom would be, by definition, elsewhere (fastened on the "bottom line" to keep up with their constant demand for funds). But, if they were juggling our eggs, Ball and his fellows concluded, we would probably opt not to jar them.[9]

It now seems that the prediction of these erstwhile-dissident corporate sovereignty theorists has at least in large part materialized in America, whether permanently or not, in the initial guise of programs such as the enormous, *no-strings-attached* tax "incentives" to produce new plants and equipment successfully sponsored by the new American federal administration in the early 1980s. Success in that particular intense corporate effort came about after years of previously futile inside lobbying. It came, not irrelevantly, in tandem with attempts by the new type of federal administration that had emerged in 1980 to overturn abruptly or de-fund costly requirements and safeguards previously mandated in the interest of public safety and long-term health.

---

9. Ball, George (1967), "The Promise of the Multinational Corporation," *Fortune*, June 1, 1975, p. 80; Brown, C., ed., *World Business: Promise and Problems*, New York: Macmillan, 1970; Kindleberger, C. P., *American Business Abroad*, New Haven: Yale Univ. Press, 1969; Modelski, George, "Multinational Business: A Global Perspective," in Modelski, G., ed., *Multinational Corporations and World Order*, Beverly Hills and London: Sage Publications, 1972, pp. 5-30.

Another specific well-known bit of evidence for the timely emergence of a genuine new power majority, thus, is the case of the previously-mandated and -funded Environmental Protection Agency emergency toxic clean-up programs that were suddenly jettisoned in the early '80s by the inaction of specially-picked Reagan appointees within the EPA itself. The state as an active participant was being unsympathetically derailed, and the broad, tested public will and its greater well-being were accordingly short-circuited to enlarge the pot of potentially available private financial capital.

In order for financial combinations to secure the requisite long-term support and freedom to act more or less independently outside the United States, in the face of badly-disposed, or at best badly-mixed overseas opinion, they must be able to count on adequate support at home. C. Wright Mills, another corporate sovereignty theorist, pointed out a generation ago that, as financially-skilled and bright as the managers and sons of dynasties behind the facades of large corporations might be, they are normally not able to constitute an effective and durable "power elite" (Mills' term) completely by themselves. They need significant allies if they are to succeed in capturing and holding political power.[10]

In the American case, corporate powers have combined efforts with at least one important, generally accepted part of the public sector that they might otherwise resent because of its non-private status. But the function of the U.S. military sector provides leading corporations with numerous lucrative production contracts and is, moreover, at least not yet a candidate for expropriation by the large companies themselves. For its part, the military sector can hardly be blamed for valuing the added consideration and relative immunity from budget constraints it has received rolled into the bargain.

In *Federalist 52*, one of his brief, cogent essays urging an earlier American public and its representatives to support the adoption of the newly-drafted Constitution, James Madison addressed, for the third time in that series, the perceived danger of majority tyranny. Obviously, from Madison's wording, the specter of being routinely out-voted and

---

10. Mills, C. Wright, *The Power Elite*, New York: Oxford Univ. Press, 1956, p. 277.

14

tyrannized by a propertyless rabble, given the new Constitution's perceived democratic cast, was a cause of concern for the mostly well-heeled local leaders who were to be delegates to the state ratifying conventions. Madison's immediate subject was, to be sure, the danger of the numeric dominance of one class. Yet, it is clear from his remarks that he was referring to a majority of power per se, viewed as a threat to the rights of a potentially out-powered effective minority. Madison, whom we have traditionally and deservedly remembered as the "Father of the Constitution," the ideological giant of the Convention, reminded the would-be state delegates in *Federalist 52* that the majority in question (i.e., the lowly of means) were themselves divided by sectional and other interests. Thus, what would seem to be a potential problem (their effective, concerted opposition to the rights of private ownership of the wealthy minority) was in fact extremely unlikely to ever occur.

What seems far more likely, given his much-repeated notion of the purpose of politics (i.e., to serve and protect the public), is that Madison would have responded indignantly to the prospect of a perennial power majority being shielded from accountability. And yet today, as I will argue in Chapters 2 and 3, organizations that are plainly the most potent and persuasive sovereign combinations of people, money and means in the Western world (i.e., the largest of the American-based corporations) are all but exempt from legal accountability and routine public oversight.

One reason for this notable but little-noted circumstance is simple. Our largest corporations are obviously both advantageous and beholden to the entire nation in numerous ways. And yet they remain, almost without exception, beholden in a legal sense, by virtue of their charters, not to the whole nation, but to carefully-selected small, relatively-weak individual *states* like Delaware. This odd circumstance saddles American society with what now amounts to a crippling limitation on the practice of Madison's public interest model of the national community: the courts have placed the most powerful of corporations off-limits to direct national-scale action. It has this effect even while the revered Madisonian vision still permeates the nation's formal constitutional structure, and has rarely and never successfully been challenged openly.

In the actual governing system, which has gradually evolved since the mid-19th century, the rule of law passed under more-or-less free institutions is still intended to govern the common individual citizen. But little more than self-interest governs the actions of the successful corporation. (Note, in this regard, that sanctions applied by the courts to large businesses today are normally so inappropriate and weak as to be meaningless, with delays in compliance granted routinely until the law can be changed. The recent, selective application of super-heavy

15

sanctions against one or two companies in extremely isolated cases gives the impression of publicly-surfaced intercorporate infighting and reprisal, which seems a logical next step in the march toward privatizing the public sphere.)

Lately, with the balance among opposing organized political interests that temporarily existed now in abeyance, the national government, viewed as the controlling large business sector's major competitor for funds, has found itself abruptly de-funded below the level necessary to provide even routine public services and maintenance of the functional infrastructure. Increasingly, federal tax revenues are now sucked up instead simply to pay perpetual, compound interest without fanfare to the mega-scale financial community, a record-smashing obligation, as we have seen already, entered into without the voting taxpayers' knowledge or consent. Majority tyranny has, thus, surfaced nationally in our day, but this time as a function of money and organization, with the power of the real, *human* majority effectively neutralized.

The manner in which this most curious reversal of roles (the large corporate sector instead governing the government) has been accomplished through the electoral system itself, will be the subject of the next two chapters. The effect of this turn-around on citizen confidence and rights has been positively devastating, as we have already begun to note.

Meanwhile, the gap between idealistic U.S. rhetoric and the reality of corporate America's libertarian financial and business activities overseas has led to periodic widespread rioting, rebellion, and reluctance to associate. Our defense of "democracy" in the larger world routinely strikes scores of millions of people as patent nonsense, given what many both here and abroad already recognize as our own system's basic repudiation of accountability. Such realities might be perilously ignored, but cannot be swept away.

- Monoscopic Vision: East and West -

The *systolic* (broadened general demand) response to the enormous wave of concentrated wealth and power generated by new high-tech applications and massively-applied debit finance is not yet clearly visible. But the conditions for it are developing: a growing rift of communications and tolerance between layers of the society, and the distressing status decline without apparent recourse of very large displaced segments of the population.

16

Surface events, even huge storms and tides, rarely herald the movement of strong undercurrents, which, while they may remain invisible, ultimately prove decisive. The democratic contagion that appeared at the beginning of the French Revolution, for instance, was effectively scattered and beaten down. This outcome was not so much due to the strength of the absolutist Old Guard as to the enthusiasts' lack of practical knowledge of how to structure a democratic society as well as the lack of a network of agreed-upon channels and means of meeting a variety of community needs. Much the same thing might be said of America's abortive, currently downplayed social revolution of the 1960s, which began in response to the quiet but billowy post-war investment expansion of the 1950s and its sponsors' monopoly over social rules and membership criteria.

The early 19th-century observer Alexis de Tocqueville closely examined the differences between the immediate result of the French Revolution (i.e., summary takeover and defeat) and that of early America's eventually-triumphant democratic revolution. He found the main reason for the difference of outcome in the fact that the Americans had had the practical experience of governing themselves since early colonial times, while the French had merely imagined what living in a democracy might be like. He noted, too, that the Americans, though coming from different backgrounds, had been able to reach agreement on a common contractual arrangement, their Constitution. This provided the modus operandi for democratic social and economic expression, while the French lacked such an objectifying instrument for sharing power, and have, by most accounts, never since been as successful as the revolutionary Americans at producing one.[11] In Chapter 2, I will discuss the significant question of how the American founders were able to arrive at the ingenious, workable, though finely-flawed formula that they left to us, notably balancing economic means with community purposes. And, further, I will demonstrate that the Constitution itself contains, in a critical and knowingly-unfinished section, a key to restoring public accountability, pride, and confidence to our political system.

But it is important to recall that, in the case of the French *systolic* (i.e., system-broadening) revolution, the Old Guard, with its control of still-predominant landed wealth, successfully recovered its position to dance on the impudent French Revolution's grave. (Even the aristocratic

---

11. Tocqueville, Alexis de, *Democracy in America*, Vol. II, (1840), New York: Knopf, 1960, p. 18.

rival British government of the time sent clandestine aid to the French absolutists to assure that such would happen). Yet, within the next 15 years, the offending aristocratic political institutions were enthusiastically swept aside. And within the next 30 years, all of the significant, once-radical aims of the diverted popular movement for broad participation and democratic control came to be adopted as routine procedure both in France and across much of Europe.[12]

As a consequence of the introduction of accountable representative government in France and Britain, a flood of necessary enactments were, at long last, passed to ease the direct impact of iron-fisted industrialism and related conditions on the lives of the neglected, wage-dependent majority. In the United States, due to the massive strength of the *diastolic* wave of early industry, coupled with the foreign immigrant status of so much of the 19th-century labor force, the *systolic* response to industrialism came a couple of decades later, though none-the-less strongly or significantly.

Thus, the wondrously fertile combination of technological solutions and finance that generated the Industrial Revolution, with by far the greatest benefits of its early years appropriated by exploiters and inventors, was followed almost everywhere at once by the beginning of an irrespressible popular movement. The theme of this second revolutionary orchestral movement was (and inevitably is) the broadening of power to fashion means by which the majority can more fully partake of the increasing benefits in order to truly improve and enrich society.

In like fashion, the definitive *diastolic* phase of what is termed the "High-Tech Revolution" is still moving ahead steadily at present, and the best wishes of its empowered entrepreneurial sponsors have just been, in large part, converted into public law. The second phase of the current revolution has not as yet occurred. Although the normal sorts of preconditions are being created within the system, the form and immediate extent of the normal *systolic* response within the context of present-day America remain a mystery.

---

12. See Gershoy, Leo, *The French Revolution, 1789-1799* (orig. pub. 1932), New York: Holt, 1960, p. 5; Croce, Benedetto, *History of Europe in the Nineteenth Century* (1933), New York: Harcourt, 1963, p. 58 ff.; For an uncommon and perhaps overoptimistic view of the place of the Reagan administration in our history, see Reeves, Richard, *The Reagan Detour*, New York: Simon and Schuster, 1985.

Crane Brinton, perhaps a worthy successor to the much better-known Tocqueville as a student of political manifestations, concluded in the early 20th century that there were "some uniformities" among conditions obtaining in different countries prior to revolutionary change. Brinton noted that popular revolutions always seem to affect "societies on the whole on the upgrade economically before the revolution came." Hence, "revolutionary movements seem to originate in the discontents of not unprosperous people, who feel restraint, cramp, annoyance, rather than down right crushing opposition. Certainly, these revolutions are not started by down-and-outers, by starving, miserable people, [but instead are] ... born of hope." It is pertinent for us to note that rebellious feelings "are roused in those who find an intolerable gap between what they have come to want -- their needs -- and what they actually get."[13]

In the present-day United States, the stage itself is somewhat different from that in most other cases. Here, the legitimacy and means of inevitable, periodic revolution are effectively institutionalized, at least on paper and traditionally, by a universally-respected, explicit but still flexible Constitution. This explains the fact that there has normally been a minimum of violence involved in the reform of conditions in America. As long as the workings of the system mandated in the Constitution are fundamentally observed and not preempted or prevented otherwise from functioning as set forth, the public is empowered to effect a so-called "rotation" of policy leadership. (The word "rotation" has, of course, the same core definition as the word "revolution".)

Still, in the absence of definitive electoral procedures made manifest in the Constitution, the means have been variously found, as we will see, to permit concentrated interest groups and interested candidacies to short-circuit the public's interest and capacity for an informed choice among programs and national candidates. Hence, our quadrennial presidential elections provide at best a murky reflection of the public will, and at worst, an outright, callous, and cynical denial.

But, on the other hand, public opinion continues to register strongly, though irregularly, when aroused. Certain clearly-perceived situations can still call forth a sufficiently powerful response from the public to bring the current controlling factions into quick compliance with the

---

13. Brinton, Crane, "A Summary of Revolutions," from *The Anatomy of Revolution* (1938), reprinted in Davis, James C., ed,. *When Men Revolt and Why*, New York: Free Press, 1971, pp. 318-19.

public's desires. But even strongly-aroused public sentiment normally avails very little in a policy sense. When public opinion is occasionally aroused, the ruling interests' surrogates in top advisory and administrative posts realize that if they will but meekly comply for the moment, the freak, adverse wind from the public side will soon subside, leaving them to regroup and continue as before.

Fairly obvious examples of the phenomenon of public arousal include the long-delayed but finally-accomplished withdrawal from the Vietnam War, President Johnson's informed decision in the late '60s not to seek re-election, and the sudden dumping of Richard Nixon. The defeat of the congressional pay increase provides a recent, forlorn instance. The public can be said to ostensibly have its way in such now-rare instances through the implied threat of unmanageable electoral behavior.

Directed Constitutional reform (most specifically, of the Constitution's uncharacteristically sketchy Article II, Section I, involving presidential elections) is sorely needed to restore the public's lost measure of control over its institutions. The possibilities and implications of such fundamental reform will be examined in their many aspects in the pages ahead.

Conditions leading to the sort of routine, determined public assertion that Crane Brinton described would seem to be gathering in the U.S. sufficiently to spark the strong power-broadening phase of the current social and economic revolution. The *systolic* tide generated may well surface irresistibly within the next two or three years, serious recession or no, and with or without the institutional channels having being cleared to adequately accommodate it.

To restate this point a bit more precisely: In keeping with Brinton's principle that society's "revolutionaries" are normally not the down-and-out, defectors from the corporatist control strategy now still being played out could be instrumental in re-orienting and decisively arousing the media-conditioned American public. Their political revolt and well-qualified leadership of others could push the balance at least temporarily in a broadly *systolic* direction. So, our "revolutionary" leaders in the short term could turn out to be certain moderately-educated, low- and mid-level corporate managers, perhaps taking a cue from David Stockman, along with small, ambitious (mostly young) operatives and technocrats, who expected when they joined the corporatist cause to have real impact on policy decisions at least inside their companies. Instead, they see others, possibly no different or smarter than themselves, but somehow a bit higher placed on the ladder, enjoying considerably more income and influence. In Russia, such obvious malcontent candidates, at least up until recently, have been periodically banished or shot. Here, their weight could be significantly felt over on the *systolic* side of the scale, persuasively championing broadened systemic participation and benefits.

Also active in leading an already restive public into self-fulfilling rebellion might be an unknown number of public-spirited, tentative one-time converts to the corporatist control cause. Such sincere followers must, gradually, be starting to realize now that many of post-modern society's most critical needs are simply not going to be met through following the straight, narrow path to super-corporate maximization.

Probably, the *boldness* of the corporatists' visible surrogates in politics (i.e., corporatist office holders and candidates, probably for the most part true believers) in publicly stating their real agenda for the American economic and social system will continue to grow as long as their current, expanded level of power in the system is maintained. But the disillusioned lower-level managers and ex-managers I mentioned, along with numerous small investors, who are profiting, but simultaneously being undercut in their ability as wage earners and deficit-ridden taxpayers, may well lead the way to the polls to vote against them. Such a reaction might serve to repudiate, at least for the moment, political control exclusively for the benefit of large business and finance. But such a public repudiation can actually happen only in the event that there can somehow still emerge a clear, broadly-based, non-corporatist nominee to support. The obscurantist nature of the current process, on the contrary, leaves the intents, allegiances, and beliefs of the two finalists for the golden grail of the Presidency extremely hard, if not outright impossible, to gauge.

Such a short-term outcome (temporary repudiation of single-sector control) would still leave the longer-term problem of constitutionally reinstating the voting public's effective check on tyranny unsolved. But, the problem could at least be more susceptible practically to genuine solution with the political grip of the corporatist would-be sovereigns temporarily abated.

The British-Austrian philosopher Sir Karl Popper, in his two-volume tract on the nature and condition of the West's open society, concedes even to *violent* revolution at least one legitimate purpose: "the establishment of democracy." By which he means "a set of institutions ... which permit public control of the rulers and their dismissal by the ruled, and which make it possible for the ruled to obtain reforms without using violence, even against the will of the rulers." Or stated another way, "the use of violence is justified only under a tyranny which makes

21

reforms without violence impossible..."[14] Let us hope against hope that violence is not again rendered necessary in order to obtain public relief and advancement in the United States.

The third known adherent I know of, of the putative *diastolic/systolic* school of social change to which I alluded earlier, is the Yugoslav dissident Milovan Djilas. Though his views remain a matter of controversy, his credentials in this particular regard are clear. "All the revolutions of the past," Djilas wrote several years ago, "originated after new economic or social relationships had begun to prevail, and the old political system had become the sole obstacle to further development. ... None of these revolutions sought anything other than the destruction of old political forms and an opening of the way for already mature social forces and relationships." In the current American case, the change in economic alignments and arrangements (a sharp narrowing and rigidizing occasioned by sweeping technological innovation) has been both fast and stunning. And here, the legally enfranchised majority are both mature enough and sufficiently capable if informed to act as citizens. All such cases, Djilas concluded, simply "had to" end in political democracy. The one noteworthy exception to this democratic imperative, in the part of the world that is today relatively advanced economically, he claimed, was the modern Communist revolution, the best-known instance being the Soviet Union. There, the revolutionary overthrow occurred not in reaction to capitalistic (*diastolic*) development and an excess of greed, but due to the society's envy of numerous other nations for whom such development had already taken place, leaving marginally-situated early 20th-century Russia uncomfortably behind.[15]

But of course, as we have seen, not all *systolic* (democratizing, wealth-sharing) movements immediately succeed. Indeed, some, like the early French Revolution, due to the ineptness of truly unready or misled masses (which cynics profess to see in all cases), have led to disaster.

---

14. Popper, Karl R., *The Open Society and Its Enemies*, Vol. 2, (1962), 5th edition, Princeton Univ. Press, 1966, p. 151.
15. Djilas, Milovan, *The New Class, An Analysis of the Communist System*, New York: Praeger, 1957, pp. 18-19.

In the Russian case, neither the economic infrastructure for operating a giant country, nor the level of awareness of the necessary human participants, seems to have been sufficient at the time of the 1917 Revolution to serve as a basis for wholesale national advancement to personal freedom and general gain. Instead, the corps of leftist ideologues who took over power at the end of 1917 actually suspended the natural operation of both the active *diastolic* and *systolic* forces. They managed to do this, on one hand, by establishing their own rule through absolutism (nothing new) in the name of the country's newly-triumphant *systolic* force (the surging, frustrated populations in urban areas). On the *diastolic* side, they placed the economic and productive machinery available firmly under their own, radically centralized control, curtailing the normal incentives to produce and innovate. This major experiment launched in hopes of achieving the benign rigid control of a social system, along with its broad implications, will be discussed in Chapter 5.

It will suffice to mention here that the official governing purpose of the Soviet system is to pointedly reject the side of the normal, vital *diastolic/systolic* balance that the U.S. system now deliberately emphasizes. And, to an increasing extent of late, vice-versa.

- Man and Tool -

A spurious objection sometimes raised by critics of the idea of actual democratic control over state policy is the notion that democracy limits freedom. That is, the notion that people are freer in some way when the society's direction-setting is abandoned by the general public to a highly-interested, politically-active and powerful few.

Alexis de Tocqueville concluded that this was not a serious argument. "It is not ... expected that the range of private independence will ever be so extensive in democratic as in aristocratic countries," he commented, "nor is this to be desired: for among aristocratic nations the mass is often sacrificed to the individual, and the prosperity of the greater number to the greatness of the few." Yet, such is the assumption we are laboring under now.

Tocqueville wrote that a genuinely democratic government needed to remain both "active and powerful" in order to carry out its public purpose. Therefore, he reasoned, "our object should not be to render it

23

weak or indolent, but solely to prevent it from *abusing* its aptitude and its strength."[16] We may conclude that to passively permit the rapid dismantling of government's machinery of vigilance and enforcement in the public interest is, for the public, to abdicate its power, although many Americans have been fooled in the 1980s into believing otherwise.

On the other side, one of Marxism's two fundamental mistakes is almost the exact opposite of this: its determined program to emasculate the *diastolic* forces by erasing economic self-interest. Thus, perfectly natural, if gradual, socioeconomic improvement is made impossible by preventing the necessary first stroke, which is self-interested progress in humankind's mastery over the material environment. Consequently, the Soviet state, for example, still has to rely on buying new technology with raw materials, and on the advanced ability of its vaunted industrial spies in the West, to maintain even its now sadly-lagging levels of production.

The role of publicly-accountable government, as most Americans up until now have abundantly realized, is not to take over or tightly control wealth-producing activities, but merely to monitor them under the law. That is, to keep them, with the larger-than-life collective power they now generate, from infringing on individual citizens' Constitutionally-guaranteed rights and sovereignty. So, to recover and continue to survive as a coherent society, we must, in effect, either throw out our Constitution, which guarantees us our rights, or restore somehow our patented ability to have it both ways. Which is to say, an enduring balance must again be struck permitting a maximum of economic initiative compatible with democratic political control.

To put it another way: If we really wish to approach our potential as a nation, to retain or regain our historic highly-positive profile, to successfully live with ourselves and our neighbors, to begin to win our struggle for survival against our current, still-determined adversaries, and to once again help lead the world for the common good with the world's blessing, we must, as a nation, once more become something more than social theorist Anthony Giddens' "appendage of a machine."[17]

Our challenge is to once more have and support an enterprising economy that operates as a great forward engine, efficiently producing for the benefit of human beings, and yet remain ultimately in charge of it.

---

16. Tocqueville, *ibid.*, p. 323 (both preceding quotes; italics mine).
17. Giddens, Anthony, *Profiles and Critiques in Social Theory*, Berkeley: Univ. of California Press, 1983, p. 212.

Hence, we simply must be able to assert, in crucial matters of direction, our collective best judgment as a people. The alternative is to allow our machine of production to manage us for its benefit.

In the pages ahead, I will discuss the purpose, origin, and subsequent career of the vital balance of interests that I believe is the heart and soul of the 1787 Constitution of the United States. I will examine its gradual overthrow by informal, extra-constitutional arrangements resulting from what I think is its critical flaw, as well as the matter of its applicability today and its surprising potential for stabilizing and improving world relations. I will then suggest a way by which its still-vital revolutionary purposes can be restored.

May its oppenents openly give their answer!

Chapter Two

AMERICA: THE BALANCED SYSTEM, ON PAPER

- American Democracy and Economics -

America's business is, and has always been, business. Tocqueville, writing in the 1830s, noted the "go ahead" attitude of the American populace, and remarked, with more than a hint of wonder, that "commercial business is there like a vast lottery, by which a small number of men continually lose, but the state is always a gainer."[1]

The *diastolic* side of the American democratic balance, which Tocqueville exalted in this passage, still seems fairly secure. But, as we have seen, a related consideration of equal importance has not been clearly resolved: *Who* is to be ultimately in control of the wealth-producing machine itself? That is, on *whose* ultimate behalf will the enterprise of the nation spin its great wealth from the uncommonly rich strands of labor, creativity, and materials that America as a cooperating whole is able to offer? Is the United States to be more of a commonwealth, with access and opportunity shared widely and deeply? Or more of a garden to be worked by servants and managers, to produce fortunes for a few?

This traditional American question has assumed even greater significance now that the three basic economic functions (capital, labor, and brain-power) so seldom operate through the same individuals, as they most frequently did in our nation's past.

Now, unlike the late pre-industrial age, when the nation's Constitution was drafted, the typical American citizen is not so much a man (or a woman) of parts in this respect. The original "We, the People" featured prominently in the Constitution tended to be either large entrepreneurs or small entrepreneurs, operating typically by applying each his own accumulated or borrowed capital, ability to labor bodily, and ability to manage and think for himself. Today's citizen tends, with

---

1. Tocqueville, *ibid.*, p. 236.

increasing frequency, to function, and to regard himself or herself, as no more than a small, interchangeable part in a vast, overall, almost galactic-scale system of invisible production. Significant ownership and control seem always to lie just beyond the typical modern American's grasp. Much of the buoyant feeling of practical control and personal value that existed for the early American freeholder or journeyman (not forgetting the unfortunate slaves and many women, who could do little to alter their condition) has long since faded.

- The Constitutional Accommodation -

Historians and their readers have frequently leaped from the correct premise that most of the delegates to the 1787 Constitutional Convention in Philadelphia were substantial property owners, to the conclusion that the document they produced must, therefore, substantially favor the interests of the "rich and well-born" over those of other citizens. But such is not really the case.

The completed document the Convention brought forth, though curiously vague on at least one crucial point (i.e., electing the president), mandates a remarkably accountable and workable system of national self-government for a nation characterized by great distances and dissimilar circumstances. The Constitution of 1787 was sufficiently democratic, let us not forget, to merit the firm support and life-long devotion of the two leading democrats of the American revolutionary age. Both Thomas Jefferson, the author of the Declaration of Independence, who had a well-deserved reputation as a radical equalitarian, but was out of the country when the Constitution was written, and the document's principal framer, Jefferson's neighbor and friend, James Madison, an outspoken apostle of majority government for wise and practical reasons, embraced the newly-framed document's tenets wholeheartedly. Hence, the argument that the Constitution was intended or originally expected to operate undemocratically rings false from the start.

Early in the Convention's deliberations, on June 18, 1787, Alexander Hamilton, an unusually eloquent speaker who was a delegate from New York, set forth his plan. Hamilton was a bona fide Revolutionary War hero, a financial genius, and a warm friend of the established business community due to its perceived ability to concentrate valuable resources. He presented his design for an aristocratic national government in a brilliant, closely-reasoned, five- or six-hour address to the assembly.

Noting, by way of background, that "the mass of the people ... seldom judge or determine right," he called for a constitution with a national President and an upper house of Congress to be elected for life ("to serve during good behavior"). He called for a lower house to be elected for a term of three years, with an absolute presidential veto over its acts. The President, in Hamilton's system, would also have appointed the governors for the states, who in turn would have had absolute veto power over the actions of the respective state legislatures.

The delegates were not unfamiliar with the system Hamilton cogently urged them to adopt: It was, after all, basically the contemporary British system of government, to be given a fresh run as a New World written constitution.

Being themselves well-born and, thus, not disfavored by the described provisions, many of the delegates tended to like such a plan. No one present spoke out against it. In fact, the assembly simply adjourned for the day without discussing it at all. Reportedly, the delegates, mutually sworn to secrecy, went their separate ways for the night, and quietly praised Hamilton's sentiments among themselves in the city's taverns and boarding houses. Hamilton's fellow delegate from New York, an able, younger man named Gouverneur Morris, was reported to have said of the day's speech that it was "the most able and impressive he had ever heard."

Yet, no one formally supported the adoption of this well-developed plan offered early on behind Independence Hall's closed doors. A few days later, Hamilton quietly left Philadelphia, missing a month of crucial deliberative sessions. He returned only at the insistence of the Convention's presiding officer, his great friend General Washington, to affix his signature to the final, drafted plan which was eventually ratified, noting as he signed it that "no plan was more remote from his own."[2]

The plan that was adopted instead of Hamilton's aristocratic system was an accommodation -- not technically a compromise -- between the cherished views of those present and perceived public opinion. It was an accommodation hammered out in session at the Convention and

---

2. Young, Alfred F., "Conservatives, the Constitution, and the Spirit of Accommodation," in Robert A. Goldwin and William A. Schambra, eds., *How Democratic is the Constitution?*, Washington: American Enterprise Institute, 1980, pp. 117-18 (both preceding quotes).

assembled in its final form mostly by a political savant, James Madison of Virginia. It deliberately accommodated a democratic sentiment nourished in the country's most-populated areas, which had burst forth in an ill-advised but nevertheless timely fashion, in Shays' Rebellion in Massachusetts a few months before. More to the point, the plan adopted was an accommodation to a frustrated public powerlessness that nearly every delegate knew first-hand and feared in his own precinct. Hence, the Constitution came to be sagely democratized.

The plan that was finally adopted by the Convention, called for a President to be elected nationally and required to stand for re-election in four years and for a House of Representatives to be popularly re-elected five times in a decade.

The Senate -- originally designed to salve aristocratic interests -- was intended to be filled by wise citizens selected by the mostly-elective state legislatures. And there was even a procedure written into the Constitution permitting Congressional preferences to overturn the externally-elected President's veto.

Compared to the starchy British model of the time, familiar and foremost in the assembled delegates' prior experience, the plan they adopted was, in fact, most amenable to democratic development and application, vesting actual, deliberative power in the electorate. Hence, it was reasoned, if grievances arose, as they inevitably would, or if there were general demands for reform or re-direction of policy on a larger-than-local scale, such matters could, as a matter of course, be accommodated within the system itself.[3] It was, further, reasoned that peculiar, more-or-less local outbursts, like Shays' Rebellion, could best be contained and confronted by respectable power vested in a broad, national community of citizens, whose organized strength was to be superior to that of the states.

Providing for the satisfaction of democratic demands in an orderly fashion in the new Constitution itself, was calculated to open the way for direct participation in productive enterprise eventually by millions of citizens, and, hence, to favor the broadly-beneficial development of the vast, new country. On paper at least, the balance of purposes thus accomplished -- of encouraging the greatest number to cooperate in doing

---

3. See Jensen, Merrill, *The Articles of Confederation*, Madison: Univ. of Wisconsin Press, 1948, p. 30; Parenti, Michael, "The Constitution as an Elitist Document," in Goldwin and Schambra, eds., *ibid.*, pp. 39-43.

the most for the benefit of each and all -- seemed close to perfect to most Americans of the time.[4]

When Jefferson first read the newly-drafted, proposed Constitution of the United States at his diplomatic post in Paris, he expressed his pleasure with it at once. He only averred that it would need "a declaration of rights" and a limit on the number of terms for the President, both of which were later added.[5] In at least one of his early letters home on the subject, this so-called "radical" Virginian assured his correspondent that, while he wanted to see a guarantee of human rights added, he was assuredly "not an anti-federalist," meaning by the phrase that the draft document outlining a federal system had his support as a plan to realize the vital purposes of 1776.[6]

It is often pointed out by latter-day, would-be aristocrats that the system set forth in the Constitution is a "republic," as somehow distinct from a "democracy," even though the only social class empowered therein to exercise any control is "the people," without distinguishing any particular sub-group or stratum.

The views and intentions of Madison, the man most responsible for engineering and shaping the precise plan of accommodation that was ratified and eventually adopted, would seem appropriate to help resolve the question of meaning that was actually attached to the word "republic." In *Federalist 10*, Madison pointed out that "the two great points of difference between a democracy and a republic are: first, the delegation of the government in the latter, to a small number of citizens elected by the rest; secondly, the greater number of citizens and greater sphere of country over which the latter may be extended."[7] Thus, Madison saw a "republic" as a specific type of "democracy," not differing from it in spirit. It is particularly worth noting in this connection that he used the word "delegation," instead of "giving over," or "preemption, or "domination by the latter." Also, the process of election "by the rest" and the status of representation, conferred for but a single, practical purpose, are paramount in his expression on the subject.

---

4. Madison explained the purpose of achieving such a balance in *Federalist 10*.
5. Jefferson to Madison, congratulating him on his co-authorship, Nov. 18, 1788; _____ to Alexander Donald, Feb. 7, 1788; _____ to Colonel Edward Carrington, May 17, 1788. It is notable that both of the reservations Jefferson stated have been satisfied through the Constitution's own amendment provision.
6. Jefferson to Francis Hopkinson, March 13, 1787.
7. Madison, *Federalist 10*.

Hence, if Madison is to be believed, he was not attached to, nor did he help create, a type of system that he would have characterized as an "oligarchy." What all of this signifies (using Madison as perhaps the best example), is that there were those in the leading ranks of power and influence who assuredly did not view republican government (or "indirect democracy," as it is sometimes called), as a thin disguise for the actual rule of a few, powerful men.

Yet, there have been ever since the Constitution was drafted, and there remain today, two contradictory views of it: First, that it was intended to create a practical, fundamentally democratic system, and second, that it was intended to permit and camouflage an oligarchy.

"What a perversion of the natural order of things!" Madison himself wrote, a mere three years after the Constitution was adopted, amazed by Secretary of the Treasury Hamilton's stubborn insistence in a series of letters to the press that government must be a strong, independent power and the people submissive. "What a perversion...!" Madison exploded in his reply, "to make power the primary and central object of the social system, and Liberty but its satellite."[8]

More than four decades later, Madison, by then an ex-President and revered elder statesman, affirmed again in a letter that "the vital principal of republican government is the *lex majoris partis*, the will of the majority."[9]

Others may have doubted it and disparaged it, but James Madison, the acknowledged intellectual leader of the 1787 Convention, wrote democracy indelibly into the Constitution of the United States, intending no deceit. And another leader of the very first order, Thomas Jefferson, who knew its leading author as well as anyone, clearly read it as such.

---

8. Madison, letter published in the *National Gazette*, Dec. 20, 1792, in response to Hamilton's published letter stating that the government must be independently strong and the people submissive, quoted in Adrienne Koch, *Jefferson and Madison*, N.Y.: Knopf, 1950, pp. 125-26.
9. Madison, 1834, quoted by Ann Stuart Diamond, in "Decent, Even Though Democratic," in Goldwin and Schambra, eds., *ibid.*, p. 18.

- Democratic Purposes and Problems -

It is a fair question why the principle of majority control over the community's destiny should have been considered the first priority for the new system of government by such brilliant and impassioned leaders as Jefferson and Madison. Born into the aristocracy themselves, they might simply have been content to maximize their own advantages: The two of them together no doubt could have swung America in a radically different direction.

The obvious answer is quite simply because, in their judgment and experience, only government by the consent of the governed turned out to be government *for* the governed in the long run. For Madison and Jefferson, as for the great majority of their fellow citizens, that was what the American Revolution was about.

Jefferson warned the majority of smallholders and relatively propertyless citizens in the America of his day to jealously guard their liberties. If they did not, he told them, with accurate foresight, they could easily lose their hard-won opportunity to participate meaningfully in the decision-making system as interested individuals, and instead become subservient to the self-serving ambitions of the powerful and super-active.[10] So, on the one hand, democracy was seen by its apostles as a matter of securing fairness to the nation.

Noted early twentieth-century jurist Learned Hand subscribed to this idea in his defense of democracy (meaning broad-based, majority rule) as an actual basis of government and law: "In a world where the stronger have always had their way," he wrote, "I am glad if I can keep them from having it without stint. ... It seems to me, with all its defects, our system does just that."

Justice Hand also saw another reason why the majoritarian system of control, despite its sometimes uncomfortable imposition of limitations on elected and even tenured officials, was as important as its originators had said it was: "Abuse it as you will," he wrote, "at least it will give a bloodless measure of social forces -- bloodless, have you thought of that? -- a means of continuity, a principle of stability, a relief from the paralyzing terror of revolution."[11]

---

10. See Jefferson to Colonel William S. Smith, Nov. 13, 1787. In his *Notes on Virginia* (1782), Jefferson wrote that "the time to guard against corruption and tryanny is before they shall have gotten hold of us, [and] it is better to keep the wolf out of the fold, than to trust to drawing his teeth and claws after he shall have entered."

11. Hand, Justice Learned, "Democracy: Its Presumptions and Realities," *Federal Bar Jl.* 1:2, March, 1932 (both preceding quotes).

Stated another way: if the control mechanism of a society is sensitively attuned, it will not discourage or prevent people from fully and meaningfully participating. Instead, it will work to provide a means for the whole society to attain its *systolic* aspirations -- for justice, broadened opportunity, responsible and not deceptive taxing and spending, and, in general, a sustainable and rising level of community well-being.

The *diastolic* changes necessary to extract more wealth more effectively per se have not posed a problem of comparable difficulty in America to date. We have passed, though not easily, from one economic revolution to the next in progressively raising our standard of material wealth. But the system's ability to distribute the new opportunities and wealth throughout the community has become increasingly problematical as a higher proportion of the ownership of resources and organizational power has, since the time of the Civil War, gradually fallen into fewer and fewer hands. And the disparity of private wealth and power between functional classes is now growing far more rapidly than earlier. This is, in part, due to a recently induced change in the tenor of our legislation, a subject to be addressed in Chapter 3.

Without actual democracy, expressed through a government with adequate authority to act in response to a public consensus in the public interest, the balancing, governing purpose of democratic institutions must inevitably be lost. And along with that must go the still-widespread value of equal justice and the once-valued example for the world of impressive, non-violent material progress. The result, if the process continues in its retreat from accountability, will inevitably be as much a system of pure force as exists anywhere in the world.

Earlier top American leaders who recognized these particular hard realities, and so passed up the temptation to simply maximize their own independent power and wealth, believed that in extending the direct benefits to be won from development of western lands, the extension of commerce, and so forth, to a progressively broader part of the general community, they were indeed securing the purposes of the Revolution and staving off tyranny. Walter Lippman once remarked that the reason for our Revolution was not to destroy authority, but to secure the right to participate in political decisions that were vital to Americans, and thereby enhance the worth of authority.[12] The post-Revolutionary

---

12. Lippman, Walter, *Essays in the Public Philosophy*, Boston: Little, Brown, 1955, pp. 67-68.

movement toward greater democracy was exemplified at its start by the charitable concessions of class power made by a profoundly wise group of community leaders in designing and installing the new Constitution. The endeavor was neither more nor less than an effort to extend the full benefits of participation to a greater part of the community in order to enlist its potential in the struggling nation's behalf.

- The Burning Question -

There still remains the question of democracy's practicality. More precisely: Can the community understand complex issues well enough, on balance, to exercise intelligent judgment? This remains a vital issue in itself, even when it is concluded that it is not in the majority's interest to have a small but singularly-powerful, self-interested minority (i.e., a *power* majority), or a series of such bolstered minorities over time, making its decisions for it.

But the question can also be reversed: Should better-informed, better-organized groups of elite specialists be permitted to exercise effective control over the system, as a sort of ruling regency, simply because the voting public is thought *by some* to be insufficiently wise or unworthy to judge and determine the broad outlines of national policy in its own behalf? Such, indeed, became the ruling position of the Federalist Party establishment in the earliest years of government under the Constitution, and discussions of these questions, as a consequence, became the reigning passion of the 1790s.

Jefferson's bald-faced statement in the Declaration of Independence that "all men are created equal" had, of course, been adopted as public currency, and, if actually true in some unambiguous way, would have sufficed to end the argument. But, obviously, people differ in every conceivable respect. Hence, many apologists in Jefferson's time and since have sought to explain what he really meant by his famous statement in order to rescue it from the bins of absurdity -- mostly without too much success.

It seems more than likely that what he meant was that there is much more intelligence and ability amidst the general population than one might be inclined to suspect. People with advantages of birth, education, or title, therefore, would have no God-given right to lord it over others who are at least as human, and have aspirations as worthy of realization, as those who could conceivably buy and sell them many times over.

35

As a matter of fact, Jefferson didn't have to look far to find intelligent men in his own time who agreed with him on the capacity of the general public. Adam Smith, the founding father of classical economics, seems to have shared Jefferson's radical, untested hunch. "The difference of natural talents in different men is, in reality, much less than we are aware of," Smith wrote in his classic *Wealth of Nations*, which he first published in 1776. "And the very different genius which appears to distinguish men of different professions, when grown up to maturity, is not upon many occasions so much the cause as the effect of the division of labour. The differences between the most dissimilar characters, between a philosopher and a common street porter, for example, seem to arise not so much from nature as from habit, custom, and education."[13]

George Washington, the nation's first President, was uncertain of the truth of the matter himself, though he confessed that his feelings were on the side of "the people." He wrote to John Jay that he was "sure that the mass of citizens in these United States mean well, and I firmly believe that they will always act well, whenever they can obtain a right understanding of matters: but it is not easy to accomplish this, especially ... when the inventors and abettors of pernicious measures are infinitely more industrious in disseminating their poison than the well-disposed part of the community to furnish the antidote."[14]

What seems most worth noting here is that Washington did not believe that the public should not rule; nor did he say that an adequately informed public was as impossibility, but rather, as Jefferson would have agreed (and actually warned), a matter of difficulty.

Federalists of Hamilton's persuasion, meanwhile, eventually resorted to a far different formula of authority, which brought forth a flood of public scorn sufficient to cause the first established party's downfall. The decisive factor, it appears, was that, however one judges the public's capacity to rule, only "the people" had been recognized as sovereign by the Constitution that they were understandably glad to support. And,

---

13. Smith, Adam, *An Inquiry Into the Nature and Causes of the Wealth of Nations* (1776), Chicago: Encyclopedia Britannica, Inc., 1952, I, ii.

14. Washington to John Jay, quoted by Walter Lippman, in Clinton Rossiter and James Lare, eds., *The Essential Lippman*, N.Y.: Random House, 1963, p. 4.

under the terms of the Constitution, no one but the public -- "the people of the United States," eventually all to be accorded suffrage -- had a defensible right to rule the country.

Alexis de Tocqueville, as we saw earlier, recognized the Constitution's value in this regard, as a legally empowering instrument that was absolutely vital to the routine practice of American popular rule.[15]

Jefferson accepted the Constitution as a legitimate instrument for the ordering of society precisely because it, in effect, laid down in the nation's fundamental law the fundamental principle of balance between the *diastolic* and *systolic* forces. As he put it, the Constitution mandated "a wise and frugal government, which shall restrain men from injuring one another, which shall leave them otherwise free to regulate their own pursuits of industry and improvement, and shall not take from the mouth of labor the bread it has earned."[16] In order to serve its legitimate purpose, government has not only to permit and accommodate enterprise, but also to be strong enough to serve as an effective instrument of public policy. In fact, its comparative strength for accomplishing the sovereign nation's purposes was recognized as one of the new Constitution's chief advantages and an overriding argument for its adoption.

- Sources of Wisdom: What Was and Was Not Intended -

The idea of the democratic community (the indispensable basis of what has come to be referred to as an "open society") was by no means first introduced to America by Madison and Jefferson. John Wise, 70 years before the Constitution was written, in fact acknowledged and defended the presence of a deep vein of popular sovereignty in New England government.

"The first human subject and original of civil power is the people," John Wise noted. "For as they have a power every man over himself in a natural state, so upon a combination they can and do bequeath this power unto others; and settle it according as their united discretion shall determine. ...A democracy is then erected, when a number of free persons do assemble together, in order to enter into a covenant for uniting

---

15. Tocqueville, *ibid.*, p. 18.
16. Jefferson, *Presidential Inauguration Address*, March 4, 1801.

37

themselves into a body, ... [and] the right of determining all matters relating to the public safety, is actually placed in a general assembly of the whole people; or [when they] by their own compact and mutual agreement, determine themselves the proper subjects for the exercise of sovereign power..."[17] Hence, the taproot of American democracy was not classical at all, but rather the early colonial experience of communities on isolated shores.

The extent to which the American founding fathers depended on classical and Renaissance philosophers for inspiration has perhaps been overstated. For instance, the French political philosopher Montesquieu, a great admirer of the British system of the earlier 18th century, is, along with the ancient Roman chronicler Polybius, often mentioned as a source of the founders' preference for a separation of power among branches of government in order to avoid tyranny emanating from a single source.

Yet Montesquieu failed to note in his celebrated treatise that the tripartate arrangement he admired, a result of the 1689 Revolution, had already been sabotaged when he wrote by the introduction of the cabinet system in Britain to re-consolidate state authority and weaken the more-popular branch. The inspiration for Madison and others on this very important point must have come largely from their direct knowledge of the effects of the changes in the British system. The American framers' decision not to have the executive be a creature of the legislature had proven -- as it was surely intended to be -- of great importance in giving "the people" a more direct check (at least potentially and sometimes in fact) on the direction taken by the national administration.

Meanwhile, concerning the republican (or representative) form of government itself, Montesquieu held, in a much-quoted passage, that such an arrangement would never work beyond the scale of a very small country.[18]

Madison reasoned, on the contrary, that the greater "sphere" of territory and interests in America would provide a check on tyranny by making it less likely that the poor, or the shopkeepers, from one locale,

---

17. Wise, John, "A Vindication of the Government of New England Churches" (1717), in James M. Smith and Paul L. Murphy, *Liberty and Justice, A Historical Record of American Constitutional Development*, N.Y.: Knopf, 1958, pp. 15-17.
18. Montesquieu, *Spirit of Laws* (1748), Book VIII, Sec. 16; Martin, Kingsley, *French Liberal Thought in the Eighteenth Century* (1929), London: Turnstile, 1955, pp. 164-65.

would combine with the poor or shopkeepers from another, different locale with different overall interests.[19]

The influence of John Locke on American Revolutionary statecraft is equally hard to gauge with any precision. The similarity of phrasing between Jefferson's *Declaration of Independence* and certain passages from the second of Locke's *Two Treatises of Government* (1690) is striking. So, also, is the similarity of ideas. Locke, like Jefferson later, specified conditions justifying rebellion against the "Arbitrary Power of the Prince" and the right of "the people" to re-form society under a new compact suiting the "common interest."[20]

Yet, Locke is also often credited with admitting special privileges and prerogatives to "property" as opposed to the mass of the people, allegedly swaying our founding fathers' judgment in that direction. Such could, it would seem, have been the case. But, if so, it probably would not have been a case of them, unlike some recent polemicists, misrepresenting what Locke had actually meant by the term "property."[21]

Locke wrote that men had left the "state of nature" and set up society, replete with political organization, to provide "for the regulating and preserving of property."[22] But, that he also expressly included in the inventory of a man's property "the Labour of his Body, and the Work of his Hands," and pointed out the fact of "this Labour being the unquestionable Property of the Labourer [which] no Man but he can have a right to," has far too often simply been ignored.[23]

Yet, obviously, the value of labor itself was thus seen by Locke as meriting all the protection and share of privileges due any legitimate property under the compact he urged; he did not anywhere suggest a distinction of prerogatives among kinds. Madison and Jefferson, along with numerous other Americans of their age, had studied Locke, and they surely knew his opinions.

---

19. Madison, *Federalist 10*.

20. Locke, John, *Two Treatises of Government* (1690), N.Y.: New Am. Lib., 1965, II: #216, #211, #212, #218.

21. For instance, see Will, George F., *Statecraft as Soulcraft*, N.Y.: Simon and Schuster, 1983, p. 39; also McDonald, Forrest, "The Constitution and Hamiltonian Capitalism", in Robert A. Goldwin and William A. Schambra, eds., *How Capitalistic is the Constitution?* Washington: American Enterprise Institute, 1982, p. 49.

22. Locke, *ibid.*, II: #124, also #222.

23. *Ibid.*, II: #27; also #28-32, #35, #40-42, etc.

Polybius' attribution of Rome's longevity (he wrote during the late Republic) to her blending of "types," meaning kingship, aristocracy, and democracy, and her contrast in this respect to Greek states that flourished brilliantly for only a brief time, may have influenced the founders, with their classical educations. But Rome was too far in the past to have had very much direct bearing.[24] The influence of other non-contemporaries (with the possible exception of Hobbes) was, for a variety of reasons, less.

Upon reflection, I must differ from the current-day fashion of identifying influences, and conclude that Madison's special genius was one of acute personal observation and skill in prescribing likely remedies for social ills. This unique sort of giftedness shows up both in the Constitution itself, which, if it was a blend of arrangements, was mostly his blend, and in the triumphant *Federalist Papers*, following closely in time.

Besides his efficient unmasking of the early bugaboo of "majority tyranny," we find Madison's indication in these essays of the hazardous "violence of faction" as sufficient reason for founding a central government with appropriate power. The particular "faction" of society wreaking violence against all the rest of society might be a propertyless rabble (as in the case of Shays' Rebellion). Or, it could involve a combination of wealthy investors set to profiteer at the early nation's needless expense by, for instance, gaining monopoly control over available western lands. *Neither* was considered tolerable.

Madison successfully opposed this second type of dangerous faction when it arose, as well as the first, while Jefferson drafted a series of public measures to defeat it, as we will see. In both instances -- that of the mob and that of the powerful land companies -- the power of a responsible central government, overarching the states as well as private interests, was clearly a necessity.[25]

Hamilton, too, in *Federalist 9*, prescribed central authority as an antidote against uncontrolled sources of power within society, or against what he, also, chose to call "anarchy."[26]

---

24. Polybius, *The Histories* (2d Century BC), transl. by M. Chambers, N.Y.: Washington Square Press, 1966, IV: 3, 11.
25. Madison, *Federalist 10.*
26. Hamilton, *Federalist 9.*

- Democracy and Its Pitfalls -

In post-Revolutionary America, corporations for manufacturing and finance were, as such, exceedingly few in number, small, and weak. They were hardly expected to pose a serious threat to either the individual's rights or the emerging democratic state. There was, however, another, seemingly more important *diastolic* element (producer of new wealth, or "growth industry") in the nation at that time: westward land development.

And, true to form, a small group of wealthy investors was arising with sufficient combined funds and desire to corner the market and control the cost, direction, and rate of trade in the main growth commodity -- western land -- at the needless and often prohibitive expense of the much larger number of potential small-holders as the nation expanded.

Many Federalists, especially in the more densely settled eastern areas of the original states, favored the private monopolization approach as a way of funneling the nation's growing wealth into the hands of its most capable investors. Private monopolization was also seen by some as an effective way of slowing the rate of western settlement in order to avoid draining the eastern seaboard of its potential labor force and market for new manufactures. Secretary of the Treasury Hamilton opposed outright the settlement of western lands (meaning to the west of Pittsburgh), which he referred to as "waste land." The slow, laborious development of new land and resources farther west, he opined, merely "diminishes or obstructs the active wealth of the country."[27]

By contrast, it seemed that Jefferson and Madison were, if anything, more democratic in the economic policies they favored than in the institutions of government they proposed. In 1776, in the draft he wrote of a new constitution for Virginia, Jefferson retained a property qualification for voting. But he also proposed that the state government be required to make certain every citizen had an opportunity to own at least 50 acres of land.[28]

Four years later, as a member of the Continental Congress from Virginia, Madison managed to persuade the government of his own state,

---

27. Lodge, Henry Cabot, ed., *Works of Alexander Hamilton*, N.Y., 1904, III: pp. 147-48.
28. Ellis, Richard E., "The Political Economy of Thomas Jefferson", in Lally Weymouth, ed., *Thomas Jefferson, The Man, His World, His Influence*, N.Y.: Putnam, 1973, p. 83.

along with New York, to cede their enormous, overlapping areas of undeveloped land in and beyond the Ohio Valley to common federal jurisdiction, and at the same time, judiciously extinguish private land company claims to vast stretches of uncleared land.[29]

In the mid-1780s, Jefferson designed a basic land policy for the Confederation government that established the subsequent American system of developing western territories in the common public domain, by making available small, even parcels of public land as individual farms. Eventually, parts of his overall plan were incorporated into the Constitution, with western federal territories thereby permitted to enter the union on an equal footing with the original seaboard states.

The implementation of this plan of greatly facilitated land tenure was sharply opposed by partisan Federalists, who supported land company claims, and who supposed that new western states formed mainly through the efforts of pioneer small landowners, would vote against them. Jefferson's plan, in simple fact, provided an important and tangible early accompaniment, giving meaning to the democratic accommodation soon to be written into the fabric of the 1787 Constitution.

Jefferson, on assignment from the Continental Congress, also devised the township and range survey system that was eventually applied to virtually all federal public land from eastern Ohio to the Pacific coast, making it easy for private citizens to acquire, locate, and sell land, which was by far the country's most important single commodity and source of wealth.[30]

The Federalists, increasingly, during their subsequent 12-year administration (1789 - 1801), tried to retard the pace of western development by setting high prices for public land and only selling in large blocks -- far larger than most aspiring western settlers would be able to buy. They thereby forced many still to buy through land companies and through wealthier individuals, who profited by breaking their direct large purchases down into individual farm units and town lots.

---

29. Brant, Irving, *James Madison and American Nationalism*, Princeton: Van Nostrand, 1968, pp. 44-48. Land companies at that time reportedly had wrested control of the politics and congressional delegations of Delaware, New Jersey and Maryland, and also exercised great power in Pennsylvania (See Brant, p. 147).

30. Ellis, *ibid.*, p. 89.

When Jefferson entered the White House at the head of an opposition "Republican" majority for the first time in 1801, he was able to reverse these anti-public, proto-corporatist policies. Even so, aristocratic interests from both the North and the South were able to block the passage of a free land policy for western settlers, which Jefferson had favored, for several more decades, until the time of Lincoln. Then, with the opposition in Congress of the southern plantation aristocracy muted, the 1862 Homestead Act was passed into law.

Still, in the case of the new nation's first major *diastolic* -- western real estate -- the sort of "anarchy" that Madison had rightly feared, with "strong individuals" able to "unite and oppress the weaker" beyond the reach of the government's means to preserve "justice, the end of government," was largely averted almost from the beginning of our independent national life. And this was primarily due to the action of the electorate in withdrawing the effective power of the Federalists.[31]

Thus, an early *diastolic* surge (the sudden, massive availability for allotment of new fertile and valuable land to the west) was followed by a strong *systolic* reaction (successful appropriation through democratic means by a much broader constituency -- in this case, nearly the whole interested public).

The potential import of the embryonic Presidency as an office above and apart from the legislative branch seems to have been fully recognized by the American founding fathers. In the 1787 Constitutional Convention, they found the matter of framing cogent rules for choosing the occupant of that office to be what we might today call political dynamite. As a result, the matter was never satisfactorily resolved. At the Convention, firm imperatives concerning the election of the President, embracing every existing shade of political faith, were, to some delegates' surprise, brandished menacingly by the normally more-amicable state delegations. In *Federalist 27*, which he wrote near the end of 1787, even Hamilton seemed to favor a popularly-chosen President. But just a few months earlier, in his address to the Convention, he had

---

31. *Ibid.*, pp. 84, 89; Madison, *Federalist 52*.

43

argued for a President to be elected for life by electors chosen by the state legislatures and, thus, to be three steps removed from the people. This apparent change in his attitude may have reflected the fact that the Convention had in the end left the procedure partly unspecified and partly fragmented, effectively leaving the door wide-open for all manner of manipulation by political operatives.[32]

In fact, according to later-published journals and reports, the attempt to determine a precise procedure for selecting the new country's chief executive nearly broke up the Convention before the document it bequeathed to us could be finished. Perhaps nowhere else in the Constitution is the politically difficult, accommodation status of the great contract of government as clearly in evidence as in the uncharacteristically vague, half-empty phrases of Article II, Section 1, entitled "President: his term of office; electors of President [etc.]." The different cast of accommodation lamely indicated in that section, providing that "each State shall appoint, in such manner as the Legislature thereof may direct, electors [for President and Vice President]," creates a sort of local option solution to a major, *national* problem, applied at the level of quasi-independent "States."

Yet, the omission of a process was itself, in effect, a compromise. On the positive side, the accommodation, simply by failing to mandate rules, left the door open for broad, democratic participation within each state, which in fact eventuated over the next several decades.

But democracy was neither mandated nor mentioned in this passage. Nor was much of anything else by way of a cogent procedure to be followed in selecting a President. All the details were simply passed down for the states to decide.

Passing the buck along to the states would, perhaps, have been as good a way as any to come up with leadership for a perpetually low-power, bankrupt confederation, which was what the newly-independent country had initially been. On the other hand, the section bequeaths a most uncertain and unsatisfactory means of selecting executive leadership for the enormous, uncommonly rich and prominent nation that the United States was by 1787 already, by act of choice, on its way to becoming.

---

32. Hamilton, *Federalist 77*; See also Hamilton, *Federalist 68*; Young, *loc. cit.*

At this most crucial point of decision, the mostly wise collective body of co-sympathizers at the Convention, believing it necessary that they agree on a prescription rather than adjourn in shambles, found themselves unable to do so. In effect, *they abdicated on the matter of electing the President.* And no one since has, at any time, succeeded in correcting the bulk of the errors of omission in the resulting odd, abbreviated section of the Constitution, although the need has often been recognized, both in the nation's early decades and later. Nor has Congress ever passed legislation to somehow correct the glaring procedural gap left by appropriate statute, although a related matter, uniform democratic participation within each state, has lately come to be recognized as a civil right properly enforceable by federal law.

Today, the questions the Constitution leaves unanswered in its incomplete section concerning presidential election could well prove to be literally earth-shaking in their implications. Two of the most important of such questions are: How shall the candidates for President be chosen? and, What sort of screening procedures should be conducted by the sovereign national public for applicants to hold its uniquely-important Presidential office?

Both of these questions have been answered informally, though not really democratically or uniformly, by various activist groups that have stepped into the gap left in the Constitution. These groups have, in fact, co-opted undelegated power by grafting onto the incomplete formal system what can only be viewed as extra-constitutional forms. The completely predictable result has been an enormous transfer of power away from the national electorate, to self-made bodies and collections of interest groups who are accordingly enabled to act as sovereigns themselves, quite apart from any attributions in the Constitution's unfortunate, half-finished mandate. Yet, though its effect is heightened today, the inevitable result of the Convention's abdication on this one issue -- the political weakening of the interested national community by the creative preemption of a vast prerogative inappropriately assigned to the subdivisions called states -- is anything but new.[33]

Madison publicly acknowledged from the outset that the provision for electing the head of the national administration was awkward and incomplete. Within the year, he wrote in *Federalist 45* (perhaps to

---

33. See Ostrogorski, M., *Democracy and the Party System in the United States: A Study in Extra-Constitutional Government*, N.Y.: Macmillan, 1910, pp. 1-2, ff.

mollify states' rights advocates, but nevertheless indicating a major deficiency in the overall plan) that "without the intervention of the state legislatures, the President of the United States cannot be elected at all."[34]

The federal government, largely as a consequence of its presidential election's peculiar legal status as a function of the *states*, has, ironically, been enjoined from enacting uniform legislation governing the procedure. Federal jurisdiction in the narrower matter of voter qualification was reclaimed only gradually, through no less than *four* amendments to the Constitution.[35]

But, because nationwide organizations have proven to be necessary after all to reasonably conduct what was, from the start, a nationwide function, various interested groups of citizens have, over the past two centuries, attempted to fill the procedural vacuum left by the Convention's neglect. At first, closed-door Congressional party caucuses and, more recently, ad hoc nominating conventions have led the long extra-constitutional parade through the vast hollows of Article II, Section 1. More recently, television networks and groups such as the League of Women Voters have -- completely apart from the Constitutional framework, and with odd, at best mixed results -- stepped into the breach left by the hapless state governments, which were, of course, individually inadequate to fulfill more than each its own fragmentary and uncoordinated mandate.

In practice, the means of Constitutionally electing the President has always been plagued with irregularities. During his presidency, Washington, along with many Federalists, denounced the ad hoc Democratic Societies' attempts to collectively nominate and influence the choice of the nation's chief executive, but without cogently suggesting how the nominating process actually should be conducted.[36]

In the second contested election in the nation's history, in 1800, the voting for president and vice president in the electoral college were still undifferentiated on the same ballot, as the Constitution originally stipulated. The results of the election were further complicated by the

---

34. Madison, *Federalist 45*; He also makes the same point in *Federalist 44*. As early as 1780, Madison had already reached the conclusion that the central government "must have a superior deciding power over the states." See Brant, *ibid.*, p. 47.

35. Amendments XV, XIX, XXIV, and XXVI.

36. See Ostrogorski, *ibid.*, p. 4.

fact that three different procedures for choosing the electors were in use in different groups of states. Some states permitted direct public participation in the process, while some did not. The result was an embarrassing tie between two candidates from the same party, one of whom had presumably only been intended as a vice-presidential choice.

Confusion of the same kind cropped up again in the four-candidate election of 1824, when none of the four achieved an outright electoral majority. The second-finishing candidate, John Quincy Adams, trailing in both the popular and electoral votes, was nevertheless elected President by the system-rescuing House of Representatives.[37] Not surprisingly, the chagrined voters turned out in much greater numbers than ever before in 1828, to overwhelmingly elect the apparently-cheated winner from the last election, Andrew Jackson.

By the mid-1820s, public sentiment against the "traditional" method of choosing the parties' nominees, in closed-door meetings of the respective parties' members of Congress, had reached the point where the prize of the one surviving major party's caucus endorsement for 1824 meant virtually nothing -- might even have been a drawback. The formal Democratic-Republican endorsement that year went to Senator William Crawford of Georgia, whose main qualification was service to the party. He was not a widely-known favorite, while three men who were rose separately to oppose him in the ensuing election.

An aroused political public soon prevailed on the members of the U.S. House and Senate to reconsider their positions on the propriety of the long-standing caucus candidate selection system. By the next election, in 1828, when over three times as many eligible voters turned out to vote than ever had before, the caucus had been scrapped completely, and presidential nominating conventions and whole new parties had arisen seemingly spontaneously, both regionally and nationally, to fill the once-again-open constitutional gap. The garish convention nominating system has met with varying degrees of success and has claimed only lukewarm general public acceptance over the century and a half that has elapsed since its inception.[38] The 20th-century addition of presidential primaries

---

37. Smith, Page, *The Shaping of America, A People's History of the Young Republic,* N.Y.: McGraw-Hill, 1980, pp. 293-94, 726-29. Hamilton's solution to this problem had called for the people to accept a "reconciling" with "the advantages of monarchy," by permitting their state legislatures to select the President without interference; See Hamilton, *Federalist 9.*

38. See Ostrogorski, *ibid.,* pp. 12-13.

-- a positive development in itself -- has been controlled judiciously to permit political election professionals, with their ties to major sources of funding, to gain even greater preempted power while generating appearances to the contrary.

Belief in the procedures of democracy has never been anything like a uniform passion driving the American system, and, in fact, has been regarded as something of a liability by politicians in every generation since the first. Hamilton, the brilliant Federalist leader and Secretary of the Treasury, was, on principle, no friend of democracy, and admittedly "not much attached to the majesty of the multitude."[39] On the contrary, his political strategy (which may be rather clearly seen to have been resurrected since 1981) was to gain solid support for the Federalist administration from those who controlled what Hamilton recognized as the "active wealth of the country." This was to be secured largely by maintaining a large and growing national debt for them to fund, with repayment at induced high interest to come from public revenues, as at present.[40] Regarding this particular strategy which, at least in Hamilton's case, no serious attempt was made to disguise, modern-day economic historian Eliot Janeway has commented that "any ... Machiavellian could have warned him that the new apparatus of Federal power designed to further the interests of the haves was liable to be taken over by the have nots."[41] And so, of course, it then was. And a better-informed electorate would, very likely, exact scathing revenge today as well.

Alexander Hamilton himself, having been born outside the country, in the West Indies, was not eligible to stand for the Presidency, in accordance with a provision in the Constitution approved during his long absence from the Convention. Hence, his schemes had to be manifested during the 1790s largely through his considerable influence on other leaders.

The Washington administration began as a national unity government, if we've ever had such a thing in America. Both Hamilton and his political and ideological nemesis, Jefferson, served in the same first cabinet. But as time passed, and the public demand for public-spirited programs began to mount against this prime minister's

---

39. Hamilton, "Ceasar", No. 2, *New York Daily Advertiser*, Oct. 17, 1787.
40. See Ellis, *ibid.*, p. 89.
41. Janeway, Eliot, *The Economics of Crisis*, N.Y.: Weybright and Talley, 1968, pp. 34-35.

unchanged aristocratic notions of government's function, Hamilton, according to his loyal friend Governeur Morris, began to consider taking action to replace the Constitution he had once signed and defended, but openly admitted he "disliked." Morris later recalled that Hamilton "detested democratical government," believing it must end in a tyranny of the majority over the rich. Morris recalled that his friend's "belief in that which he called an impending crisis arose from a conviction that the kind of government most suitable, in his opinion," could be introduced "as a result of a civil war," and, in fact, "could be established in no other way."[42]

Jefferson, whom Hamilton characterized as a "fanatic," gained the Presidency in 1800, due largely to public reaction against Hamilton's own measures, which included the elitist land policy and jailing people who spoke out against the Federalist government or its officials. Hamilton reacted to Jefferson's election by appealing to his long-time friend, New York Governor John Jay, to call a special legislative session in order to change the state election law to nullify the opposition's popular and electoral majority.

"In times like this...," the distraught Hamilton wrote to the Governor, "it will not do to be overscrupulous. It is easy to sacrifice the substantial interest of society by strict adherence to ordinary rules...."[43] Jay, who had been the third, minor author of the *Federalist Papers* explaining the Constitution, along with Madison and Hamilton, declined.

Writing to his friend Dr. Benjamin Rush 11 years later and several years after Hamilton's death, Thomas Jefferson recalled how the Federalists had tried at that earlier time "to beat down the friends to the real principles of our Constitution, to silence by terror every expression in their favor." And he noted that "the nation at length passed condemnation on the principles of the federalists, by refusing to continue Mr. Adams [actually, a Federalist, but no friend of Hamilton himself] in the Presidency."[44]

---

42. Governeur Morris, quoted in Page Smith, *ibid.*, pp. 796-97.
43. Smith, *ibid.*, p. 293.
44. Jefferson to Dr. Benjamin Rush, Jan. 16, 1811. The voters simultaneously changed the membership of Congress from 64 Federalists and 42 Republicans in the House and 19 Federalists and 13 Republicans in the Senate in 1799/1800, to 69 Republicans and 36 Federalists in the House and 18 Republicans and 14 Federalists in the Senate in the session of 1801, the year Jefferson assumed the Presidency.

Jefferson's remarkable balance of concern for the interests of the new nation, working to aid the establishment of the active economic structure of the country (the *diastolic* side of the necessary balance), as well as promoting democracy and widely-distributed opportunity (the *systolic* side), is well-attested. His attitude is reflected, among other places, in his campaign as Secretary of State for patent legislation. His avowed dual purpose was to protect the rights of inventors while serving the public interest through offering, as he put it, "an encouragement to men to pursue ideas which may produce utility." While "inventions [as communicable thoughts] cannot, in nature, be a subject of property," he wrote to explain his thinking, "society may give an exclusive right to profits arising from them."[45]

Some interpreters have accepted as decisive the fact that we are not now living in a Jeffersonian, but a Hamiltonian world, typified by great manufactures and banks.[46] Yet, it is to be hoped that we, too, will somehow find the sense to repudiate Hamilton's partial and unfair, unrepresentative governing system in order that we, also, might keep the *diastolic* advancement he favored as an accessible, and thus sustainable, public benefit.

- Industry: The New *Diastolic* -

Well into the 19th century, manufacturing contributed only a minor portion to the value of commercial production in the United States. Up to 1816, the last year of James Madison's presidency, manufacturing's high-water mark as a proportion of America's exports had been 6.6 percent. Through 1810, the nation's manufacturing industries remained in fourth place, behind the products of agriculture, the forest, and the sea, in the value of production traded abroad to contribute directly to the growth of American wealth.[47]

45. Jefferson to Isaac McPherson (a Baltimore inventor who had written to him), Aug. 13, 1813, in Adrienne Koch and William Peden, eds., *Life and Selected Writings of Thomas Jefferson*, N.Y.: Modern Library, 1944, pp. 629-30; Wall, Joseph Frazier, *Iowa, A History*, N.Y.: Norton, 1978, p. 118.

46. For instance, see Will, *ibid.*, pp. 101, 103-106; Brown, Stuart Gerry, *Alexander Hamilton*, N.Y.: Washington Square Press, 1967, pp. 73-74; Hamilton, *Report on Manufactures*, delivered to Congress, Dec. 5, 1791.

47. See Nettels, Curtis P., *The Emergence of a National Economy, 1775-1815*, N.Y.: Harper & Row, 1969, p. 397.

As late as the mid-1850s, in fact, manufactured goods barely surpassed 10 percent of the total value of the nation's crucial export trade, even though, in absolute terms, the value sold had grown to 15 times the 1810 level. Yet, by virtue of industrial production undertaken expressly for the purpose of expanding the country's resource base westward to and beyond the valley of the Mississippi, we had by then become the world's second-ranking industrial nation behind Great Britain.[48] Iron rails, fence posts, boots and blouses, kettles, buggies, locomotives, and steamboats had to be manufactured to accommodate the nation's unmatched internal growth, and were. Coal and iron were mined in increasing amounts, and commercial and transportation volumes grew apace.

The effects of the new concentrations of capital needed to fund such new, vital growth industries on the country's still-developing system of self-government were visible at first only to those who were looking for them. Madison warned even before the dawn of American industrialization, in 1791, citing problems of control encountered earlier in Europe, that peril as well as promise lay ahead as America's developing economy began to undergo rapid change. "Incorporated societies ... are powerful machines," he declared in the U.S. House of Representatives, "which have always been found competent to effect objects or principles in a great measure independent of the people."[49]

And Jefferson complained in pen and ink a few years later, in 1814, of "the aristocracy of our moneyed corporations, which dare already to bid defiance to the laws of our country."[50] By the late 1830s, Tocqueville sounded a warning concerning the America he came to know intimately, writing that "the manufacturing aristocracy which is growing under our eyes is one of the harshest that ever existed in the world." Harsh, from the standpoint of relations with its growing force of employees. He warned that "the friends of democracy should keep their eyes anxiously fixed in this direction; for if ever a permanent inequality of conditions and aristocracy again penetrate into the world, it may be predicted that this is the gate by which they will enter."[51]

---

48. North, Douglass C., *The Economic Growth of the United States, 1790-1860*, N.Y.: Norton, 1966, pp. v., 165, 284.

49. Madison, speech in the House of Representatives, lst Congress, 2d Session, Feb. 8, 1791, quoted in Adrienne Koch, *Jefferson and Madison*, N.Y.: Knopf, 1950, p. 110.

50. Thomas Jefferson, 1814, quoted in Jeremy Rifkin et al, *Common Sense II*, N.Y.: Bantam, 1975, cover.

51. Tocqueville, *ibid.*, p. 161.

Finally, the nearly-cataclysmic mid-century Civil War simultaneously mobilized and matured the previously underdeveloped industrial sector and removed effective opposition to a little-known new political party, whose post-war leaders turned around radically to serve the highly financed demands of rich, growing industry, while openly denigrating those still classed together in the public mind as "working men."

That latter, de-emphasized and often-reviled large and growing part of the industrializing nation's population included the still greatly numerous but scattered and relatively isolated, sometimes "radical" farmers and many urban and rural foreign born. As these somewhat disparate groups sought in common to gain access to the new levels of wealth generated by growing industry, frequently resorting to collective bargaining to confront collective ownership of manufacturing and service industries, they were branded by the dominant political establishment and its press as "dangerous classes." Those with foreign-sounding names were often additionally villified as "anarchists," the later epithet "communist" not yet having entered the American vocabulary.

The apparent "danger" lay in the fact that the disparaged "working men" potentially controlled over half the nation's votes, if not its money, so could, in theory, seriously condition the content of its laws. Hence, the leaders of the more militant farmers and workers who sought to effectively organize to effectively defend their interests were branded as unpatriotic and subversive. Through the spread of such now-transparent disinformation, political and economic power was maintained and coddled in the hands of the so-called "respectable elements". The patriotic if unreflective native-born middle class responded by repeatedly more-or-less uniting at the polls to keep in power the party avowedly opposed to any of the demands of heavily-accented immigrant workers, recently-rebellious southerners, and paradoxically "anarchic" organized farmers.

At one point, in the 1876 election, the normally-dominant post-war party in Congress mysteriously bypassed the Constitution's mandated procedure for concluding indecisive elections, and invented an "Electoral Commission" to deliver the then-debased Presidency to their nominee, Rutherford Hayes, rather than let it go to the "radical" candidate Samuel Tilden, who had amassed a quarter of a million more popular votes, and seemed to have amassed several more electoral votes as well. Meeting in joint session, Congress then voted to award the disputed electoral votes of four states, including three still half-militarized reconstruction states in the South, to Hayes, giving him an artificial one-vote victory. But it must be noted that the competition in those Victorian-age elections was normally only between similar rival "factions" and their respective candidates; the public was, in reality, distant and involved only rather perfunctorily, not having chosen the candidates. The conclusive proof of the unrepresentativeness of this cornered system lay in the monopolistic purposes that were served.[52]

An astute visitor, political sociologist M. Ostrogorski, writing in 1910 about the changed America he discovered, labeled most aptly the peculiar combination of wealthy, governed ownership sector and ruling party that had formed to control democracy. He called it a "conquering plutocracy."[53] The fear Madison had voiced of a selective "anarchy" under the new Constitution, with "strong individuals" finding a way to "unite and oppress the weaker," was gradually realized in the rise of unlimited corporate political financing and bribes. The described adverse result was due, in the first instance, to federal relinquishment of legal jurisdiction over corporate activities, under the unprecedented political influence of the relatively-new collective creatures that Madison had still referred to in his day as "incorporated societies."[54]

In the entire United States, during the Federalist era of government that came to an abrupt end in 1800, only some 300 joint stock ventures had as yet applied for and been granted corporate status, and not over half a dozen of these were manufacturing companies. Charters of incorporation were issued in early America mainly by state legislatures, normally assuming that the bulk of the new firm's activities in commerce and production would not extend beyond the limits of the granting state. Until the demand for charters become too great, long after 1800, each new grant of incorporation occasioned a separate enabling act, with enforceable provisions appropriate to both the company's expressed purposes and the interest of the public. The prevailing reason for issuing charters at that time was embodied in the so-called "public purpose theory" of incorporation.[55]

---

52. Smith, Page, *The Rise of Industrial America, A People's History of the Post-Reconstruction Era*, N.Y.: McGraw-Hill, 1984, pp. 924-26. The emergence of Lincoln as an early, earnest exception to this trend and the only strong, independent President of this whole late-middle period, has much to do with the fact that he won election from a field of four major candidates when the political establishment had fractured North and South; almost exactly the same thing that had occurred with the decline of the controlling caucus system in 1824, producing the slightly-delayed emergence then of a strong, willful, and unmanageable popular President, Andrew Jackson.

53. Ostrogorski, *ibid.*, pp. 1, 92, 100-101.

54. Madison, *Federalist 52*; Koch, *loc. cit.*

55. Nadel, Mark V., *Corporations and Public Accountability*, Lexington, MA: Heath, 1976, pp. 209-210.

The early federal government, on rare occasion, granted corporate charters for particular, large-scale purposes, as in the cases of the First and eventually-disfranchised Second Bank of the United States. Hence, direct, national-scale public authority was not unknown -- or unfelt -- in the early corporate community. Perhaps as a result, the main area of related legal controversy at the time involved the right of the federal government (in most other respects, the higher arbiter) to review the provisions of a charter granted by a state or other jurisdiction.

A landmark case in this uncharted area was that of Dartmouth College v. Woodward, argued before the U.S. Supreme Court in 1819 under Chief Justice John Marshall, a tenured Federalist appointee. In the Dartmouth case, the Court ruled that the federal government could not review any part of the college's charter, even though the charter had been issued by the earlier, colonial regime.

Yet, the Chief Justice's remarks, in ruling to extend immunity to the charter's holder from the authority of the general community, somehow still managed to express the prevalent public purpose theory quite well. "A corporation," Marshall wrote, "is an artificial being, invisible, intangible, and existing only in contemplation of the law. Being the mere creature of the law, it possesses only those properties which the charter of its creation confers upon it ..."[56] Since the granting colonial government no longer existed, the implication of Marshall's decision, rather at variance with his stated reasoning, was that the charter-holder was really beholden to *no one*.

Jefferson, 10 years in retirement by this time, but yet firm in his belief that the law had to be flexible in order to accommodate changing needs of the community, was alarmed at the seeming discrepancy between the Chief Justice's stated reasoning and his decision in this signal case. The philosophical founder commented in a letter to Governor Plummer of New Hampshire that "the idea that institutions established for the use of the Nation cannot be touched or modified, even to make them answer their end, because of a right gratuitously [granted], is most absurd against the Nation..."[57] The Dartmouth case's implications as a

---

56. Chief Justice John Marshall, *Trustees of Dartmouth v. Woodward*, 4 Wheaton 518, 636 (1819).

57. Jefferson to Gov. William Plummer (1819), quoted in Page Smith, *Shaping of America*, p. 701.

legal precedent, though then still of minor import, were clear and distressing to fore-sighted Americans who valued democratic control.

During the 19th century, the dramatic enhancement that took place in the role of and means available to American corporations produced two fundamentally important results. First, most of the largest chartered companies eventually far transcended state boundaries in their operations, and thus outgrew that level of jurisdiction in any practical governmental sense. Second, faced with vastly-increased numbers of charter applications as the century wore on, the state governments, with varying but limited capacities to cope, began to compromise their vested responsibility to their own and, arguably, other states' citizens. The besieged states, faced with the Promethean task of chartering hundreds of what were by that time essentially nation-wide corporations, began to approve paid applications more or less automatically, granting standardized privileges without the old leavening of public interest requirements.

Hence, new corporate entities, eventually being mass-produced by nearly every state from Maine to Texas, were being turned loose to operate commercially in other states as distant as Missouri and California -- out of sight and presumably out of mind. This expedient concession of nearly-automatic licenses for the growing number of units involved in the new leading growth sector produced, partly out of bureaucratic necessity, a new "general incorporation theory," gradually replacing the more demanding "public purpose" rationale in American law. After the Civil War, states that still tried to apply and enforce more than minimal standards found that they were rapidly losing valued chartering clients to states more willing to relax the earlier standards.

Eventually, in the all-out bidding wars that ensued, first New Jersey, and then tiny Delaware -- the latter holding perhaps less that one one-thousandth of the nation's productive resources and means in the normal sense -- offered to let prospective or re-organizing corporations draft their own terms of charter. The intended and realized effect was to attract a very large share of the nation's major fast-growing companies, many without any significant part of their actual operations transpiring in, or even anywhere near, the adopted home state.[58]

---

58. See Hurst, James Willard, *The Legitimacy of the Business Corporation in the Law of the United States, 1780-1970* , Charlottesville: Univ. of Virginia Press, 1970, pp. 69-70, 109-110; Nadel, *ibid.*, p. 210.

In the context of the modern, enormously-expanded scale of activity, the major licensing states, representing their own interests and only by the merest coincidence the national interest, quite clearly lack the appropriate scope of jurisdiction and power to govern all of their varied, far-flung "corporate citizens" as they do their resident human communities. Further, the federal government, in so far as it might be so inclined, is enjoined by 19th-century legal decisions from in any way *directly* chastising even the worst corporate offenders. Thus, the basis of corporate license accountability, applied earlier to protect and serve the public, has been lost entirely, except perhaps in a single ancillary domestic industry, broadcasting, due to anti-democratic ideology, corporatist political influence, and the competition for revenue.

Today's efforts at controlling inevitable abuses against the public trust by powerful, mega-scale corporations must, as a result, concentrate entirely on *incidental* criteria, such as ambient air quality or the payment of contracted obligations. This modern-day strategy of attempting to legally combat serious symptoms of what is frequently anti-socially inclined power, undertaken as a last resort in the twentieth century, has, predictably, proven ineffective at achieving and protecting community purposes, because, at most, a few incidents of symptoms are enjoined by fines or fees which, if the misbehavior is truly profitable for the company, can be regarded as a routine and transferable cost of doing business. And this already-compromised strategy of prosecuting incidentals suffers further from notoriously lax enforcement of the law in the 1980s. Such a dismal outcome, from a pro-public, or law and order point of view, is due not only to the current super-influence of the regulated concerns, but also to the rapid proliferation of serious cases of abuse, owing to the absence in the law of effective primary sanctions to insure compliance. And, finally, the failure to even begin to adequately police corporate behavior at the designated *state* level of jurisdiction is due as well to the recently-intensified competition among scores or even hundreds of economically depressed and fearful localities and states to attract and retain jobs and enterprise. Thus, the modern general purpose theory of chartering has placed the citizen public literally in thrall to legally-coddled collectives and reduced the American individual to a remote, second-class citizenship, by discarding the traditional basis of corporate accountability to the community at large.

Few important corporate decision makers are, as such, ever jailed for even gross violations of the law as a responsible individual would be, in good part because of the degree of protection from accountability not undeliberately extended to large corporate enterprise by a beholden political system. In addition, some firms are now managing to escape irksome contractual obligations and agreements through technical reorganization and bankruptcy; countless others continue to gain interminable stays of compliance and enforcement, while their lobbyists and propagandists work tirelessly and successfully to strip from the law the scant public protection that still remains. Great business corporations have contributed inestimably to American life, and surely merit every consideration of a non-extortionary sort. Yet, placing them effectively above the level of community sanctions that we routinely apply to infinitely less-powerful genuine citizens, starting in earnest in the late nineteenth century, has proven disastrous for America in a myriad of ways.

Unless we expect state governments like Delaware's to reach justly and effectively to Chicago and Bhopal, the public's only remedy for its deepening morass of powerlessness must be exactly the same as when the Constitution finally replaced the grossly inadequate Articles of Confederation in 1789. That is, we need to place the dangerously and irresponsibly self-willed (this time corporate) citizens back under the routine legal authority of a publicly-accountable national government. Only thus can we hope to successfully confront the looming hazard posed to the entire community by selective anarchy involving the kind of "strong individuals" who now quite clearly can "unite and oppress the weaker."[59] But, unfortunately, a national government itself accountable to the nation must be recovered first. So, that must be the nation's next main object.

Manufacturing and commercial stock companies, on the scale called for by the territorially-expanding economy of the U.S. in the 1800s, were literally something new under the sun. Meanwhile, the somnolent, post-medieval British economy was also just then being revolutionized into an urban-industrial one, largely within a single generation. And the lives of nearly everyone on that teeming, smallish "isle of Mars" were directly transformed by the change.

---

59. Madison, *Federalist 52*.

The great majority of Britons were much more likely to be employees than large entrepreneurs. Thus, their indignant and surprisingly powerful reaction to the squalid, intolerable working and wage situations provided by prosperous owners left to their own devices, resulted directly in effective political democracy and badly-needed reforms through mandated legislation.

Still, it took some time for the changes gradually brought about in Britain's power structure to express the mounting demands of the greater society. The conditions that resulted when the entrepreneurial "class" wielded tyrannical, unchecked power have been forever recorded by such contemporary writers as Charles Dickens and the irascible social chronicler William Hazlitt.

Mr. Hazlitt, writing in 1824, stated that the immorality of the corporations' behavior toward their numerous employees was mainly due to their lack of an individual judgment and an individual's regard for reputation. "Corporate bodies are more corrupt and profligate than individuals," he wrote, "because they have more power to do mischief, and are less amenable to disgrace or punishment. They feel neither shame, remorse, gratitude, nor good-will. The refinements of private judgment are referred to and negatived in a committee of the whole body, while the projects and interests of the corporation meet with secret but powerful support. ..."[60]

Twenty years later, the conditions in Great Britain's manufacturing centers were just as bad as those Hazlitt had lamented, or perhaps even worse, because, by then, they were projected on a far grander scale. The historian Andre Maurois recorded that when the notorious social philosopher Friedrich Engels first ventured to Manchester in 1844, "he found 350,000 workers crushed and crowded into damp, dirty, broken-down houses where they breathed an atmosphere resembling a mixture of water and coal. In the mines, he saw half-naked women, who were treated like the lowest of draft animals. Children spent the day in dark tunnels, where they were employed in opening and closing the primitive openings for ventilation. .... In the lace industry, exploitation reached such a point that four-year-old children worked for virtually no pay."[61]

---

60. Hazlitt, William, *Table Talk* (1824), London: Everyman Edition, 1952, p. 264.
61. Maurois, Andre, *The History of England*, N.Y.: Praeger, 1953, quoted in Djilas, *ibid.*, p. 10.

Engels himself lived to see an entirely different situation in industrial Britain; but the sweeping social changes that occurred were only due to increasingly heavy public and labor pressure and the social reform movement that in the end turned the British political power system upside down.

To put it another way, one could say that the inevitable *systolic* (benefit-circulating) phase of the Industrial Revolution naturally followed the *diastolic* (wealth-originating) phase, some two or three decades later during those years, and that it operated with unprecedented thoroughness to transform the narrowed, class government of the United Kingdom into a functioning democracy.

In the United States, where a high percentage of the growing numbers of industrial workers in the 19th century were themselves immigrants, substantial reforms of the abysmal early conditions of industrial employment came much more slowly, through legislation demanded by a sporadically-scandalized public, coupled with a long series of nearly-ambivalent court rulings. A characteristic, but fairly well-known, early labor decision was rendered in the case of Commonwealth v. Hunt in 1842, in which Judge Shaw of the Massachusetts bench ruled that "the labor union in and of itself" was "not illegal."[62]

Since the citizenship responsibilities of corporations were never effectively established in American law, related reforms in the interest of actual human beings co-existing in the community have come only very gradually, and usually after a hard, sometimes perilous, struggle for a hearing. Yet, the broader public force (i.e., the *systolic* side) generally progressed in the wake of the *diastolic*, in sporadic, rather than continuous, forward progress.

---

62. *Commonwealth v. Hunt*, 4 Metcalf III (Mass., 1842), discussed in Robert Evans, Jr., *Public Policy Toward Labor*, N.Y.: Harper & Row, 1965, p. 50. The right of organized labor to bargain with ownership/management as an equal partner was finally secured almost a century later by the passage of the federal Wagner Act in 1935. See Rockefeller, John D. III, *The Second American Revolution, Some Personal Observations*, N.Y.: Harper & Row, 1973, p. 104; also noted in Evans, *ibid.*, pp. 6-8.

After the Civil War, rising, war-enhanced industrial leaders, wishing to consolidate and legitimize their emerging dominance over American politics, found a neat formulation of their claims in the theory of "Social Darwinism" promulgated by British sociologist Herbert Spencer. Spencer wrote that times of serious engagement, such as wars and the struggle to transform a new continent through industrial improvement, tend to stratify society into its more- and its less-able members. The "fittest" (financially ablest) members of society, he argued, have not only the right, but the moral obligation (a sort of post-medieval *noblesse oblige*) to lead and to decide public issues according to their best lights, for the benefit of all. And the rest of the society was, naturally, obliged to conform to the judgment of the best-qualified few. In less-stressful times, Spencer conceded, the social rankings and their restrictions might be relaxed somewhat.[63]

Spencer's writings were permeated with the sense that to interfere with the free social evolution worked out for the society through the competitive activities of the society's "fittest" members would be to wrongfully weaken society by obstructing its course of development.[64] He wrote that compulsory cooperation with the absolute freedom of "the fittest," which he would have required, could be supplanted by wholly voluntary cooperation once it was discovered that society's needs would be met completely through uncontrolled competition. The aroma of anarchism in this historically-debunked and once-relegated but resurrected doctrine of faith has not gone unnoticed.[65] But, how quickly we forget!

Ostrogorski, very likely the most insightful scholarly Americanist of his time, described the late 19th- and early 20th-century subversion of America's democratic system in graphic terms: "Members of a degenerate ruling class, high dignitaries of State, nay, even tribunes of the people might be bought," he wrote. "But how was it possible to buy the people itself, a whole sovereign people? Party organization in the

---

63. Spencer, Herbert, *The Evolution of Society*, selections from "Principles of Sociology" (1885-86), R. L. Carneiro, ed., Univ. of Chicago Press, 1967, p. 92.
64. See Lea, James F., *Political Consciousness and American Democracy*, Jackson: Univ. Press of Mississippi, 1982, p. 9.
65. See Dunning, William Archibald, *A History of Political Theories, From Rousseau to Spencer*, N.Y.: Macmillan, 1920, pp. 395-402. Dunning refers specifically here to Spencer's *Data of Ethics and Justice*.

United States supplied the answer: all the corrupters who try to bend the power of the State to their own selfish ends have but to identify their interests with those of the party organization which is the conscience keeper of the sovereign demos; they have only to become its financial supporters. It is in this way that the party organization has served as a lever to all great private interests..."[66]

The long-overdue solution to this persistent American problem, decked out somewhat differently now than in Madison's or Ostrogorski's time, lies not in negatively restricting the parties or the financial interests. Instead, the public's remedy lies in reclaiming, by law, the paralyzing extra-constitutional power inadvertently left to those yet-unborn interests by a devilish accommodation of the moment in 1787.

---

66. Ostrogorski, *ibid.*, pp. 396-97.

Chapter Three

AMERICA: THE NEW CORPORATIST STATE

- Twentieth Century Currents of Change -

In little more than the blink of an eye in the 1970s, the fortunate approximate balance of contending interests in America of over two generations was at an end as one of the runners lost wind and started to fade back.

The broader-based, outwardly more democratic fonts of organized political power had revived in the 20th century to challenge the still-burgeoning corporatist forces in two related ways: through the growth of labor unions and consumer organizations, and by the rapid spread of social knowledge and awareness via non-technical, so-called liberal education.

The philosophically opposed corporatist sources of organizational strength continued to thrive independently. Their continued power was due to the continuation of rapid overall economic growth and the continuous, competitive weeding-out among major business corporations themselves. The more resourceful surviving units of major business remained bent on clearing their paths still further of serious public interference. The mega-scale corporate sector itself, as distinguished from smaller-scale private business, also clearly benefited from the removal of the sanction of public law over its members that stemmed from the growing incongruity of *state*-level chartering and consequent legal jurisdiction over businesses that were becoming increasingly world-scale entities. And, in part, the large corporate sector also owed its relative prosperity to the courts' correctly shielding it, in response to the newer general purpose theory of the law, from direct federal authority.[1]

---

1. See Hurst, *ibid.*, pp. 109-110; Galbraith, *ibid.*, p. xv., points out that by the late 1970s, the two thousand or so largest corporations in the U.S. comprised about half of the economy measured by value of product. He referred to these in all seriousness as the "planning system" of the U.S.

These undeniable boons, at least to specific very large-scale business combinations historically, must be set against the background of their effects on the rights and quality of life of individuals and of other politically-interested segments and levels of society.

The relative strength of the two distinct forces (represented by those favoring increased concentration of power and those ostensibly favoring broad power-sharing) shifted significantly from time to time throughout the middle half of this century. Such shifts of influence were due to corporatist avarice and libertarian stock-trading laws (contributing, at least in the public mind, to the 1930s Depression), and to the outwardly more-democratic side's ineptness in social experimentation in the 1960s and '70s (again, in the eyes of the voting, tax-paying public).[2] Yet, since the 1930s, the relative power of the two forces had, until fairly recently, either remained close to even, or else quickly returned after only a brief lapse to a balanced position, demanding a high degree of effective bipartisanship and the practical rejection of dogmatic one-sided economic programs.[3]

But, by the mid-1970s, a trend of relative decline in heavy industry, and more so in its vast, organized labor force inside the United States, had clearly emerged. Such results were, of course, due in large part to tremendous inroads made by new, better and cheaper foreign competition in many industries, and, more especially, to the sudden outbreak in America and elsewhere of a new high-tech, low-labor "revolution," requiring far fewer industrial workers within the country. A simple result of the sudden collapse of organized labor and allied interests was a surprisingly abrupt end to the largely accidental political balance that had long prevailed.[4]

---

2. George F. Will discussed such pendulum swings in the relative strength of libertarian and communitarian attitudes as tantamount to popular fads in his daily column some time back. See *El Paso Sun*, Dec. 27, 1984. Andrew Hacker, writing in 1957, attributed a lessening of the power of the old American (corporatist) ruling class over the previous half-century to "the Americanization of the immigrant and the expansion of the economy." See Hacker, Andrew, "Liberal Democracy and Social Control," in Fein, Leonard J., *American Democracy, Essays in Image and Realities*, N.Y.: Holt, Rinehart and Winston, 1964, pp. 113-122.

3. For example, political sociologist Adolf A. Berle, writing in 1963, eulogized the remarkable long-term freedom in America from narrow, ideologically-based solutions, in favor of a more pragmatic approach to common problems. See Berle, *loc.cit.*

4. This signalled the simultaneous downfall of the interpretive "Industrial Society theory" discussed in Chapter 1. See Giddens, *Sociology*, pp. 60-62.

During the time when the long balance of forces had spelled a broader, in effect more public-spirited coalition of interests in the formation of national public policy, bitter enmity continued to exist among frustrated, narrow ideologues, still scheming in the boiler rooms on both sides. Those who favored a freer and more prominent corporate role I will refer to, and have been referring to, as "corporatists." These quintessential vested-interest politicos, most of them no doubt sincere in their beliefs, longed for a chance to further advance and consolidate their enormous 19th century gains in the law. The corporate operatives of the recent past fought relentlessly to shake completely free from the expensive, though relatively ineffective, indirect regulatory approach to curbing the more dangerous and destructive aspects of certain lucrative business/industrial practices on behalf of an otherwise unprotected public. They blamed politically-interested educators and the rising mass media for selectively informing society of the broader, adverse effects of some of their practices and activities, which were, they at least claimed, either overblown in media coverage, or else only their concern and nobody else's business.

Political writer Michael Novak summed up many of the corporatists' frustrations shortly before they at last successfully out-maneuvered and out-distanced their combined competition at the ballot box at the beginning of the 1980s. He noted that the core of the still-strong "liberal" opposition to corporate political power was "a new social class ... whose main business is not business," and that the growth in influence of "national organs of daily news" meant that "'the rules of the game' have been changed." Novak explained: "Not many decades ago, for the purposes of real power, many believed that no news is good news." He recalled, interestingly, how "the vote of the bright, young, technically expert professionals ... was carefully exploited by the new frontier."[5]

Corporatist idealogues were, meanwhile, at work on a winning strategy. A book co-authored by Samuel P. Huntington, entitled *The Crisis of Democracy*, which was commissioned by the corporate elitist Trilateral Commission in the mid-'70s, reflected that "democracy is only one way of constituting authority, and it is not necessarily a universally applicable one." It should give way, in many instances, the book said, to "the claims of expertise." The example that was cited in the segment of the book by Huntington, focusing on what he called "the surge of the

---

5. Novak, Michael, *The American Vison, An Essay on the Future of Democratic Capitalism*, Washington: American Enterprise Institute, 1978, pp. 29-30.

1960s" when students sometimes ruled on university faculty appointments, seems to miss the point, though, in claiming to portray an allegedly rampant democracy. Such a publicly irresponsible practice in one institution within society would, properly speaking, be a clear example not of rampant democracy as claimed, but rather of *anarchy*, or absence of the rule of law. This landmark book's subjective observation that "dissatisfaction with and lack of confidence in the functioning of the institutions of democratic government have thus now become widespread in Trilateral countries" seems far more ominous, given the caliber of its sponsors. It is reminiscent of, but more pervasive and more effectively dangerous than, the narrow genius Hamilton's shadowy, collaborative schemes from the top of the early-American power structure designed to overturn "democratical government."[6]

Since the late '70s, some pundits, writing in an outwardly more majoritarian vein, have warned of a self-interested "new elite" of narrowly-educated young professionals now permeating all levels of American politics, whose members believe themselves to be uniquely qualified to govern the society, and are openly contemptuous of democratic rules and values. As noted earlier, a small group of influential social analysts announced over two decades ago that the nation state, as a genuine instrument of governance, was, due to its loss of ability to function in a major way as an economic actor, about to become, for practical purposes, irrelevant.

That prediction seems now to be rapidly materializing. In the case of the more recent "new elite" theorists, the loss of democratic control in society they warn of clearly merits more focused and widespread attention. But their complaint that people engage in politics to further their own interests strikes many as hollow in today's ambience and rings of sour grapes. The only likely purpose of such a senseless argument from them is, ironically, partisan advantage.[7]

The problem posed by the exclusivism and mutual intolerance of the two opposing fundamental ideologies (the elitist and the rule-by-the-proletarian camps) is, upon close examination, evident. Each of the two

---

6. Huntington, Samuel P., in Huntington, M. J. Crozier, and Joji Watanuki, *The Crisis of Democracy, Report on the Governability of Democracies to the Trilateral Commission*, New York Univ. Press, 1975, pp. 113-14, 158-59. Treasury Secretary Hamilton's schemes are discussed in Chapter 2, supra.
7. See Lebedoff, David, *The New Elite, The Death of Democracy*, Chicago: Contemporary Books, 1983, pp. 67 ff.; Modelski, *loc.cit.*; Ball, *loc.cit.*

extremist, one-sided classical ideologies separately poses its own thinly-veiled form of threat to public order and well-being, were it to exclusively dominate. And this is, of course, because each separate side represents only an essential half-truth image of the life of a functional society.

James Madison, in recognition of his authorship of *Federalist 10* and *Federalist 51*, is often cited as a main source of the modern theory of pluralist democracy. Modern pluralism, seemingly true to its name and tradition, encourages the apparent striving together of numerous distinct interest groups to produce an American policy consensus that on balance will accrue to the public good. This general, mostly descriptive theory of democratic government, along with the less-precise but perhaps more-insightful theory of industrial society cited in Chapter One, currently lies in ruins.

Both have been stripped of credibility, at least for now, by the impressive triumph of one of the vying interest groups, large corporate business. The corporatists' political triumph, as we have seen, followed the organizational decline of their combined rivals, produced by the rapid shift away from labor-intensive industries.[8]

But, importantly, the discredited pluralist theory's apparent perceptual error does not lie in some newly-discovered weakness in the purposes of the balance of interests embedded in the Constitution, which Madison labored to establish and then to explain in the two key, frequently-mentioned passages from the *Federalist Papers*. Instead, the fateful error would seem to lie in the modern pluralists' failure to put Madison's (and the Constitution's) political purpose, of accommodating the mutually offsetting interest groups, ahead of the misperceived identity of such groups in front organizations. Modern pluralists seemingly have failed to recognize that the United Auto Workers, the National Association of Manufacturers, National Rifle Association, environmental and education lobbies, etc., do not nearly add up to American society. These are only fragmentary, at best partially-representative organizations. Hence, this twisting of what Madison and

---

8. G. William Domhoff, *Who Rules America Now?* Englewood Cliffs, N.J.: Prentice Hall, 1983, pp. 130, 203-210, discusses the limitations of modern pluralist theory. Also see Miller, Arthur Selwyn, *The Modern Corporate State, Private Governments and the American Constitution*, Westport, CT: Greenwood Press, 1976, pp. 216-17.

the other still-revered framers of the system actually meant by "factions" and "interests" is the modern pluralist theory's enormous conceptual flaw. According to Madison, the value of having a wide variety of personal interests and points of view represented politically, was the protection of the public by its own unfragmented action from domination by any faction or combination narrower than itself. The modern pluralists, conversely, have tried without ceasing to form a dominating combination of factions narrower than society.

In sum: Madison's avowed objective was incomparably broader and more public-spirited than that of the modern pluralists who have invoked his name. He wrote, characteristically, in *Federalist 51* that "a coalition of a majority of the whole society could seldom take place on any other principles than those of justice and the general good."[9]

Moreover, when Madison wrote of "interests," he demonstrably did not have wealthy, incorporated lobbies and professional activist groups in mind, as do the partisan present-day "pluralists." In fact, when such self-interested combinations became a threat to the public interest in his time, as in the case of the powerful land companies that tried to gain control of the country's western lands, he stood opposed. Instead, he asserted in the two much-quoted passages of the *Federalist Papers* cited here, the common observation that the public's safety would be best secured by individual citizens and their elected representatives making decisions in an open system such as the Constitution was intended to establish. The practical basis for such a system in America was simply the coherent nation-wide community of varying viewpoints and differing interests. And this scheme worked as long as the interested public remained the system's main constituency.

As explained in Chapter 2, probably the only practical way this indispensable notion of pluralism as Madison, the Constitution's principal author, understood it can be made operational again in our time, is by the fortunately relatively-uncomplicated expedient of deliberately repairing the gap left in the procedure inadequately sketched in Article II, Section 1 of the document. This would have to be done in such a way as to effectively permit the American people as a whole -- our system's sole legal body of sovereigns -- to themselves make a reasonably-informed choice of and among nominees for the directionally vital office of the Presidency.

---

9. Madison, *Federalist 51.*

The currently-dominant large corporate interests very probably no longer need fear competition for control of the system as now constituted from rival interest groups (municipalities, labor organizations, ecologists and consumer groups and the like). Being relatively free of accountability under law and increasingly in control of mass imagery via media advertising, they have for years held a sizable edge over such competitors. Instead, they now fear surges of *public* reaction beyond the normal workings of institutional politics. The danger they perceive is that such surges of public feeling, which they purport to view as irrational and counter-productive, might arise unexpectedly over some unforeseen, non-corporatist issue or issue area. Such surges of public passion can only serve to interrupt their present objective of steadily eliminating the capacity of government, whether otherwise publicly-accountable or not, to act as an independent competing agent by imposing agenda items with a price tag from the outside.

The continued existence of power-sharing machinery in the now-less-than-convenient 1787 Constitution still makes such untoward interruptions possible as (in the corporatists' view) the short-lived Carter presidency with its genuine mixed agenda. The strategists in the corporatist camp would like to impose a politically deodorized program to protect against costly, "wasteful" systematic diversions of resources for public purposes. And the surest means clearly seem to involve, first, positively *eliminating* the government's remaining capacity to regulate business activity and allocate the public's money, and second, establishing *firm* corporatist control over the disposition of government and of society's available funds in the meantime.

The large business community's political surrogates, leading the nation of late, have draped themselves in democratic rhetoric and super-patriotic images, to viscerally appeal to a vast army of followers. This is, of course, because although they do not actually represent the interests of a broad constituency in advancing their single-criterion policy program, they still need to enlist the active and willing support of scores of millions of Americans as followers.[10] Corporatist ideologues, quite understandably, tend to disrespect and disdain the structure of the essentially democratic political process that is still formally in place, just as their spiritual forebears Alexander Hamilton and Herbert Spencer did.

---

10. John Plamenatz discusses this pseudo-democratic mode of leadership, dating back at least to Napoleon's use of plebiscites and an elected legislature, in *Democracy and Illusion*, London: Longman, 1973, p. 90.

For example, M.I.T. political scientist Walter Dean Burnham likens the loyalty of Americans to what he considers an antiquated and highly inefficient form of government to the continued following of religion by many in this day and age. "The United States has a constitutional regime," he has written, "which is of almost incredible antiquity and cumbersomeness." Burnham quotes approvingly the assessment of Samuel P. Huntington, the sometime Trilateral Commission scribe, which characterizes the American Constitution as a "Tudor polity," resting, as did attempts at balancing arrangements under Elizabeth I, on a "*consensus rei publicae*," thus making it harder for sheer economic power to prevail. Burham criticizes Americans for expecting "benefits coming to them personally" from the political system. This is presumably because he would prefer to see benefits applied instead exclusively to the super collective entities at the top of the economic hierarchy, for *them* to allocate.[11]

Huntington noted back in 1975, not without palpable hope, that "dissatisfaction with and lack of confidence in the functioning of the institutions of democratic government have thus now become widespread in Trilateral countries. Yet, with all this dissatisfaction, no significant support has yet developed for any alternative image of how to organize the politics of a highly industrialized society."[12]

In summary, the more extreme publicly exposed corporatists, who find their views a bit more than marginally more acceptable just now, are both testing the waters and seeking ways to safely dismantle the remaining vestiges of what has been, for them, a cumbersome and needlessly perilous system for maintaining practical control over policy that affects them. Unless their steadily unfolding plans should somehow fail, due perhaps to an outright depression, war, or true ecological catastrophe, I believe we may expect to see an initially startling, but concerted rhetorical and advertising campaign within the coming decade, seeking public support to "streamline" our system of government. Such can be done, the President or, perhaps more likely, key members of his administration or his congressional allies may inform us, by partially replacing what will no doubt be lavishly memorialized as our current, long-faithful, but now-outmoded, *procedural* Constitution. To take its

---

11. Burnham, Walter Dean, "The 1980 Earthquake: Realignment, Reaction, or What?" in Thomas Ferguson and Joel Rogers, eds., *The Hidden Election*, N.Y.: Pantheon, 1981, pp. 120-21.

12. Huntington, *ibid.*, pp. 158-59.

place, I expect that corporate sector surrogates in power positions will suggest an apparently closely-related, but more "flexible" formulation establishing much more "standby power" unequivocally in a single high office, thus arguably better befitting new, higher technical realities and 21st-century needs for fast, decisive action, and in fact bypassing Congress on most pressing matters.

In the meantime, leading corporatists and their political surrogates will no doubt continue to blast away at such inert regulatory machinery as the federal government has left. They will also continue working to push more of the offending regulatory functions, even the incidental ones, down to the states, a level of government whose limited jurisdiction and enforcement power and limitless desire to maintain a competitive local "business climate" make it infinitely easier and less costly to deal with.

In this withering away of the effective, federal state that they invariably firmly believe in, modern corporatists are, it seems, neglecting the profoundly wise warning of one of their very earliest mentors. Adam Smith reminded his readers in the 18th century that the necessity of civil government grows up with the acquisition of valuable property."[13] Eventually, given the sweeping, sudden changes in our day, even corporatists may find themselves in need of a level of protection and support unavailable from a seriously-weakened democratic state. Eventually, frustrated, institutionally powerless masses of citizens will most assuredly again demand the rights of citizenship and justice no longer secured for them by a balanced, fully-operative Constitution. They may not even know why their condition has so changed. But, economically and environmentally strapped, they may very well demand unavailable rights en mass, irrationally as it were, rather than accept the inevitable diminution in living standard entailed.

Political scientist Moshe Czudnowski, in a recent essay on the importance of who is in control, identifies three stages of leadership style that Western-type societies sequentially pass through. Since modern societies stem from feudal or autocratic beginnings, the first stage is one "where social stratification is relatively rigid and social change relatively slow," so that "the social background of a ruling elite is still a valid predictor of policies." But, "in increasingly pluralistic societies, where mobility and change are relatively high, the social background of decision-makers becomes a diminishing indicator of political affiliation

---

13. Adam Smith, *ibid.*, p. 309.

and attitudes." As a result, a wider, more public-spirited attitude tends to prevail when dominant power is not a foregone conclusion for any one class. And, finally, "under the impact of social and economic crises" (such as the first really serious international competition for means and markets encountered by America's techno-industrial sector,) "ideologies and party platforms reclaim their predominance and reflect social differences or cleavages."[14]

In our formative Revolutionary age, American society, followed shortly by nations in Western Europe, moved beyond the first of these situations and entered the second. Madison and Jefferson, among other contemporary leaders, seized the opportunity afforded by the foundation of a new government to forge a set of rules to insure against the society's movement (actually, a reversion) into the third, confrontational stage that Czudnowski describes. This they accomplished by constitutionally vesting sovereignty in the whole, inclusively broad body of citizens, mandating the nation as a whole, in so far as was possible, to select and review the holders of civil power.

Nevertheless, in great part due to the original Constitution's understandable lack of specificity on the single most important procedural point, and because of the long spate of extra-constitutional medicine show since filling the vacuum thus created, we are now emerging rapidly into a phased socioeconomic leadership situation of the unglorious *third*, unfortunately most common, kind.

- The Triumph of Managerial Ideology -

Democracy is not precisely the mode of governance practiced by most major corporations in their own internal affairs. Individuals might object to this fact in some instances, but, if they do, they are presumably free to take their money and invest it elsewhere, or to not invest it at all. Or, they can try their hand at business on their own. That is certainly their privilege. The owner-authoritarianism practiced in-house in corporate decision making is, in and of itself, probably not a matter of public concern.

---

14. Czudnowski, Moshe M., in Czudnowski, ed., *Does Who Governs Matter? Elite Circulation in Contemporary Societies*, DeKalb: Northern Illinois Press, 1982, pp. 5-6.

But attempts to co-opt the nation's political system, using new technical means and concentrated wealth to hamstring the government's ability to carry out its very serious Constitutional mandate of promoting the general welfare and establishing justice, *are* matters for public concern. As are continuing attempts to restructure the nation's system of public authority via corporate patronage to ultimately approximate the corporate power model of the boardroom and the street. In the remainder of this chapter, I will try to explain how such "streamlining" objectives are being gradually but surely realized within the current, still remediably birth-flawed American political system.

What is at stake, from one point of view, is the future pattern of what is called America's "ideology of management." This matter, critical to establishing the boundary between absolute ownership and public accountability, ultimately relates to the position and rights of the country's citizenry vis-à-vis the major owners and managers of its economic enterprises. The latter as a group are, now fairly confidently, working through the political system to achieve full and secure immunity from public interference, ostensibly to permit them to successfully rise to stem the challenge of world economic competition.[15]

The productive wealth of the United States is inarguably concentrated today in the hands of far fewer (and far greater and richer) commercial and financial firms than ever before. Due to the traditional American prejudice against monopolies in various sectors (a condition that probably would have developed long ago in every major industry if nature had been left completely free to take its course), the prevalent pattern is one of *oligopoly*. There are from three to five giant surviving firms dominating in each of a large number of key industries. These survivors, in many cases now diversifying and shifting into greener endeavors, scarcely compete with each other in a really cutthroat fashion, because the law and the unwritten rules conspire to keep their ranks from shrinking further. (Attest: federal aid to Chrysler, Lockheed, U.S. Steel).

Hence, the biggest participants are, for the most part, amicable competitors domestically, able to unite in bewailing the "unfairness" of effectively-organized foreign competition and to stand firmly together on

---

15. See Bendix, Reinhard, "Industrialization, Ideologies, and Social Structure," in Etzimi, Amitai and Eva Etzimi-Halevy, eds., *Social Change, Sources, Patterns, and Consequences*, N.Y.: Basic Books, 1973, p. 315.

the issue of government-industry relations. This cooperation on political matters among the key participants forging what Galbraith has recognized as the American planning system, ostensibly tends toward a stable cost-price structure and more predictable conditions for company operation.[16] Despite the image at times projected to the public that the corporate community is seriously divided, there is virtual or absolute unanimity within the top layers of the corporate establishment on the most important substantive matter in the present discussion, which is the demand for basic immunity of the corporate world from government sanctions and censure.[17]

By its nature, large-scale industrial activity involves establishments of one sort or another in which many subordinate employees follow the routine directions of a small handful of managers. To the extent that business owners and managers choose to view society as merely a vast business arena, well-suited to the fulfillment of the ends of business (i.e., increasing profits and power of control over the resource environment), they tend to view politics in a way analogous to Wall Street. That is, the active part of society is seen as a pool of potential clients or patrons of the few who occupy the seats of power.[18] From this point of view, no one could be a more helpful or welcome client for a successful politician than a large firm or a politically-united industry.

After all, whose long-term success is more important to the national good than the auto or electronics industry? The fact that the Constitution seems a bit outmoded and cumbersome in its procedural requirements, and that the laws regulating political access might sometimes be naive or ill-contrived, poses no real barrier to influence-trading, but is instead more of an irritant. The important thing, from the standpoint of the corporate client, is generally that business proceed smoothly, not that well-meaning but naive laws be strictly observed in every instance.[19] Most long-term government officials at least understand these imperatives. Many reputedly owe their political lives to favorable

---

16. Berle, Adolf A., *Power Without Property, A New Development in American Political Economy*, N.Y.: Harcourt, 1959, pp. 88-90.

17. See Galbraith, *ibid.*, p. 71, xv.; Domhoff, *ibid.*, p. 130. Disagreements, of course, arise from time to time concerning other issues, such as tariff protection.

18. There is an apparent close resemblance between such an active interpretation of power in a republic and the actual constitution of the later Roman Republic, a matter to be explored in Chapter 4.

19. John Z. De Lorean, who was a long-time General Motors executive, commented in an interview in 1979 that "the system has a different morality as a group than the people do as individuals," permitting it, for instance, to "tamper with the democratic process of government through illegal political contributions." Quoted in Herman, Edward S., *Corporate Control, Corporate Power*, Cambridge, UK: Cambridge Univ. Press, 1981, p. 259.

74

works and approved voting records, just as companies owe their continued existence to pleasing their investors.

Thus, unchecked economics, seeking only efficiency, steadily erodes the publicly-supported political structure just as irrigation water steadily erodes and dismantles its essential, man-made channels, which may be repaired and re-adjusted or not, according to preference.[20] But today, the relative power and influence of the corporate giants has so increased that the once scarcely-conceivable opinion, first ventured little more than three decades ago, that the nation-state system of the West, led by the United States, is steadily being displaced by multinational corporate power and functions, no longer surprises anyone.[21]

Yet, surely, anyone can think of public purposes that could not, or would not -- because of their inherent unprofitability -- be well-served by private companies without public subsidy or oversight. The dogmatic corporatist claim that pure business competition alone will lead to a just and amply-supplied society simply cannot be taken very seriously by community-minded people. Further, it is reasonable to assume that unaccountable corporate power tends to corrupt private and public institutions, and that it tries to undo government's crucial ability to function, not primarily for public-spirited reasons, but mostly to gain selfish advantage. The chips must then fall on the hapless citizen public where they may.

Irresponsible wielders of corporate power want, above all, to maximize their own competitive situations, to minimize the risk of losing even part of the time in struggles over policy, and to avoid expending the resources available from economic production for any other purposes besides the promotion of gross economic increase and its elite accoutrements. In other words, the present-day corporatists' singular real objective and their means are consistent: through unchecked competition, to foster the survival of the strongest units at the dependent public's expense. They blindly rationalize that the public's sacrifices will be more than made up. Herbert Spencer would have cheered.

---

20. See Ostrogorski, *ibid.*, p. 92. Corporate executives, partly in recognition of their too-frequent "revolving door" relations with regulatory agencies, in effect often applying public money to achieve private purposes, have been described as America's "commissars". See Harrington, Michael, "Corporate Collectivism: A System of Social Injustice," in De George, Richard J., and Joseph A. Pichler., eds., *Ethics, Free Enterprise, and Public Policy*, N.Y.: Oxford Univ. Press, 1978, p. 251.

21. For instance, see Modelski, *loc. cit.*

Conversely, Albert Einstein, a man who is reputed to have grasped the notion of efficiency in nature, nevertheless anguished over the steady erosion of public spirit by rampant vested interests in Germany near the end of the Weimar Republic in the early 1930s. In his writings, he quoted Nietzsche's remark that "only individuals have a sense of responsibility." And, realizing the absolute need for a balance of purposes in human society, he declared it "the chief duty of the State to protect the individual and give him the opportunity to develop into a creative personality."[22] Modern corporations, nearly everyone would agree, have earned their place; yet, though powerful self-maximizing agents, they voluntarily claim no responsibility whatever to the individual or the multitude per se.

As a result, it is plain that if America is ever going to recover the admittedly fortuitous, long-embattled, but durable balance of economic and social priorities that literally made it a society worth dying for in the recent past, we must find a way to bring corporate behavior back under the mutually-defensive aegis of public law. Until that event happens, Einstein's humane vision will no longer be possible for society's many, and public values and human resources will be continually and systematically deprioritized. In the meantime, it appears certain that sociologist Anthony Giddens' observation that "the more a worker comes close to being an appendage of a machine, the more he or she ceases to be a human agent" will become increasingly more apt in America instead.[23]

Of course, not every member of the large business community favors large business domination of public policy. Businessmen at all levels can certainly also be community-spirited and content to accept their place as responsible co-citizens with the rest of the nation. Many businessmen deplore special influence and avoid compromised practices. As is the case with any group, pro- and anti-social alike need to live under the benevolent authority of a common law in order for the community to operate most advantageously.

Businessman Robert Hessen, in his 1979 book *In Defense of the Corporation*, holds that "people rightly fear that corporations, alone or in

---

22. Einstein, Albert, *The World As I See It*, ('Mein Weltbild', transl. by Alan Harris), N.Y.: Philosophical Library, 1979, pp. vi., 57.
23. Giddens, *Profiles and Critiques in Social Theory, op. cit.*

76

clusters, can exercise political power and manipulate the government in order to obtain special favors and privileges at the expense both of other companies and consumers; [and] corporate power is to be feared only when it involves attempts to secure favors and achieve results that could never be obtained in a free market." He concludes, I think laudably, that "there is no justification for allowing any private individual or business organization, including corporations of any size, to achieve its goals by means of political power. ...Economic power is the only power that corporations, large or small, should be able to wield in a capitalist system."[24]

In a similar vein, General Motors President Thomas Murphy observed that "our society ... has some situations which bear upon the health and welfare of both the individual and the general populace where regulation of some sort is not only desirable but absolutely necessary. ...Government regulation of business, or of any other activity, becomes objectionable only when that regulation is excessive and unwarranted."[25] The only remaining question, then, is whether the businesses to be regulated should be permitted to finally decide for the society whether its regulation standards are excessive or warranted.[26]

The key participants in the process of stalemating the publicly accountable power of government under the finely-flawed American constitutional system I am describing can be grouped into at least six broad categories.

---

24. Hessen, Robert, *In Defense of the Corporation*, Stamford, CT: Hanover Institution Press, 1979, pp. 110-111.
25. Murphy, Thomas A., "The Distressing Relationship Between Government and Business," in Gatti, James F., ed., *The Limits of Government Regulation*, N.Y.: Academic Press, 1981, p. 135.
26. There have also been cases of business leaders opposing publicly-irresponsible power on principle, yet buckling when the chips were down. For instance, Roger Blough, Chairman of U.S. Steel, once wrote that the leaders of giant labor unions spend much of their time trying to influence "how over-all society should manage its affairs. ...People become wary of too much power;" see Blough, Roger M., *Free Man and the Corporation*, N.Y. McGraw-Hill, 1959, pp. 62-63; Also: "In a free society, there is no other way than the voluntary corporate way" (p. 123). Blough's voluntary restraint in agreeing to hold back steel prices for a time in the early '60s at the request of President Kennedy is legend.

First, there are those who possess political skills among the leading wealthy and well-connected industrialists and financiers themselves. They are often the current heads of prominent old families whose names are recognizable to the public. Commonly, their own direct political involvement extends to their active membership on one or more of the highly-prestigious and influential "nonpartisan," quasi-governmental advisory councils or committees, such as Business Council and Business Roundtable.[27]

But today, unlike earlier times when men like Andrew Carnegie and J. Pierpont Morgan personally dominated the management of great business enterprises they had founded, the functions of management and effective control (traditionally called "rights of ownership") normally are exercised by highly-paid, specialized chief executive officers and boards. Many of these leading executives, as individuals, actually own little, if any, of their company's stock. These people, who are in effect the top employees of the corporate world and serve only during "good behavior," now exert, indisputably, the most influence on the ongoing, collective policy of the enormously powerful American business establishment.[28]

These top management people are, thus, surrogates of the rightful owners. And they manage what Galbraith has, in all seriousness, referred to as the American business "planning system" comprising the nation's largest and most powerful companies. The top strata of management operate politically through financial relationships with political specialists who are, in effect, also paid surrogates of the politically-interested companies. Surrogates of this description include, among significant others, people in public office at all levels.[29] This de facto "planning system" is much better able to succeed politically inside the country now than ever before, for two related reasons. First, as noted at the start of this chapter, the financial and organizational means of their long-time organizational rivals (labor, municipal, and agricultural organizations, etc.) has faded very much due to the structural effect on employment

27. Domhoff, *ibid.*, pp. 131-32.
28. See Kristol, Irving, *The Public Interest*, quoted in Cox, Allen, *The Cox Report on the American Corporation*, N.Y.: Delacorte, 1982, p. v.; Galbraith, *ibid*, pp. 86 ff; Berle, *Power Without Property*, p. 153. Berle (1959) concluded that the corporate organization in the U.S. was then still "actually controlled" by "the public consensus" in many respects.
29. Galbraith, *ibid.*, pp. xvii., 1-9, discusses the concept of the planning system, which he, in fact, had introduced previously.

patterns of the massive influx of the revolutionary new technology. And second, the nation's techno-structure, developed and operated principally by large business, gives that ownership sector a decided edge over opposition groups in initiating and employing new technical capabilities. These new capabilities include a goodly number, as we will see, that lend themselves to gaining control over the ill-defined, and hence particularly susceptible, American electoral system.

In no area of life is Jacques Ellul's claim that "technology represents a center of polarization for all 20th-century mankind, and that technology feeds on everything that people can want, try, or dream," more true than in modern politics.[30] Hence, the corporate community's agents in the American electoral system at present are mostly not employees of the companies themselves, but independent technical specialists with a refined and highly valuable service to sell.

These agents work as middlemen to establish mutually-rewarding alliances. Their clients are, on the one hand, politicians (who are also usually ideologues to at least a certain extent themselves) and, on the other, well-heeled interest groups of a familiar stripe that can provide the necessary sophisticated organizational skills, financial help, and political feedback for the candidate selected to best represent their agenda. Without large doses of such institutional help, most high-level campaigns quickly bomb, their messages never reaching the public.

Major business interests are, obviously, not the only organized interests to be taken on as clients by the small number of highly-touted, technically advanced specialist agencies. But nowadays, as I have already indicated, the large corporate interests far outdistance any potential rivals on the scene in their seasoned ability to judge and pay for performance, provide useful contacts, and render technical assistance. Hence, it is they who are best able to retain and equip the superstar organizations in this small, extremely highly motivated field.

Voluntarily declaring a principled truce and leaving the nationwide electoral system free of competitive, muscled vested-interest influence would pose an unacceptable level of risk to both the wealthy institutional clients and the most competitive and best-connected candidates. Competition for influence in managing the informally-structured system of national leadership selection is too great for the rival interests to forego maximum involvement on their own behalf. Hence, at least four

---

30. Ellul, Jacques, *The Technological System*, (transl. by Joachim Neugroschel), N.Y.: Continuum, 1980, p. 209.

major categories of surrogates are heavily involved on behalf of large corporate interests and other special interest groups.

Perhaps the single most powerful category of political technicians are the specialized pollsters, who are able at present to do far more than simply inform a candidate for Congress or the Presidency where he or she lags and where to concentrate his or her resources. Pat Caddell, the chief pollster for a number of surprisingly successful recent Democratic campaigns (including that of Jimmy Carter in 1976 and Gary Hart's dramatic rise from a pack of also-rans in 1984), has openly lamented the enormous power he and his peers wield in the electoral process. "We [the tiny cadre of top candidate pollsters] have pre-empted the political system," he stated flatly in an interview some years ago. "We decide who are the best and most likely people to be successful, and so we have contributed to the decline of political parties [as the self-constituted selectors of candidates]. I'm not sure it's healthy at all, and it's a question that bothers me greatly."

What sorts of candidates do these high-percentage pollsters, who are rightfully regarded as high tech wizards of virtually-assured success, either in nomination and attendant influence or election itself, pick to back in building their solid, winning reputations? "We look for people," says Pat Caddell, "who give quick and often facile answers. People who look good on TV and who can project the kinds of messages we want to project. Whether or not they understand them is a different question. ...We don't look for people who have deep, thoughtful, complex and complicated approaches to life, because we wouldn't be able to put them on TV. ...We determine who shall run for office."[31]

What kind of messages do pollsters, often employed as operatives also of another kind (i.e., image designers), look for candidates to project? Messages of potential popular winners, to be sure. But, more importantly, messages that will suit a sufficiently wealthy, interested body of contributors ideologically and convince them that the candidate can and probably will win and thus multiply, rather than liquidate, their carefully apportioned, high-stakes investment. Popular appeal can then be, to a very amazing extent, engineered.

---

31. Pat Caddell, from an interview with journalist Edwin Graham, quoted and discussed in Perry, Roland, *Hidden Power, The Programming of the President*, N.Y.: Beaufort Books, 1984, pp. 175-76, 230 (both preceding quotes).

Once the acknowledged champion at this sort of political game, Caddell seems, in the business/finance-dominated '80s, to have more than met his match the person of candidate Ronald Reagan's pollster Richard Wirthlin, with his almost infinitely-refined PINS computer simulation program, *20 years* in the making.

The basic idea behind PINS was to telephone at intervals several hundred likely voters in every congressional district in the country, starting literally years before the targeted election. The extensive, specialized interview team was to record, through a series of friendly and relaxed, anonymous, half-hour calls at regular intervals to the same carefully-chosen households, what virtually every sort of voter everywhere was thinking about every conceivable issue and trend: What they would want a leader to be like, to look like, to say, what definitely not to say. Then, computerized public profiles were to be created for each telecommunications media market in the country and the candidate to be briefed accordingly, with continuous, pinpoint updates. In other words, the right candidate could be *unfailingly* cast, scripted, and edited. That was the idea.

An ideal candidate for such a sophisticated electoral-management system would thus be able to assume and adeptly perform a subtly-different role conforming to varying shades of expectation and concern in any state or part of any state, involving any special type of audience, over local or nationwide media or in person. The selected, closest-possible-to-ideal candidate could be specially scripted to appeal without fail, and necessarily without specifics, to a majority of the likely voters wherever his or her managers, consulting Wirthlin's accurate profiles, had knowingly scheduled an appearance.

A man of glib, earthy, slightly-humorous sayings, seasoned, yet with cameo good-looks and charm, disgusted with failed and expensive government bureaucracy but not boring anyone with too many details. An apparently-warm man with a seemingly-natural aura of glamour whom people had observed in a relaxed mode for years. This was the man of the clear majority in 1980 and, after an apparent turn-around from an early severe recession, again in 1984.

Wirthlin, of course, knew all of this very well. His simulation model was so accurate that, in 1980, when most respected nationwide polls found the presidential race too close to call, Wirthlin confidently called it precisely to the percentage point. His prediction was based on closely-monitored and controlled long-term trends of preference, and made several days before the election. Two years later, out of more than five hundred congressional and gubernatorial seats being contested, he was able, using his advanced monitoring of trends, to correctly predict the winner in all but three contests.[32]

Wirthlin's team, the Reagan team of campaign managers, were, strangely enough, preceded in their essential strategy by the managers serving the successful Whig candidate for president in 1840, the weathered but dignified-looking old Indian fighter William Henry Harrison. These managers ordered this hand-picked old General to say nothing, but instead, to let local Whig advance men everywhere tell the people what they wanted to hear and arrange flashy parades dominated by popular symbols such as 26-star flags, hard cider barrels, and log cabins. Harrison thus won 80% of the electoral vote; Reagan captured 91% in 1980.[33]

Media advertisers are the third category of high-level American political surrogates. In modern America, we are surrounded by the glitsy, beguiling art of commercial advertising, now subtly or profoundly enhanced by still-rapidly-advancing video techniques as well as trendy folk themes, much as medieval men and women were surrounded and daily imposed upon by their saints and icons.[34] The reason we are so put-upon (as well as amused, etc.) is that we so overwhelmingly respond. Quite obviously, no united group of interests manages to have its political candidates advertised to the American public more successfully or skillfully than large business interests. They have beyond comparison the most and the most-successful experience at screening and hiring effective media promotion. They, uniquely, know how to sell to their public. And it shows in the qualitative difference in the national parties' political ads.

A fourth, indispensable type of surrogate for leading special interest groups in the electoral process is, of course, their chosen *candidate*. A candidate so honored can, as we have seen, now be subtly programmed to convey successfully the most advantageous and reassuring messages, as well as to remain silent on a great many important agreed points. One must keep in mind that the grossly underspecified formal, Constitution-based system does not require a candidate for president to do anything more to acquaint voters with his or her qualifications, ideas, or habits of

---

32. Perry, *ibid.*, pp. 191, 226.
33. See Smith, Page, *The Nation Comes of Age, A People's History of the Ante-Bellum Years*, N.Y.: McGraw-Hill, 1981, p. 180 ff.
34. Schudson, Michael, "Advertising Says 'Let Us Feel Good About Ourselves'", *U.S. News & World Report*, Jan 28, 1985, p. 62.

thought than meet simple filing deadlines in order to appear on the ballot.

I will explore the implied fertile vacuum of guidelines and procedures in the law and suggest a possible remedy in Chapter 7. For now, let us simply ponder one basic question: Does it seem likely that any major *company* in the United States would permit serious, competing candidates for any of its top executive positions to set the entire agenda and timetable for all appearances during the time of consideration, to routinely turn aside the directors' vital concerns with a line or a joke, or to select the company's handful of interviewers personally on the basis of congeniality and mild repute? And if so, *under what conditions?* Such has, in fact, been precisely the lot of America's legal sovereigns, the nation's voters, in all recent presidential elections.

A fifth, irregular type of surrogate for special business and related interests would seem to be the so-called political "new elite" at the grass-roots level, as ably identified and described by political author David Lebedoff. Its members are identified as combination party stalwarts and arrogant, local-level caucus leaders and participants who favor decision-making by moderately educated, specialized technicians and mid- to lower-eschelon managers from the ranks of business and government like themselves. Therefore, they attempt to block wide participation at the precinct and district convention levels by introducing needlessly tedious rules and procedures. Generally, these para-professional, self-anointed local operatives tend to ignore public voter preferences expressed in their party's primaries, unless the local results favor those whom higher wisdom and endorsements from appropriate interests indicate should be nominated.[35]

To the extent that the six types of specialists described here continue to succeed in deleting the vastly greater public from the deliberative electoral process, our nation will continue to lose the fruits of its Constitutional birthright. Predictably, participatory democracy, since the beginning of the still unanswered new *diastolic*, high-tech revolution, has receded yet further toward the status of a polite sophistry, an

---

35. A conspicuous example of this sort of behavior occurred in the Wisconsin Democratic nominating process in 1984, when the more limited and tedious caucus procedure reversed the win by candidate Gary Hart in the slightly earlier state primary and awarded *almost all* of the state's national convention delegates to Walter Mondale. For a more thorough description of the so-called "new elite" operating in politics, see Lebedoff, *loc. cit.*

objectively-meaningless word to pose against diabolical socialism in rhetoric.

- The Two-Part Corporatist Objective: 1 -

The political objective of the *corporatists* in America (those who favor control over our political system and discretionary allocation of our nation's entire stock of resources by mega-scale private business) is to produce at all costs what have been called "facilitations" for the business sector. Facilitations sought politically can take the form of either immediately and directly improved profitability, or enhanced conditions for assured efficiency to lead to improved profitability.[36] While there is often disagreement on details of policy among corporatists, since the situations of even the largest of business interests greatly differ, they tend to strongly favor any measures that will further these two permanent goals, especially the first. And they generally oppose as one *any* measure that disfavors or detracts from these two goals, regardless of other merit. The efficiency of income production is the main point, because it suits both the short-term and longer-term goal of the corporatist political program and the perceived interest of the corporatists themselves.

It is important to realize that the problem with the single, compound objective, which is assuredly advantageous and desirable to a considerable degree in and of itself, is that, once adopted as national policy, it excludes all other definite goals as economically inefficient and therefore unworthy ciphers unremuneratively claiming a share of the system's capital funds. The corporatists claim to believe, based on the blindest and most forgetful of known faiths, that all legitimate social goals can be achieved by the American (and world!) public simply by reasonably turning society's most valuable resources and its future solely over to *them* and relinquishing responsibility.[37]

---

36. Jacques Ellul, *ibid.*, pp. 111-117, introduces the term "facilitations" and discusses its ultimate implications. Berle, *Power Without Property*, p. 90, cites efficiency and profitability as the systemic goals of American business.

37. Galbraith, *ibid.*, p. 117, makes this point. I am reminded of an episode in Brazilian author Machado de Assis' 1883 story translated as "The Devil's Church," in a book by the same name (Austin: Univ. of Texas Press, 1984), in which the devil reinstates avarice as a virtue and proclaims it the "mother of economy".

This sole corporatist objective of facilitating the growth of large-scale business, applied politically, produces a single-criterion program that *must* promise to meet all of society's needs through the operation of the unregulated competitive marketplace, because it has nothing else to offer. As long as large business interests face effective political competition from a mix of other interests roughly as resourceful as themselves, a pluralistic mix of blended and mutually-enhanced outcomes can result in the construction of true public policy. Under such balanced social-political conditions, the business viewpoint's leading contribution, tempered by others, is critical to our national well-being. But if the business interests are somehow either discredited and vanquished, as has happened in certain doctrinaire socialist states like Ethiopia, *or* manage to dominate competing interests under a captured system of representation in the United States, the results are bound to be dangerous for society.

A relevant question posed to Americans again today is the accuracy of the corporatists' claims that the unfettered marketplace will take good care of everything, or, to state it slightly differently, the question of the validity of the corporate oligopoly's interpretation of the public good. Economist Milton Friedman has made the point, citing as an example Henry Ford's financial support of an anti-Semitic newspaper, that a given corporate chief executive officer's notion of social responsibility will not necessarily conform either to the general public's view or its interest.[38] Surely, the net public value of an unbridled corporatist program, or anything very close, should be more than suspect. One primary objective of American government should, indeed, be the facilitation of economic growth; but probably not at the cost, even in circumstances up to and including imminent national emergency, of the public's ultimate control, under public law, over all sectors of society, no matter how wealthy or advantageous. For therein lies our hope of maintaining an open society in the United States.

I believe it is eminently arguable that much of the productivity and public spirit that has been increasingly lost in this country to a syndrome

---

38. In dismissing the insistence of corporate critics that business corporations should balance their profit motives with social purposes, Friedman cited Henry Ford's financing of the Dearborn *Independent*, an anti-Semitic newspaper, as one business leader's notion of social responsibility. See Friedman, Milton, in Friedman and Eli Goldston, a dialog, "'Responsible' Corporation: Benefactor or Monopolist?" *Fortune*, 88:56, Nov. 1973.

of personal alienation and isolation, leading to such social problems as pandemic chemical dependence and the all-but-complete lack of respect for public authority, is yet recoverable. It might well be that these values could be substantially recovered by restoring the prospect of meaningful, pervasive, candidly informed public participation and universal accountability, starting with the national electoral process.[39]

The inability of America's great corporate interests to act reliably in the public interest, apart from the sanction of unblocked, democratic law, can be clearly discerned from other vantage points besides Friedman's concerning the eccentricities of individuals and cliques. Thomas Jefferson identified one aspect of the current problem more than a century and half ago. He observed, in a blunt manner uncharacteristic of necessarily-compromised politicians in our present system, that "merchants have no country of their own. ...All they are interested in is the source of their profits [and] the mere spot they stand on does not constitute so strong an attachment as that from which they draw their gain."[40]

If such was the case in Jefferson's time, it is without a doubt equally true today, in an age more or less dominated by multinational businesses. President Eisenhower made this same essential point in a speech in Rio de Janeiro shortly before bowing out, back in 1960: "Capital is a curious thing with perhaps no nationality. It flows where it is served best."[41] U.S. companies rarely remove manufacturing operations to Thailand or Mexico in order to aid any other Americans besides themselves, however skillfully they may argue that it would have that effect. As I will try to explain in brief a few pages farther on, no country, including our supposedly democratic one, can long afford, even from a strictly economic standpoint, to allow the single-criterion corporatist program to rule and transform its society. Technostructural input into national decision making is quite obviously indispensable, but in no wise requires the heavy expense of voiding other, albeit less wealthy and aggressive, elements of

---

39. I am bothered by Richard J. Barnet and Ronald E. Muller's point in *Global Reach, The Power of the Multinational Corporations*, (N.Y.: Simon & Schuster, 1974, p. 348), that "no government dedicated to steady, spectacular economic growth as the prime tool for maintaining social peace can afford to take a tough line with big business," only to the extent that I question the consistency of such a tool with the reality of a democratic society.

40. Thomas Jefferson, quoted in Barnet and Muller, *ibid.*, pp. 77, 307.

41. Dwight D. Eisenhower, quoted in Barnet and Muller, *ibid.*, p. 77.

the society in favor of a specially-imposed, all-consuming single-criterion strategy to empower and clandestinely subsidize American-based multinationals. Just to start with, we cannot afford the monumental economic losses *this* "competitive" national strategy continually entails.

The question of how American society was induced to relinquish its effective legal control over large-scale American business is apropos, and can be answered from two vantage points earlier in our history.

First, as I have already suggested, the procedural gap in the formally mandated electoral process has permitted powerful and well-organized interests to dominate when such interests grew strong enough to wield inordinate influence. (I will demonstrate later that the founding fathers probably could not have designed a way to prevent this most mundane of eventualities, while we probably can).

The second front of public authority's slippage was no doubt strongly influenced by the progressive effect of the Constitutional deficiency in point on the perennial character of national leadership. This front of public retreat was the gradual accession by the states, and acquiescence at the federal level, to the argument of the assumed general utility of corporations. Accordingly, the public purpose criterion for corporations was permitted to wane and disappear altogether, rather than placing the hundreds of new, national-scale, and eventually multinational corporate entities, starting in the 19th century, under broad, adequately strong federal jurisdiction. The states, it is true, would have lost much of their lucrative licensing business if the latter course had been followed.[42] But, in the final analysis, the now cosmically-answerable public officials in charge at the time were simply willing to swallow the early corporatists' arguments.

George Cabot Lodge, confronting this fact in his 1975 book, comments that "we can only marvel at how completely our faith in the ability of the corporate structure by itself to undertake economic action for the good of the community obscured and obliterated the procedures for making that

---

42. Hurst, *ibid.*, p. 110. Currently, over 50 percent of the 500 largest U.S. corporations are legally chartered to operate by the singularly permissive, tiny state of Delaware, which most of them dwarf in terms of means and budget. Under the sponsorship of Senators Joseph O'Mahoney and William Borah, the idea of federal licensing of companies engaged in interstate commerce came fairly close to Senate passage in the late 1930s, before being eclipsed by events leading into World War II. See Hawley, Ellis W., *The New Deal and the Problem of Monopoly*, Princeton Univ. Press, 1971, pp. 371-72, 427n.

structure legitimate."[43] Jacques Ellul identifies the corporations' mystique in successfully appealing for immunity from sanctions as their appeal to the common idea of progress toward achieving "wants" and "dreams" and urging the extreme fragility of progress, within a technologically attuned society. This sequence has led, dreamlike, to what Ellul has called the technological system's "self-augmentation" within the broader social context.[44]

Michael Harrington complained that what he perceived as an unwritten political rule to the effect that "government shall on all major decisions maximize corporate priorities" defines, in his own phrase, a "hidden agenda." In order for such a policy criterion to really be legitimate, he contends, it would have to be posed honestly to the public as the platform of a major party, to be voted up or down.[45] The winning, corporatist campaigns of the '80s instead focused on tax cuts treated as welfare payments to the masses, when in fact large, overwhelmingly-corporate investors (direct buyers of million-dollar-plus denomination guaranteed-rate high-interest bonds) were the only true, net winners. Meanwhile, the mass of citizens were quietly burdened, perhaps permanently, on an ever-revolving basis, with history's heaviest bill.

It is very obvious that corporate interests suffer defeat on issues from time to time, though very rarely now. Commonly cited examples of measures passed despite the heavily-financed objections of at least part of the corporate community include stringent water quality standards, auto and job safety standards, strong (though perhaps not very well-enforced) strip-mining legislation, and an end to government subsidies for supersonic transport construction.[46] These particular measures were all passed when the national public consensus on the rapidly worsening threat to our total environment, and hence ourselves, still translated into

---

43. Lodge, George C., *The New American Ideology*, N.Y.: Knopf, 1975, pp. 139-140; he concludes (p. 141) that "today what legitimacy the corporation has derives principally from its own self-perpetuating management..." I strongly suspect that the general public would go farther than Lodge does in granting corporations legitimacy per se.
44. Ellul, *ibid.*, p. 209.
45. Harrington, *ibid.*, p. 50.
46. See Domhoff, *ibid.*, p. 130.

an effective national political consensus for environmental maintenance. On the other hand, corporate campaigns at the time strongly *opposed* these pro-public measures that are still today generally believed to be in the public's best interest. This suggests that a fair share of the corporate sector's still-growing list of successful political efforts, especially the broad effort to permanently remove itself from the rigors and necessary costs of public oversight that it has long tended to view as harassment, might serve to oppose and defeat the public interest. Responsibility without accountability, we are finally seeing revealed, is tripe.

- The Two-Part Corporatist Objective: 2 -

John D. Rockefeller III, in his mid-1970s book supporting broad community decision-making on matters affecting the community, reminds us that, while "an authoritarian system is often more efficient for the accomplishment of specific tasks in the short run..., a heavy price can be paid for short-term efficiency in a loss of creativity, a build-up of resentment, a weakening of initiative." He concludes, in a practical vein, that "democracy works better in a dynamic and changing situation," where an open procedure for eliciting public support can accomplish more than the harsh law of the jungle toward producing the long-term stability needed for confidence and growth.[47] Which is precisely the same thing Madison concluded.[48]

But today's newly-fortified corporatist operatives and surrogates do not afford themselves the "luxury" of viewing society broadly or objectively. It is now evident that they are far advanced in establishing their blindered, single-criterion program in the law, and have perhaps already weakened popular government to the extent that it will be unable by reason of institutional incapacity and budgetary commitments, almost regardless of election outcomes, to compromise their cherished interests and exemptions from oversight or claim any sizable share of society's once-discretionary wealth for public purposes. The inevitable *systolic* reaction to regain broad, general access to tangible benefits may, when it comes, shake the now multiply-plundered American system to its core. The first prerequisite for a relatively gentle and beneficial

---

47. Rockefeller, John D. 3rd, *The Second American Revolution, Some Personal Observations*, N.Y.: Harper & Row, 1973, p. 171.
48. See Madison, *Federalist 52.*

completion of the revolutionary socioeconomic cycle we are now unexpectedly experiencing is for the public to see through the imperfectly made-up corporatist rhetoric referring to anarchy as democracy and to large corporations as freedom-loving individuals. Then, this century may end in somewhat the same way it began: with a thoughtful step back from "robber baron" law. But we may find it impossible to extricate ourselves from one-sector tyranny this time without finally curing the Constitution's unfortunate practical silence on executive selection.

One political goal of the corporate interests, in their newly-productive effort to create a situation conducive to unlimited profit taking and long-term control of investments, is, as we have already seen, to control the mechanism of the state in order to neutralize its remaining capacity for regulatory action. Another, longer-term goal, only recently possible in reality, is to disassemble the central government's machinery for most purposes, in effect causing an artificial and public-mystifying return to the mythologized pre-societal stage that both Locke and Rousseau called the "state of nature."

The corporatists' appeal to limitless "free enterprise" as a patriotic American virtue epitomizes this amazing ideological plunge. William Simon, a well-known economist and former Treasury Secretary, has been an eloquent spokesman for the notion that the technostructural element (or *diastolic*) is single-handedly responsible for the development of positive, distinctly American values. "The material abundance, the freedoms of choice, the opportunities for meaningful work are all largely the result of the creativity and productivity of our free and competitive economic system," he has written. "This is the crucial theme that must be communicated to all Americans until they understand it." He adds to this the not-insignificant insight that "the Soviet system provides much less for its people. They must turn to the U.S. ... for our technology and capital," and concludes, impeccably, that the "crucial factor has been our national commitment to liberty and personal dignity."[49]

It should be noted that while the lifestyle preferences Simon expresses certainly ring true, they are not attainable or defensible by the Spartan,

---

49. Simon, William E., "Government Regulation and a Free Society," in Gatti, ed., *ibid.*, p. 63.

90

purely-muscular means he prescribes. The vision of democracy he seeks to communicate is that it is more a self-evident function of the marketplace, of voting by consumers among commercial and job choices posed by a sovereign industrial and financial sector, than of the free and decisive voting booth. His vision of an industrial open society ignores which of the desirable elements actually came first and produced the other.

Philosopher Karl Popper warns in his book supporting the Western open-society concept that this sort of appeal for single-minded commercial autonomy and sovereignty has a long line of antecedents. Referring to the situation of early 19th-century Britain, Popper reminds us that "using the slogan equal and free competition for all, the unrestrained capitalism of this period resisted successfully all labour legislation until the year 1833, and its practical execution for many years more. The consequence was a life of desolation and misery which can hardly be imagined in our day."[50]

America also has its own squalid history of sweatshops and abstemious wages to recall. The American term "free enterprise," to denote the same sort of ungoverned capitalism, appears to have originated as part of the late 19th-century neo-Darwinian theory of the social economy. Its subscribers' concept of society has been said to go very much like this: "We'll all engage in competition, a war of all against all, and some of us will do better and some of us will survive; others will do worse and won't survive. That's tough and that's all there is to it. Of course, the majority will not survive." The author of this summation, Irving Kristol, notes that "the majority, on the whole, thought that this was not a very good way to live, that human society should not be so constituted under the law of the jungle."[51] Hence, the effective political practice of corporatism would seem to require an uncommonly large measure of public deception in place of candor concerning its real objectives. If the truth be told, a democratic society is unlikely to consciously select unmitigated single-interest domination.

Yet corporatists, perhaps owing to a sort of no-nonsense naivete, often seem to be genuinely mystified by continued opposition to their more extreme views in the United States. John Hospers, in an article entitled

---

50. Popper, *ibid.*, p. 122.
51. Kristol, Irving, "A Capitalist Conception of Justice," in De George and Pichler, eds., *ibid.*, p. 63.

"Free Enterprise as the Embodiment of Justice," notes, in much the same vein as William Simon, that "many people, who are its beneficiaries, rail against it; yet it has provided more people with a high standard of living than any other system ever devised by man. ...When no restrictions are placed on these things [i.e., liberty to think, to invent, to produce, to trade], the ingenuity of man knows no bounds."[52] Yet, the point is missed here, too that the undoubted *diastolic* benefits mentioned must accrue, if they are long to continue as benefits, within the context of an entire, still-sovereign society.

Corporatists once in power strive to exclude informed public participation from actual decision-making by obscuring policy choices, to preserve their much-understated, strong and uncompromising one-track purpose. It has been pointed out that, because of the particularly-specialized nature of the regime's program, even other types of formerly competent specialists, besides friendly, corporatist economists, were also excluded from the policy circles of the corporatist Reagan administration. And the main policy tendencies of that administration are being determinedly continued. Noting the corporatist state's tendency to dismiss all other goals as impertinent, or at least not pertinent enough to fund, Galbraith explained that "that is why its affirmation [i.e., that of profit maximization] is so necessary for holding discussion of corporate behavior within the ambit of the economist. That is why it is so urgently defended."[53] That is why the question inevitably asked in the just-ended, and yet very much still-breathing administration, was whether a practice would result in corporate enhancement, or in net cost. One need not exaggerate to say that only corporatist real policies have been pushed through to adoption of late, since single-mindedness reigns.

Back before 1930, Spanish social philosopher Jose Ortega y Gasset decried the new breed of specialized technicians whom he recognized already as the group most likely to exercise power over society throughout the 20th century. He objected to their then-increasing influence because he realized that, by themselves, they tended to share only the same narrow and limited gamut of wordly knowledge on which

---

52. Hospers, John, "Free Enterprise as the Embodiment of Justice," in De George and Pichler, eds., *ibid.*, pp. 70-71.

53. Galbraith, *loc. cit.*

to draw. Yet, they were supremely confident, Ortega concluded, because they were so naive: Hence, he felt, they would be doubly-dangerous as leaders.[54]

The implication that others, not technical specialists of like training and experience, were, consequently, unable to judge modern policy questions, served, in the Spaniard's opinion, as a ruse to enhance their own social worth. In fact, it could hardly be denied that all the rest of society combined is immeasurably more knowledgeable and able in general to determine broad questions of public concern than a strata of narrowly-trained, thoughly like-minded specialists, who no doubt should be looked upon as helpful technical advisors to the public and its duly-elected officials, but not as policy overlords.

The American founding fathers' hard-won and much-celebrated Constitutional safeguards, to which I have made ample reference already, are simply inoperable inside a closed room of like-minded individuals. In fact, if the national government is effectively rendered docile and safe in order to rid corporate power of an irritating and costly adversary, the procedural safeguards in the Constitution (especially, a real and operable separation of powers) will not be available to provide the public recourse or safety in any situation. And the result, as Madison noted, must necessarily be unmitigated tyranny, achieved by what would be properly seen as a *regression* from progressive, civilized order marked by pluralistic cooperation, into a pre-social-contract "state of nature," marked by public powerlessness. As a preventive for this sort of dire circumstance, Madison explicity urged "controlling" by law the "factions" that could otherwise manage to monopolize the system.[55]

Meanwhile, the customary "revolving door" for interested top corporate managers into key bureaucratic posts and back again has long helped keep all that remains of independent government economic policy benign: Democrats have their well-known and lesser-known executive retainers, and Republican administrations have theirs.[56]

---

54. Ortega y Gasset, Jose, *The Revolt of the Masses* (1930), anon. authorized transl., N.Y.: Norton, 1957, pp. 110-111. Winston Churchill used to say that "experts should be on tap but never on top;" quoted in an interview by British writer Paul Johnson, *U.S. News and World Report*, March 27, 1989, p. 73.

55. Madison, *Federalist 52*, and *Federalist 10*; Locke, *ibid.*, II: #3, #124.

56. This problem is explored at some length in Lowi, Theordore J., *The End of Liberalism, Ideology, Policy and the Crisis of Public Authority*, N.Y.: Norton, 1969; A shorter discussion is found in Harrington, *ibid.*, p. 51.

Professor John Hospers, whom I cited earlier, like perhaps most "free enterprise" ideologues, believes, with regard to matters of business, that government should simply learn to mind its own, theorizing that there really is no proper role for government in society except "to keep the peace."[57] Non-corporatist writer George Modelski noted that under an actual, purely corporatist administration, "there still would be need for keeping order, for creating and maintaining good corporate citizenship."[58] *Some* corporatists would probably include the creation and maintenance of a mega-scale physical infrastructure -- highways, harbors, etc. -- and perhaps certain, direct subsidies to key industries and emergency wealth transfers, to counter the ravages of "unfair" foreign competition from time to time, as appropriate public contributions to our greatest mediators of wealth. But the vital role in maintaining a background of public order would assuredly top most corporate short lists of government's proper activities. If police or military work were ever to become directly profitable, then the last reason for having a state, in the view of many corporatists, would likewise wither away.

The government's chief role, according to true corporatists, then, is in keeping *all other* sorts of people, both foreign and domestic, respectfully orderly, and in guarding against *their* (i.e. *counterproductive*) violence, while leaving the most powerful and self-aggrandizing units in the largely-emerged new world society ungoverned.

So, then, what are the results for other people of the corporate interests' steadily-growing monopoly on actual power? Social scholar Max Scheler, writing in Europe back in 1912, already perceived a "ruling ethos of industrialism: the exaltation of utility values and instrumental values over vital and organic values." The eventual result for society at large, he found, was a form of alienation, a crippling "*resentiment* of the vitally unfit against the fit, of those who are partially [i.e., functionally] dead against the living!"[59] Jacques Ellul, in the early 1980s, saw within the intensifying concentration on the values and skills of the current advanced technology, a growing marginalization of "countless young, old, and semi-capable people" into economic powerlessness and, by implication, irrelevance for the serious purposes of society.[60]

---

57. Hospers, *ibid.*, p. 70.
58. Modelski, *ibid*, p. 25.
59. Scheler, Max, *Resentiment* (1912), transl. by William W. Holdheim, N.Y.: Schocken, 1972, pp. 162-63.
60. Ellul, *ibid.*, pp. 111 ff.

The new technical virtuosi have, meanwhile, jelled into a new social leadership class marked by an increasingly recognized ability to discern and to cope. These, the apparent savants of the post-modern age, we might reasonably feel obliged to trust to forward our interests.

Yet, if we really hope to regain our collective national health and social coherence at this juncture, people in America of every sort must instead begin to *insist* on applying our own human values and judgments -- which we all, as individuals, know and trust most because they are the values that pertain to our own life experiences and feelings. Far too much these days, we are permitting ourselves to be ruled by omnipresent, mediacast "new age"-type values that, blind to their effect on us personally, are corporately designed and honed to facilitate the operations of mass-marketing machines and amoral sales strategies. Unless I am mistaken, such have precious little to do with conservative American values in the traditional sense.

On a wider scale, we must very soon begin to realize that, instead of representing progress, the new, elite corporatism that is forging its way through politics actually represents a fundamental *regression* of human worth per se. Our ancestors in medieval Europe and elsewhere already had the reality of unlimited knowledge and freedom for the few. To maintain that our founding Revolution was undertaken to achieve such a purpose as that is, at best, a fundamental error. Indeed, corporatist Americans have more in common with the Revolution's loyalists than its much broader-based patriot side on that account. Yet, with our greater economic interdependence, the stakes are perhaps higher and the deceptions more subtle today than in earlier times.

We have seen it amply demonstrated before, in the early American South and in early 19th-century Britain, that pure, unleavened economic power will lead to the enslavement and arbitrary use of human beings to support the ownership rights and freedoms of large-scale economic units. We are seeing this still in South Africa and, Chapter 5 will argue, in the enigmatic Soviet realm today, where power and privilege continue to belong to so few individuals.[61] In our society as well, if broad public

---

61. In the U.S.S.R., productive property is by definition and normal practice a state monopoly, maintained in the name of the public. But what Westerners would think of as rights of ownership, including the right of direction, disposal, allocation, prestige, and other perquisites of economic authority are the monopoly of a small class of state managers. An actual difference is that the Soviet authority structure remains monolithic, whereas that now rapidly emerging basically unchallenged in America is, in most important respects, oligopolistic, with cosmetic and pragmatic concessions still made to the legal and potentially powerful sovereigns, the common and theoretically equal citizenry.

control is systematically rubbed out rather than revitalized, the results will inevitably be tragic.

George F. Will perhaps expressed this point best not too long ago in his daily column: "A society in which the public turns to the dust of mere interests is reduced to hoping the wind will not rise. Prudence requires measures to encourage citizens to be linked by ideas that give public content to the public mind, and give it in a shape and substance that deflect idle winds. ...De Tocqueville warned that individualism 'at first, only saps the virtues of public life; but in the long run it attacks and destroys all others and is at length absorbed in down right selfishness'."[62]

- *Realpolitik*: American-Style -

When Charles Louis de Secondat, Baron of Montesquieu, wrote his *Spirit of Laws* in the 1740s, he argued that the chief officer of the government should, following the earlier English example, be chosen separately from the legislature and not be its member and head, in order to avoid a monolithic tyranny in government. The American founding fathers had read Montesquieu and tended to agree on this point, creating a genuinely powerful but circumscribed American Presidency that became, at least superficially, dependent on popular election.

Thus, the presidential office normally provides the main focus of common attention, consolidated authority, and political direction for the entire society. Not surprisingly, the real and symbolic power of the Presidency has made it the leading target of aspiration for special interest organizations of every sort.

It has, of course, long been the dream of the perennially most-powerful single interest group in the country, a dream reluctantly deferred since the advent of the approximate balance among pluralistic interests back in the 1930s, to have an able spokesman specifically and consistently representing its particular socioeconomic views in the Presidency. Leading business operatives had been watching the political rise of Ronald Reagan and knew that he had for a number of years advocated, with corporate sponsorship, what was essentially their agenda,

---

62. Will, *Statecraft.*, p. 149, quoting Tocqueville, *ibid.*, II, p. 98.

to reduce government's capacity to act and cut away every program requiring governmental action that they saw as detracting from their exclusive objective. By 1980, the rapid, simultaneous fading of rival organized special interests, wrought by the overwhelming structural impact of the new wave of high technology, finally permitted them to realize their dream.

Ronald Reagan became the first true surrogate of large corporate business to occupy the White House at least since the gray dawn of the 1930s, when neither the corporate sector nor the Presidency possessed anything like the pervading power in society of today's versions. Indeed, the change in prevailing social values in the United States since Ronald Reagan's ascension in 1981 has disproven earlier assertions that even the president was now hardly more than a figurehead in the real American system.[63]

Of course, if that assertion had been completely accurate, the interest groups' efforts to secure funds and favor for candidates of their choice would probably never have attained the astonishing level of volume and complexity they have attained. But, in fact, taking advantage of the present, largely extra-Constitutional system of election, the wealthiest corporate interests may be able, now that they can single-handedly hold the stage against their structurally weakened special interest competitors, to screen and propel into the Oval Office a long series of true corporate sector surrogates. With these high-level managers securely in place, they can complete their goal of streamlining the American system, by tuning and systematically factoring out unwanted friction and opposition, over the next several years.

And there is little obvious reason why the now effectively unrivaled major corporate interests should not be able eventually to deftly outbid their comparatively understrength special interest rivals in order to orchestrate the majority of financing and technical support to field candidates from *both* major parties. They could by so doing further reduce the risk of both effective competition and public backlash and lessen substantially the perceived danger of a genuinely public-spirited administration with a broad agenda coming to power. In the meantime, continuing improvement in the technological means available to professional surrogates of major interest groups can only result in still further reducing the public equation in any given nationwide election

---

63. For instance, see Miller, *loc. cit.*

toward that of a quadrennial runoff between ultra-smooth, air-tight video advertising campaigns.

At least outwardly, Ronald Reagan's presidential campaigns embraced the issues of the large, intense constituency of the religious New Right. There is no apparent evidence that this productive alliance cost the candidate, either in 1980 or '84, any support, or drew any public reaction whatever, from the solid corps of gin-sipping Reagan corporatists in the major boardrooms and up along Wall Street.

Significantly, the highly persuasive and lucrative support from this immense, not-necessarily-business-related, new lobbying, financing, and voting group, was answered thereafter mainly by occasional rhetorical flurries from the President and one or two of his subordinates. Items of the so-called Reagan social agenda were somehow never pushed as high-priority objectives by the administration once in office on a level even remotely comparable to the dogged campaigns waged for such *corporatist imperatives* as social spending cuts, the shifting and scattering of programs downward to states and localities, slashing taxes in effect to increase the government's dependence on high-interest borrowing, or elaborate and archane military procurement schemes.[64] Further, the oft-stated hope of actually attaining the so-called Reagan social objectives indirectly, through the Supreme Court appointments that assumably would and did occur in the recent President's second term, still seems speculative at best. That slow, very unsure strategy itself, in fact, seems to fly directly in the face of the fastidious New Right's earlier stated opposition to "judicial legislation" as an anti-democratic means. And, for whatever reason, few if any New Right social activists themselves have appeared on the Supreme Court.

Nevertheless, the effect of candidate programming on dream-candidate Reagan's overall campaign performance was successful to an unsettling degree. The President's one, very memorable, bad performance in his second successful campaign occurred when he briefly deviated from the close, moment-by-moment scripting by his precisely-informed directors. His slip came when he agreed independently, against

---

64. The government's much-fought-for "Baby Jane Rule" seems a curious partial exception. Reagan, it should be remembered, had actually, *supported* abortion as Governor of California. See Evans, Rowland and Robert Novak, *The Reagan Revolution*, N.Y.: Dutton, 1981, pp. 33, 211.

nearly unanimous informed advice, to launch himself into the mostly-controlled tumble of the September, 1984 televised presidential debate against his opponent Walter Mondale. In the course of the debate, the general public gained the eerie sense firsthand for almost the first time ever that this popular public man could not operate publicly without a written script.

With that single, major, nearly-disastrous exception, all other publicly-made statements by the candidate were again, as in 1980, carefully developed and tested for ready acceptance by a high percentage of the audience.[65] Which is not at all to say that Reagan himself lacked principles or bona fide political objectives. On the contrary, his program turned out in practice to *be* the single-criterion program of bottom-line maximization espoused by the corporate community, one-liners and kudos to other strata of society notwithstanding.

It seems virtually inarguable that President Reagan, in line with this exclusive core objective, deliberately created a fiscal crisis in his first term by doubling the national debt within four years, through drastically and suddenly interrupting the government's flow of income. Senator Daniel Patrick Moynahan, for one, openly ventured on various occasions that the President took this dramatic course of action in order to force the abandonment of costly non-business-related programs by severely crippling the government's means to pay its obligations.[66]

But equally important would seem to have been the political motive, because the certain immediate effect of the dramatic action could hardly have gone unforeseen at the White House and in the Treasury Department. The surefire effect politically was that of simultaneously making ecstatic mega-scale financiers, who welcomed the new, enormous and guaranteed high-return opportunity afforded to them, and the vast majority of strugging taxpayers and billpayers, who naively rejoiced in the hidden-purpose gambit of deferring liability on a fearsome scale at soaring interest. The audacity behind that single momentous instance of public deception seems so monumental that the administration surely deserves to be memorialized by it alone. Indeed, the effect is such that the living may never completely recover.

---

65. See Perry, *ibid.*, previous references.
66. Paraphrase from interview with Sen. Moynahan (D - N.Y.), *MacNeil-Lehrer Newshour*, PBS, May 2, 1985.

If such is the character of supply side economics, it seems more than appropriate for the public to ask, from whose sides is the funding to richly and continually supply the new, controlling interests intended to come? From whose hands and into whose hands is roughly the charitable tithe of the nation now annually being compulsorily passed? And, finally, when was the public ever openly urged by *any* corporatist candidate to consider supporting such a compulsory financial sacrifice to giant lenders, in exchange for its loss of accustomed government services? If we continue to find in coming years that we cannot, as a community or as individuals, afford to do much of anything except pay interest on interest to supply effectively sovereign mega-lenders, our home-grown American financial community will no doubt agree to redeem our national credit with another, new government-guaranteed bill-payer loan, payable this time at interest upon interest upon interest, by "we, the people." Hence, the public must, eventually, begin to ask, whatever happened to the government *of*, *by*, and *for* the people that Abraham Lincoln once eulogized? And, more important, how can we get it back?

Congress, in Ronald Reagan's second term, resisted still-deeper cuts in the nation's human resource programs to a much greater extent than the administration expected. Even then, when his gambit to personally decimate the federal government's *systolic* purpose had apparently came up short, the President, conspicuously alone among prominent elected officials, was in no hurry to take positive action aimed at closing the enormous budgetary gap.[67] An additional, not-often-mentioned reason may have been that an original, engendering transfer-of-wealth commitment of Ronald Reagan to background financial institution sponsors was being kept. The evidence for such a notion is still perhaps circumstantial, but certainly not lacking; and a matter of such terrific magnitude and national impact is surely significant enough to bear a bit more careful probing. Undeniably, Secretary Alexander Hamilton's age-old point regarding the utility of a perpetual, heavy national debt to weld the wealthy to the state still has its business community and political advocates. And simple greed still flourishes as well.

---

67. For an instructive account of the handling of an earlier public debt-private windfall crisis, see Schachner, Nathan, *The Founding Fathers*, South Brunswick: Barnes, 1954, pp. 89-91. The present administration's main tendency so far has been to conceal the full size of the annual budget deficit.

The Reagan administration's all-out effort to slash the mandate of every governmental function not directly benefiting the large corporate sector (examples are legion and well-known) clearly demonstrates the application of the single-criterion program. The purpose of this ground-breaking, at first inadvertently-mandated initiative has been precisely two-fold: to free up virtually all available wealth in the society to be funneled into corporate hands as quietly and efficiently as possible, while weakening the public sector's position as a potential competitor for capital. Neither need nor merit in terms purely of human or natural resources was considered of overriding importance, though politics may occasionally have demanded just the tiniest deviation to confound critics.

Instead, it was repeatedly echoed that unleashed "free enterprise" would respond to all genuine needs beyond the level of indigents' bare biological survival. The newly-restricted criterion being imposed was simply that all available money in the society must be channeled to quickly make money. Hence, if a way were found to make subway safety or environmental detoxification directly profitable, these things would have been deemed unquestionably worth doing, and the inflated costs passed along.

The induced shifting of public programs down from the federal to state and local levels was intended to serve two distinct corporatist purposes, and emphatically was not initiated by its corporatist advocates for the purpose of nurturing local-level democracy, as sometimes advertised. Their purposes were instead consistent with the single-criterion objective. First, the actual headquarters and majority of operations of most mega-scale corporations lie within certain large, wealthy states and regions, while the bulk of public assistance and urban problems fall proportionately within other, less-affluent states and localities. Thus, shifting the cost burden downward below the federal level is similar, from the large corporate point of view, to the earlier phenomenon of "white flight" from central cities to more affluent suburbs to escape financial responsibility for maintaining the legally-contained city. In both cases, the burden is shifted much more heavily onto citizens and localities much less able to bear it, an approach *diametrically opposite* to investing in human resources to promote the general welfare. Secondly, shifting the burden of social responsibility downward weakens the federal government as an entity with the potential to threaten the corporate sector's newly-enhanced control over society's purpose and the flow of its wealth. Hence, government assistance programs were ridiculed by the corporatists in the new-style government, as "throwing money at problems." Meanwhile, the tax system's channeling of an endless flood of the public's harder-than-before

101

earned money as a direct windfall to corporations and large financial houses, whose intended use of it was entirely unrelated, was somehow supposed to answer even the most persistent needs of the greater community. We need to stop and ask ourselves whether this is what has resulted.

Not surprisingly, given what we know from earlier experiments of this kind, the most profound results experienced thus far within the heavily-materialistic ambience produced are the economic slippage of the middle class and the further alienation from the economically advantaged community of the relatively less advantaged. Those at the bottom end receive more from private charity now, mostly because their need has grown visibly and shockingly apparent.

With gross profitability the sole focus of the captive government's active attention, the dictum "out of sight, out of mind," once reserved for the overseas poor, became a flesh and blood reality embracing literally millions more unfortunate American citizens than earlier. This was a reality, we were told by the President himself in 1985, shortly following his re-election, that we could "no longer afford" to come to grips with. Meanwhile, corporate profits soared and continued to soar on citizens' re-channeled tax dollars to unprecedented heights and the stock market balooned even while the nation's productivity continued to seriously lag.[68] Such, then, are the main results of the induced, rapidly accelerated erosion of the inconvenient *diastolic/systolic* balance that was deliberately, though imperfectly, woven into our Constitution.

---

68. I mentioned earlier (in Chapter One) the Reagan administration's celebrated unwillingness to carry out previously-mandated toxic waste clean-up legislation by impounding EPA Superfund allocations and sponsoring a policy of internal sabotage within the agency. Perhaps the President continued to willfully believe, in effect, that "trees cause pollution," as he insisted during his 1980 campaign. Additionally, while he is certainly not alone among Presidents in this, his executive orders to mandate activities against enemies of the administration include a blatant 1981 example, permitting the CIA to employ surveilence on U.S. soil, along with the FBI, a clear violation of the CIA's careful formative mandate, and also another of more recent date, requiring 120,000 federal employees to agree to a lifetime ban on speaking out against administration policy using a vast new body of artibrarily "classified" information, in an apparent effort to counter the Carter administration's Freedom of Information Act. The President also issued a conveniently-unilateral executive order in 1983 to permit the FBI to begin an investigation against a citizen without any evidence, if the person is arbitrarily named a "security risk". Interview with Frank Wilkinson, President of "National Committee Against Oppressive Legislation", PBS, *Latenight America*, April 24, 1985.

Political economist A.A. Berle surmised in 1963 that the non-ideological, non-rigid balance that still characterized economic policy up until quite recently, which he referred to as "the American economic republic," had come into existence "only because of the conjunction of [certain] conditions." Regarding the pro-public results of the creative balance of interests involved, he added that "no better vindication, perhaps, of the American democratic process (irritating as it often is) can be found than the history of the past thirty years [i.e., from the 1930s to the 1960s]. It nailed its flag to no dogma. It evolved instruments adapted to problems. It never deserted its primary promise of a free society designed to permit free men to realize themselves."[69]

It is, as I have demonstrated, no accident that in 1980, just when the rough balance of power among organized interests had come crashing down, a remarkably rigid, ideological administration emerged for the first time in decades, clearing the way for its less-robust successors. It is not insignificant that its leader, a professed ideologue, would have to agree with the stigmatized Eastern Bloc ideological patron Karl Marx on two key points. First, we would have to agree with Marx's dictum that "changing the world is more important than understanding it correctly."[70] Relatedly, he would have to privately concede that democracy's essential premise, the effective representation of all interests and citizens, since it entails giving and not directing, is something which, unfortunately, cannot be afforded. Such, for us, are the results of our choosing blindly, and especially from among posed and pre-selected choices. The most logical -- although illogical -- alternative for many millions of only normally-informed Americans -- now almost a majority of the eligible population in their own right -- has been to simply abstain on their one-day-in-four-years chance to choose and decide. The right of national self-direction established by America's founding Revolution has been finally re-reduced to that.

Most careful observers have, accordingly, reached the sobering conclusion that, in America, as political analyst William Domhoff put it, "there is very little relationship between politics [open, visible politics] and policy."[71] Some, including Domhoff and political socialist Theodore Lowi, blame this on the present two-party system.[72] My own view is that

---

69. Berle, *The American Economic Republic*, pp. 14-15.
70. Novak, Michael, *ibid.*, p. 11.
71. Domhoff, *ibid.*, p. 121.
72. *Ibid.*; Lowi, Theodore J., *American Government: Incomplete Conquest*, N.Y.: Dryden, 1976, p. 299.

the main problem is instead rooted in the enduring long-ago abdication concerning the basic electoral process that still lies embedded in the Constitution.

Without a doubt, if the resulting gap in the Constitution, *were* conscienciously filled in to bring the promise of a workable, pro-public order to what is by far the most crucial routine process for setting the direction and establishing the agenda of our system, selfishness and self-interest would still continue to operate. And these facets of normal human nature *must*, in fact, continue to operate in order for democracy to be self-government, as Madison, the principal author of the Constitution, quite obviously recognized. But, at least as long as a multitude of genuine public and private interests remained opposed at fairly sharp angles, as they would, no group would be able to walk off with the whole loaf at others' total, and often unknowing, expense. And we would again have to respect one another in order to continue; and we would have to live as a whole community, which in fact we are.

That much, I believe, can still be repaired. If we would sincerely endeavor to re-empower the nation as a whole to actually select its leadership, we need not labor under a system of domination. As long as the rest of the Constitution's profoundly wise procedural and rights protection guidelines exist in place, the curious, deceptively small lacuna, a long-forgotten, impolitic accession to the jealous, sovereign states of the first and failed Confederation, could be advantageously closed. I will explain how I think it could be done at the end of this book.

Chapter Four

SOCIETIES AND NATURAL HISTORY

- Is American Society Unique? -

Up to now, in unraveling the fortunes of the two leading elements of America's mystique, we have seen many of the basic outlines of our larger-than-life nation's history emerge with a certain intrinsic clarity.

One of these two once widely-heralded elements is, of course, our country's fabled economic productivity, gained through intense application of technology to abundant resources. This aspect of America, in fact, eventually introduced an unexampled kind of self-conscious international leadership (i.e., *diastolic* leadership) to nearly the entire globe, including the relatively new and always-lagging Soviet bloc.

The other prominent facet of America's renown has been its allegedly unique degree of democratic access to wealth and personal achievement through what I have referred to as its *systolic* tradition, institutionally integrated as a regular and officially recognized feature of this society by the separation of powers and other carefully crafted features of our Constitution.

But gradually, over the past century or more, as I explained in the previous chapters, professionally-organized and -financed interest groups have been able to replace the country's citizenry as the main body of political constituency. And, as a very recent side effect of accelerated rapid change in the country's technological base, one supremely powerful and well-organized sector, the large business community, has found itself able to systematically control and hence selectively phase down the organs of the federal government into conformance with its own single-criterion political objective.

The whole, multi-interested public (i.e., the Constitution's "We, the people...") still remain legally the sovereigns of the United States. But given the inevitable exploitation by a swarm of well-financed interests of the odd, two-centuries-old gap in the Constitution's mandated electoral process, it is completely impossible now for the American people to select and competently review their own top leaders, and thus to basically govern themselves, as was clearly envisaged by Madison and his fellow nationalists in founding the new system. The legal sovereigns' judgment is, in fact, systematically avoided by the primarily extra-constitutional workings of the actual executive selection process.

Yet, it still may be possible to stem, peacefully and without heavy-handed legal restrictions, the resulting tide of obscurantism and financial interest domination with which we have become familiar and regretfully complacent, in order to reclaim the fast-disappearing genuine democratic element of our national birthright.

Ahead, in Chapter Six, I will discuss how a restored democracy, once more reflecting the expressed interests of the nation as a whole, could tremendously improve our current reputation and standing in the world, to our own very considerable, long-term benefit. In part, the effect of a restoration of popular rule would be to restore the *psychological* advantage we need to more fully realize our relative advantage in material resources and location.

But first, let us consider, for comparison's sake, some instances, in the careers of societies beyond America and the present, of the emergence, development, and loss of roughly the same focused vision of economic growth accompanying a new breadth of participation and freedom, that we ourselves have experienced. Then, we will consider the instructive career of the Eastern or Soviet Bloc in this same light. Even a modest survey will, I believe, suffice to suggest the pervasiveness and persistence, across cultural boundaries and time, of what I have referred to as the *diastolic/systolic* dynamic in human affairs.

While the survey here must be cursory, with perhaps as many important examples left out as discussed, I think it will indicate enough parallels to suggest a general life cycle pattern for democratic regimes, featuring a multiple repetition of causes and effects. I hasten to add that the healthy and productive stage of maturity resulting in a workable *diastolic/systolic* accommodation and compact seems to be anything but universal in the experience of societies. Apparently, the majority of historic nations have not been permitted, for one reason or another, to complete the groundwork or develop the public vision required. And none has retained the crucial balance permitting both sustained economic strength and an open society indefinitely.

Yet, everything must have its first time, and our own case has been uncommon from the start. At least, we ought not abandon our heroic and storied effort now.

- Ancient Days and Nights -

For every known instance of notable success by a society in the ancient world, a *diastolic* explanation has been suggested. The Sumerians' advanced irrigation works and their maintenance of a dispersed community of dependent farmers in what is now Iraq created the first recorded urban, commercial state in the late fourth millenium BC. Iron weapons, harnesses and stirrups, wheeled chariots that brought stability and accuracy to animal-borne warfare, and, later, bronze alloys, naval ships and formations, and local supplies of resources for trade, are suggested as mainsprings of the dramatic military and commercial careers of the Hittites, Medes, Assyrians, Phoenicians, and early Egyptians. Such developments might be compared to the initial advantages given to North America by bountiful agricultural and energy resources and the enterprise to harness them. Each new threshold of development, in the ancient world as now, brought to the innovators a fresh round of success.[1]

Much of the preparation and background for early Greek democracy, which arose simultaneously in a number of small states in the region of the Aegean Sea, appears to have been provided by a new, widespread experience. Starting in the eighth century BC, many thousands of previously land-bound peasants started to find employment in the burgeoning trade with new Greek colonies along a dozen distant coasts. This experience provided common Greeks with exposure to the larger world, greater affluence, and independence from the dominating landholding class. A wave of revolutions followed, aimed at sharing political power more broadly among the large new middle class, when the tyrant families' rule was found to be too restrictive and self-serving.[2]

---

1. See Nef, John U., *Cultural Foundations of Industrial Civilization*, Cambridge Univ. Press, 1958, for a more thorough discussion of the importance of *organizational* superiority.
2. See Forrest, W. G., *The Emergence of Greek Democracy, 800-400 B.C.*, New York: McGraw-Hill, 1966, pp. 93-97.

After a similar fashion, early American democracy was seen by Tocqueville to have emerged along the western shore of the Atlantic due to remoteness and the indifference of the preoccupied colonizing power to urgent opportunities and needs facing the colonists.[3]

The misnamed "Old Oligarch" of ancient Athens, a figure whose identity is now unknown, defended the advantages of democracy in his city (the system of direct democracy called the *demos*) from the attacks of critics. Whoever this Athenian was, he was a practical and not a sentimental or purely idealistic believer in democracy. "...The *demos*," he declared according to his contemporary, Xenophon, "in fact is wise to let low-class characters speak. For if only the upper class did so it would produce good results for itself but not for ordinary men. As things are, when some low-class fellow gets to his feet, he lights upon a policy which is good for himself and others like him. But again it may be argued that such a man is incapable of devising a profitable policy. Perhaps, but the *demos* knows that even his stupidity and vulgarity, so long as it is combined with good will, will bring more profit in the end than all the aristocrats' nobility and wisdom, coupled as it is with hostility."[4] Historian W. G. Forrest adds in interpreting this passage, that, without deliberate intervention, "the bulk of new riches finds its way into the pockets of those who are already rich."[5]

British historian C. Hignett notes that members of the *demos* in Athens in the somewhat earlier time of Kleisthenes "still looked up to the members of the great families for leadership and guidance, but they were fully conscious of their own powers and were prepared to exact a heavy reckoning from statesmen who forgot that they were now no more than servants of the *demos*."[6]

It seems unlikely that modern Americans in general will ever recover a positive attitude toward those placed in authority (whom we still prefer to call "public servants") unless the general public is somehow restored as their principal constituency and reason for holding office. Unlike the

---

3. Tocqueville, *ibid.*, II, p. 18.
4. Xenophon, *The Athenian Constitution* (5th century BC), i: 6-8.
5. Forrest, *ibid.*, p. 98.
6. Hignett, C., *A History of the Athenian Constitution to the End of the Fifth Century BC*, Oxford: Clarendon, 1962, p. 157.

democratic Athenians of Xenophon's time, modern-day American citizens often feel completely powerless against the grave threats and challenges they perceive to their society, originating both outside and inside the country. Their sense of frustration and fear, much in evidence both in poll results and in a number of self-destructive habits and patterns of behavior that are most common in America, is not unrelated to the fact that, in the normal course of things, the present-day U.S. public really *is* powerless.

In contrast with Athens' celebrated form of government, imperfect and relatively fleeting though it actually was, the description by an early Roman historian, Polybius, of the political situation on the ancient Mediterranean island of Crete is much more reminiscent of the direction in which American society still seems undauntedly impelled at present. "Their laws," Polybius wrote of the Cretans, "allow them to acquire as much land as they can -- to infinity, as one might say; they honor money so much that gaining money is considered not only necessary but the finest of arts. Speaking generally, their behavior concerning rapacity and avarice is so much a part of their particular way of life that among Cretans alone of all mankind, no sort of profit is considered disgraceful. Again, their rules concerning office call for early rotation and are democratic in form. ... [Yet they are] caught up in the greatest number of private and public factions, murders, and wars because of their innate avarice. ... One could find few examples of private character more deceitful than those of the Cretans, or of public scheming more criminal."[7]

Polybius' sober account reads like a melodrama: a flawed constitutional democracy, subverted and reduced to anarchy. And the Cretans' put-upon neighbors were not quick to forget, either: Cretans are still frequently reminded by other Greeks of their remote ancestors' 2,000-year-old reputation. By contrast, Polybius found the actual system of the Roman Republic in his day (later seen to be no utopia itself, in terms of results for its citizens) to be one of "fairness and propriety."[8]

---

7. Polybius, *The Histories* (2nd century BC), transl. by M. Chambers, New York: Washington Square Press, 1966, VI:3; Also see Paul, in Titus 1:2, *New Testament*.
8. Polybius, *ibid.*, VI:11.

The impressive rise of Rome to international power, viewed later as a major watershed in world history, is, like that of the United States, impossible to attribute to a single *diastolic* event or event sequence. But an unusually large part of Rome's great success, like that of modern Japan or the late British Empire, seems to be more attributable to organizational and psychological factors that led to wealth and control of international resources, than to any set of initial material advantages.

Rome's republican revolution occurred, according to tradition, in 509 BC, overthrowing an earlier tyrannical kingship in favor not of the common people, but of an aristocracy. After a later (287 BC) popular revolt by a reportedly sorely oppressed great majority of commoners, an annually-elected body was created to represent common citizens, to stand alongside the aristocratic Roman Senate.

In practice, by the time of Cicero in the first century BC, the two residual, annually-elected people's Tribunes were subject to heavy punishment, oftentimes death, by a vote of the Senate at the end of their terms if they had "erred" in a so-called "matter of principle." The vast majority of Romans who were commoners could, at best, hope to gain a hearing as bargaining clients of one of these largely-hamstrung Tribunes they had elected or, far less likely, one or another of the aloof Senatorial families.[9]

It is worth noting in passing that this system of token representation and clientage under the late Roman Republic at least outwardly resembles the model of common stockholders in the direction of financial matters vis-à-vis the corporate holders of market seats on Wall Street today. The idea that such a model could also be applied politically, with interest groups and other entities being the private clients of office holders, thus has an ancient if not entirely noble precedent.

As for the results of the Roman Republic's clientage system, British historian P. A. Brunt concludes that "for its oppressive character, patrician rule must have lasted longer" than the tradition accepted by Roman historians allowed. "We must believe," he goes on, "in the tradition that there was grave discontent among the masses. Small farmers were constantly falling into debt. Under the Twelve Tables [the Roman common law] the debtor who would not or could not pay was liable in the end to be sold into slavery abroad by his creditor. ...We

---

9. See Brunt, P. A., *Social Conflict in the Roman Republic*, New York: Norton, 1971, pp. 45-46.

hear much of a mysterious contract called *nexum*, whereby the poor, in return for loans had to work in bondage to the rich. We are told of a persistent demand for distributions of land. Much land, it is said, was owned by the state (*ager publicus*) but exploited almost wholly by those who controlled the state, the patricians, for their own benefit."[10] The people's elected representatives, the Tribunes, were, not surprisingly within this narrow class-dominated system, interested mainly in increasing their own influence with the all-powerful Senate.

Finally, in Caesar's time, even the oligarchic patrician Roman Senate was overthrown by a handful of its own, on the excuse of unifying and thus streamlining the capability of the Roman military command to defend the Empire against threats from non-Roman "barbarians" to the north and east. Thereafter, the highly checkered series of successive Roman emperors themselves got caught up in webs of unbridled turmoil and military intrigue. They repeatedly and dangerously bought time for the patrician Roman state by packing the over-extended armies and especially their officer ranks with the manifestly non-Roman but martial "barbarians" themselves. Thus, no great gain in public well-being or security seems to have ultimately resulted.[11]

On the contrary, it is discernible from the record here, too, that the slide away from the mooring of public accountability, once underway, was very treacherous and steep. It should not particularly surprise us, given their respective notions of government as a preserver of common rights, that among America's founders, both Madison and Jefferson were avid students of ancient history. Their early colleague Hamilton, whose gift was finance, manifestly was not.[12]

A world of information has come to light during the past two centuries, illuminating the careers of much more ancient civilized societies and states, of which Madison and Jefferson knew nothing. But unmistakable evidence of a widespread belief in freedom and the value of individual opinion, alongside the ubiquitous appetite for material prosperity, arises from the records of the very oldest literate society yet

---

10. *Ibid.*, p. 58.
11. See Boak, A.E.R., *Manpower Shortage in the Fall of the Roman Empire in the West*, Ann Arbor: Univ. of Michigan Press, 1955, pp. 109 ff.; Luttwak, Edward N., *The Grand Strategy of the Roman Empire*, Baltimore: Johns Hopkins Univ. Press, 1976, p. 111 ff.
12. For instance, see Jefferson's interesting reminiscence to Dr. Benjamin Rush regarding Hamilton's conception of Julius Caesar, Feb. 16, 1811.

discovered. And, surprisingly, the political course of ancient Sumer, reconstructed from its wondrous archives on clay starting near the end of the fourth millenium BC, would seem to bear out Ortega y Gasset's reasoned dread of a society taken over by technical experts.[13]

A well-known scholar of Sumer, Samuel Noah Kramer, explains that while the temple with its noble priestly caste was the largest and most important building in the urban environment 5,000 years ago, much of the fertile, alluvial land that was the basis of the wealth belonged in practice to common individuals. "In early days," he tells us, "political power lay in the hands of these free citizens and a city-governor known as *ensi*, who was no more than a peer among peers. In case of decisions vital to the city as a whole, these free citizens met in a bicameral assembly consisting of an upper house of 'elders' and a lower house of 'men'. [But] as the struggle between the city-states grew more violent and bitter, and as the pressures from the barbaric peoples to the east and west of Sumer increased, military leadership loomed as an apparent pressing need, and the king, or as he is known in Sumerian, the 'big man', came to hold a superior place.

"At first he was probably selected and appointed by the assembly at a critical moment for a specific military task," Kramer tells us. "But gradually kingship with all its privileges and prerogatives became a hereditary institution and was even considered the very hallmark of civilization."[14]

Kramer's fellow orientalist Henri Frankfort adds that the loss of Sumer's democracy was in no small part due to a surprisingly simple constitutional deficiency: It seems that the practice of taking a vote to resolve issues by majority decision had not yet been invented. Instead, discussions in the open assembly had to continue until absolute unanimity was reached, crippling the state's capacity to act in the common interest in times of danger.[15] One can only hope that modern American democracy will not likewise be given up in practice for want of

---

13. See Ortega y Gasset, *loc. cit.*; Discussion in Chapter Three, supra.
14. Kramer, Samuel Noah, *The Sumerians, Their History, Culture, and Character*, Univ. of Chicago Press, 1963, pp. 73-74. Moscati, Sabatino, *The Face of the Ancient Orient*, New York: Doubleday Anchor, 1962, pp. 18-19, and Jacobsen, T., "Primitive Democracy in Ancient Mesopotamia," *Journal of Near Eastern Studies*, 2 (1943), p. 172, essentially corroborate this picture.
15. Frankfort, Henri, *The Birth of Civilization in the Near East*, New York: Doubleday Anchor, 1956, p. 77.

a relative simple and workable democratic mechanism that it now sorely lacks.[16]

- Modern Instances -

Subversion of a relatively open system of government by a few key people has often occurred behind the scenes, with the former free institutions maintained outwardly intact at least until the re-consolidation of power was complete.

The commercial revolution of the late Middle Ages led to the replacement of feudal kingships based on the old, agrarian economy in a number of north Italian city states, by a new, elected communal council form of administration. But eventually, in Venice and Florence, short lists of repeatedly-offered candidates were drawn up in private conclave to retain a majority under the control of a despotic *signor*, a single ruling individual, while every constitutionally eligible citizen still retained an equal vote among the chosen nominees. Cooperating candidates were, however, then voted for or against, not in secret, but by each eligible voter openly dropping a white or a black bean.

The unofficial ruling *signories* of the subverted states would often eventually become hereditary within a single, dominant family. Dante, for one, greatly lamented the prevalence of this cynical form of subversion in the otherwise brilliant and wealthy Renaissance "republics" of his day.[17]

A basic tradition that most Americans still without a doubt prefer, is that of keeping the actions of every member of society, up to and including the chief of state, under the authority of the law. This tradition of public accountability stems in a formal sense from the English *Magna Carta* (Great Charter) of 1215. The reputedly churlish, inscrutable King John was forced by his rebellious barons, at a field called Runnymede, to accept an agreement limiting somewhat the scope of and increasing his accountability for his actions, so as not to violate *their* conception of the society's interests. For his part, King John was so

---

16. See discussion in Chapters Two and Three, supra.
17. Martines, Lauro, *Power and Imagination, City States in Renaissance Italy*, New York: Vintage, 1980, pp. 94 ff, 110, 150.

113

little accustomed to viewing himself as anything remotely resembling a public servant that he is reported to have grumbled that he was being made a slave.[18]

Even so, the fundamental principle of constitutional government, that of universal accountability under the law, was routinely applied, although less than perfectly, in much of the English-speaking world for centuries thereafter. It is still effectively invoked against major challenges by strong individuals on occasion, most frequently prodded by insistent public opinion threatening severe civil or uncivil retribution in cases that seem particularly clear-cut.[19]

In general, for fairly obvious reasons, the interest of common citizens no matter where in maintaining an essentially fair society of laws, is honored as a routine matter only when the public is fully empowered to act incisively as an electorate. Otherwise, apathy prevails in normal times, and the increasingly bold and frequent abuses of power that follow for an extended time, only result in sporadic, frustrated violence or anti-social withdrawal and non-involvement on the part of the oppressed general public.

In 19th-century Britain and France, as noted before, the degree of public frustration necessary to force enactments mandating full and decisive public participation and hence leading to relief was not reached until the unchecked storm of abuses against the dependent laboring class that accompanied full-scale industrialization had become an intolerable public affront.[20] Legitimate public needs are only met through responsive government when either the level of public outrage, or actual representation of the public, become sufficient. And continuous public outrage is far less bearable than is direct accountability through fair elections, which finally became standard both in Britain and in France before the century's end.

---

18. See Brooke, Christopher, *From Alfred to Henry III, 871-1272*, New York: Norton, 1966, p. 220; Stenton, Doris Mary, *English Society in the Early Middle Ages*, Baltimore: Penguin, 1965, p. 49.

19. The degree of moral indignation that crippled Gerald Ford's chances of election in 1976, following the Nixon pardon, provided a fairly recent major test of this critical attitude in the United States.

20. This point is made in greater detail in Chapters One and Two, above.

Oddly enough, the sensibilities of Russians were heated white hot in 1917 not in response to the effects of industrialization inside Russia, but in frustrated longing for industrialization in a stagnant peasant society as the way to duplicate the great material advances of industrial societies in the West. But no legal channels for significant public expression as yet existed in the country. Nor, for that matter, were such devised by the successive leaders of the ultimately triumphant Bolshevik revolution that followed.

Instead, the *systolic* function (in the form of actual participation in decision making), and the country's *diastolic* (production control) function were both conveniently retained by a small group of philosophically "correct" leaders who were to act as the public's permanent guardians. Thus was born the clearest and most informative example to date of government purely by technical management specialists. The results of the Soviet experiment in intensely concentrating the control of *both* of society's vital forces will be reviewed in Chapter Five.[21]

The classic 20th-century instance of a death of democracy under stress is that of the German Weimar Republic in 1933. Its aftermath of special horror may somehow seem to set this particular case of public demise apart. Yet many of the conditions that pertained in other examples that we have already glimpsed are evident here as well, leading to initial results of a more-or-less familiar cast following public authority's subversion and downfall.

The modern democratic tradition had at that time not yet become firmly-rooted in Germany. Yet the republic that was founded after World War I, when a sharp turn from autocracy had been viewed as imperative, still enjoyed much support within the country and very likely could have survived in calmer times. However, given the notorious inflation and unemployment rates in Germany early in the 1930s Depression, along with festering anger over the broken nation's treatment by the European victors of the First World War, tides of authoritarian sentiment rose again on both the right and left. But this time, the

---

21. The reality of the original broadly-based general revolution in Russia in the midst of the First World War is beyond dispute. See the discussion of the public mood, exploited by the leaders of various stripes, in Crankshaw, Edward, *The Shadow of the Winter Palace*. Harmondsworth, U.K.: Penguin, 1978, Chapter Twenty, "Impossible to Live Thus Any Longer," pp. 392-416. That the forces which ultimately triumphed so completely excluded popular participation in decisions (as was also the case in late eighteenth century France) is instructive, by its absence, of the value of a fundamental law. By comparison, the American Revolution, from its inception, was more complete and thus yielded the public far more.

authoritarian choice lacked the accustomed probity of a strong traditional monarch which had lent it its former aura of legitimacy. The German Communists were numerous and might have come to power, had not the broad right wing, with instrumental backing from a huge heavy industrial sector that naturally sought to control and stabilize the chaotic financial situation, stepped into the breach to take over first.

The titular leader of the German right was, of course, Adolf Hitler, a magic crowd-builder, a little-known, rakish-looking former sign painter from Austria. His role was widely expected to be for the most part benign, that of a symbolic front man and firm, no-nonsense rally-leader.

Hitler's biting, insinuating rhetoric had a sense of unreality about it, preventing most participants from taking the message he proclaimed at face value. Yet, the eventual Fuhrer was not a newcomer, but instead a man with tested instincts in the struggle for power. The swelling hysteria for German assertiveness that he fanned swept away the fumbling, deliberative bodies the industrialists and the military despised, leaving power seemingly beyond effective challenge in the actually-fragile new Nazi administration's hands. For the undecided, old Marshal Hindenburg was prominently seated in the midst of the new Reich cabinet, seeming to assure the critical stability demanded.[22]

Present-day West German political scientist and historian Karl Dietrich Bracher has described Hitler's so-called "National Socialism" as an "elitist movement seeking mass support yet not considering the masses sufficiently knowledgeable politically to share in the decision-making process." Bracher stated further that the owners of Germany's heavy industries at the beginning assigned to the Nazi party "the function of 'finding and uniting the most capable persons in Germany through a selection conditioned by day-to-day struggle' to carry out the elitist training for leadership and to serve as the 'political selection organization' for the authoritarian regime."

---

22. Bracher, Karl Dietrich, *The German Dictatorship, The Origins, Structure, and Effects of National Socialism*, transl. by Jean Steinberg, New York: Praeger, 1970, p. 169; Peter Gay, in his characteristically insightful study, *Weimar Culture, The Outsider as Insider*, New York: Harper Torchbooks, 1970, discusses the impetus behind the founding of and opposition to the Weimar state and traces its subsequent hard career; pp. 1-22 and 147-164.

Bracher added, in explaining the Nazi phenomenon not as an individual, but an orchestrated triumph, that Hitler "would never have crashed the gates of power without outside help; he would have remained a would-be tyrant..."[23] But Hitler's capacity for independent leadership once in power was widely misjudged, while the legal signposts and checks on authority previously established in the system were either removed or ignored to permit the consolidation of control well-calculated to restore to Germany unity, balance, and international prominence.

But even the Nazis were not entirely lacking in candor before their takeover at democracy's expense. In 1928, before the onslaught of the catastrophic crisis of the Depression, when members of the Nazi Party were successfully standing for election to the Weimar Reichstag in what they called their "legal revolution," Goebbels, who would soon be Hitler's propaganda minister, announced their intention openly in an article in the partisan press. "We go into the Reichstag in order to acquire the weapons of democracy from its arsenal," he wrote. "We become Reichstag deputies in order to paralyze the Weimar democracy with its own assistance. The state itself will supply and finance our fighting machinery... We come as enemies! Like the wolf tearing into the flock of sheep, that is how we come."[24]

By contrast, with the exception of the much ostracized Hamilton two centuries ago, few of political democracy's opponents in the United States have ever been this candid in public in their opposition to the idealized open, considered government of all and for all that almost all Americans have learned to revere from their earliest days in school. For a public figure to openly oppose such a resistant and wonderful popular myth invites an opprobrium equal to Hamilton's.

Systemic control, rather than outright abolishment of democratic institutions, meanwhile, remains the order of the day for America's corporatist "realists". Most American opponents of open democracy would probably still be stridently opposed to the latter course (i.e., outright institutional abolishment) for now, if only because of the perils of the powerful backlash it would most likely still involve.

But patience not being the strong suit of the powerful drivers of present-day American large enterprise of whatever political bent, I

---

23. *Ibid.*, pp. 86-87, 230-31.
24. Goebbels, Joseph, "What Do We Want in the Reichstag?" in *Der Angriff*, April 30, 1928, quoted in Bracher, *ibid.*, pp. 141-42.

personally look for this uneasy situation to change rapidly. Within the next one to five years, depending on the corporatists' assessments of their political fortunes, I expect to see the previously inconspicuous yet highly-placed criticism of the Constitution's frustrating and expensive separation of powers features that has already hatched out in the literature of business policy (see the discussion in Chapter Three), begin to trickle down into mainstream media commentary, and then break suddenly into general informed conversation.

This initially jarring development will most likely be followed by a set of actual measures, in the form of proposed amendments backed by prominent officials in both the executive and legislative branch, to "streamline" and "up-date" the so-called "unrepresentative" American procedural system. The proposed changes will, I believe, be linked publicly to the "symptomatic" fiscal crises and the exigencies of ruthless and mounting world economic competition, requiring much more executive discretion and flexibility than are currently available. Such a strong move in the near future to further consolidate the flow of power for greater efficiency of action via Constitutional change, is predictable, given corporatist rhetoric, an unprecedented volume of secret, currently illegitimate foreign policy actions by the current and recent corporatist executive branch of the government, and the progression of proposed system changes under the still-new and incomplete corporatist political dominance up to now. (Prominent examples of the above, a number of which are almost daily emerging out of obscurity, include the secret Iran-Contra affair and the innocent-sounding request for a "line-item veto," which would beyond any doubt seriously weaken the representative role of Congress by permitting the President to alter the legislative branch's intent in approving a bill.)

The basic purpose of the persistently-marketed and -demanded changes, though they will have to be pleaded to the public 90 degrees off from the real purpose to have the requisite all-but-certain chance of at least gradual success, will be to permit the single now-dominant well-organized interest to control American policy much more surely, responsively, and with less costly competition from other interests and viewpoints. The proposals will probably be rejected out of hand by Congress, following public opinion, at first. But their backers will continue and persist until the public, too, will come to accept the rationale that, in these changed times, their government's hands are actually tied without such fundamental, streamlining "reforms." Extended and bitter congressional wrangling and foot-dragging over the "reforms" put forth will, in fact, be cited to demonstrate their need.

Precisely how the corporatist amendment or, much more likely, amendments will actually read is impossible to say, although I fully expect the powers of the Presidency, particularly concerning the use of executive orders, to be very considerably strengthened at the expense of the Congress. It is simply infinitely easier for multinational business and finance to secure perennial control via the one, much smaller branch; and Congress, notoriously, contains far too many so-called "populist" mavericks. Though the coming corporatist "reform" effort's success is not yet completely assured, the signs of imminent, radical change are in the wind.[25]

As the foregoing survey of earlier societies indicates, American society may be close to unique in the world only in the long-lasting potential of its frequently ill-served, now seriously compromised self-governing system. That important potential for continued American longevity aside, we may conclude that there is a definite family resemblance among the causes and effects in the life cycles of sometime-democratic societies, ancient and modern. None show particularly unique origins, susceptibilities, or immunities. All achieved democracy at a certain point because the desire and real need to fully participate in society is universal.

The Spanish aristocrat Ortega y Gasset protested in the early 1930s, mainly because he was not a democrat, that, "in a right ordering of public affairs, the mass is that part which does not act of itself. ...It has come into the world in order to be directed, influenced, represented, organized.... For the mass to claim to act of itself is then a rebellion against its own destiny."[26]

---

25. For instance, the staid Kiplinger organization has gotten a whiff of this chemically-new scent. In his *Washington Letter* back on May 3, 1985, Austin Kiplinger announced with an uncharacteristic note of worry that "Our Constitution will be in the news during the next few years. It's almost 200 years old, and some folks feel it needs changing. ...Economic concerns are the stimulus, as they were in the 1780s... A new convention would draft a balanced-budget amendment.... Meanwhile, a group is digging into [other] changes that may be necessary. ...This involves the BASICS of our system. ...Scares Congress, so it may OK the amendment if a convention appears sure." But the drive for what will be represented as "streamlining" won't be stopped quite so easily. A related widespread defamation of the counterbalancing *institution* of the Congress has, meanwhile, already begun.

26. Ortega y Gasset, *op. cit.*, pp. 115-16.

In other words, Ortega knew instinctively that the people *en mass* should not be permitted to decide the society's direction. They should be managed, used, guided by ... *someone*. And on this, Joseph Goebbels and Joseph Stalin could have easily agreed. Indeed, a particularly fascinating feature of oligarchy (rule by an exclusive, like-interested few, for whatever purpose) is that the management becomes an interchangeable part.

Ortega y Gasset goes on to say that "when the mass acts on its own, it does so only in one way, for it has no other: it lynches." This Spaniard, too, is really referring to the chaos of anarchy, and not democracy, though, significantly, he doesn't notice the difference. He adds: "It is not altogether by chance that lynch law comes from America, for America is, in a fashion, the paradise of the masses."[27]

We who have known and accept democracy because it serves us, as a nation, best, can easily amend his statement to say that the "mass" will resort to illegal action only if it has no other way. And then we need to make sure that it *does* have a way; that is, that the procedural system will continue to exist to serve the sovereign nation and not a faction. Let us not wait too long to act on this.

Corporate financial and technical domination of national politics has already muted and mooted most significant public controversy in America at the national level. The volume of the public voice has now been lowered on most vital issues to an unobtrusive murmur in the background. It is not that Americans don't *care* enough anymore; lacking the necessary deference by national politicians and corresponding reasonably-defined choices, they simply don't know how to begin to respond. Their reactions are accordingly almost always unfocused and, without an attainable meaningful object, futile. Under corporate-sector dominance, the legally-sovereign public has been managed out of sovereign significance. If dictatorship is entailed by a loss of meaningful democratic choice, that's what we have. And it ought to feel chilling.

Let us turn now and look at the changing management system and surprising prospects of the West's chief, abiding rival for influence and power in the world, the patiently cunning, momentarily retooling, realigning, and regearing Soviet Union.

---

27. *Ibid.*, p. 116.

Chapter Five

THE SOVIET EXPERIMENT: A DOUBLE BIND

- Dismal Origins, Unrealized Potential -

It would be a stupendous error, even at this point, to count the Soviet Union and its allies out of serious, world-scale political and ideological competition. The long-lasting allure of the Soviet collective system of social organization for relatively underdeveloped nations up to now has stemmed not from comparison of the relative success of their economic system and ours, but, paradoxically, from the bitter beginnings of the creation of the Soviet Union itself. While we in the West tend to emphasize the concept of underdeveloped *countries*, suggesting that the physical resources of certain places are not being fully exploited, the perceived neglect of chances for the fuller development of human resources is of greater concern to most inhabitants of poorer countries. And the fact is that many more people and nations worldwide are at present being left farther and farther behind.

The Soviet system's general rejection of capitalist development has retained a certain attraction, then, because in the experience of most "Third World" nationals, effective funds to develop resources in their countries have tended to come from abroad. And such highly-selective development financed elsewhere has frequently tended to avail Third World citizens only the less-rewarding forms of commercial participation, such as menial, scantily paid jobs for a relatively small number of workers, on a permanent and unchanging basis.

Such indeed had been the prospect, by and large, of Russians themselves during the peak years of early Western industrialization three and four generations ago. Their resources then were being exported to supply mechanized industries in the more highly-developed countries of the West, whose "capitalists" were developing Russia's resource industries, at that time actively exporting mainly minerals and timber products. Such concentrated wealth as then existed *within* the vast, resource-rich country was, meanwhile, still tied up in large, feudal landed estates. Because of this similarity of intransigent starting conditions, Soviet Marxism, the proffered remedy that convincingly enough removed foreign domination from Russia for succeeding generations and positively led the way to relatively advanced industrialization in that once remote, backward country, is still seen by most Third World populist leaders as worth examining, and by many as worthy of emulating. The fact that the Soviets' current President may now succeed in channeling Western development capital eastward under special terms hardly threatens to diminish his huge, still autonomous bargaining bloc's allure in areas of the world that have painfully endured centuries of outside domination and repressive internal influence.

Yet, a very peculiar set of governing procedures that was introduced in the Soviet Union not by Stalin, but under the leadership of the founder Lenin himself in the years after 1917, has been continued in basic form up to the present. The purpose of these procedures has been to induce rapid industrial development while avoiding the thoroughly documented evils for those not owners of uninhibited, raw capitalism. These standardized Marxist-Leninist measures, though successful at the beginning, have, because of their stultifying effect on people as individuals, generated problems of at least equal severity.

So, despite the allure of the Leninist system as a functioning alternative to foreign and class domination, the special new difficulties generated by the Marxist-Leninist system are far from being a secret in the world at large. This circumstance leaves the worldwide ideological field still open for a more prudent and farsighted West than at present to win peacefully, although the long-term competition is actually still far from over and, due to rapidly exacerbating Third World problems, promises to heat up more in the future instead of fading away.

Let us examine this critical point in more detail. The Soviets, starting with Lenin and his view of man in society, have sought to ban the troublesome, frequently anti-social incentive of private accumulation by banning private ownership. They have, thereby, in effect capped the generative springs of pride in ownership and the incentive of possible future ownership and reward that might normally lead to sustained productive efforts and creative improvements.

Applying the same quality of insight, the Marxist-Leninist view finds the multitudinous masses of humanity, ostensibly the beneficiaries of the Marxist system, to be ineffectual, complacent, easily-duped dullards.

Thus has been rationalized the unchanging, or insignificantly-changing, status of the masses in the Soviet Union as subjects of the governing Communist Party Central Committee and its Politburo, rather than actual citizens empowered within the system to hire and fire their top leaders and thereby effect state policy. (It is notable that President Gorbachov's recent reforms have successfully, contrary to most reports, garnered *more* power within the system for himself and his immediate successors.)

Lenin, through suffering personal trials, finally came to trust no one but himself. Likewise, the ruling Central Committee elite since his time, however constituted, has entrusted no element outside of itself with even a scrap of substantive independent power. The succession and patronage of key party and government posts at all levels is still retained strictly in-house. And the masses of Russia and its enormous, consolidated empire are *still*, in actuality, more effectively subjugated, regulated, and reformulated at present than in any of the past, autocratic centuries.

To state this point another way: the *basis* of the Soviet totalitarian experiment, at least up to now, has been the effort to achieve the total or near total blockage of what I have referred to as the natural *diastolic* as well as the *systolic* dynamic of human development within the society. To say nothing of the very interesting results, never before has an authoritarian state been sufficiently ambitious, ruthless, and capable of almost totally displacing the natural functions of *both* progressive mainsprings of the society.

And the results of thus arbitrarily and as totally as possibly denying and replacing normal human by ideological state action have turned out as badly overall as might reasonably be expected. Indeed, the violent measures necessary to insure the simultaneous short-circuiting of *both* great, irrepressible natural forces of development in the society have entailed results more drastic and far-reaching for the hundreds of millions of individuals involved up to now than I have so far suggested.

Both of the basic, negating features of Soviet action have stemmed from a concept of Lenin's that he chose, for reasons of his own, to refer to as "democratic centralism;" and neither feature has as yet been altered greatly in the applied doctrine of the U.S.S.R. The two principles involved -- retention of full political power in the lone active component, the Central Committee of the Communist Party, and the full retention of productive property rights in the state -- appear, in fact, to be necessary features of the peculiar Leninist vision of a controlled, justly-organized society. They are seen as "correct" reform doctrine, and so to be fundamentally maintained, if not openly heralded, regardless what their maintenance may require, until such time as the reformed human prototype, denominated "homo Sovieticus," becomes the standard working model. Though cosmetic and morale-building touches and internal juggling can be affected with great care by Gorbachov and other ingenious leaders in the interim, the abandonment of Soviet competitive ambitions and the actual basis of state communism is far more problematical and not presently in view.

Persistent claims by Western intellectuals that the Marxist-Leninist system is not "true Marxism" have, likewise, missed the main point. The Leninst system being cogently and now more softly urged on economically-weakened nations around the world, is what it is. And what it is demands a major sacrifice of individual human aspirations in pursuit of the ironic promise of collective-level independence from a dominating world owner class. Neither that glittering purpose nor the natural allure of it for the growing ranks of the world's desperate will disappear by magic.

- Lenin's Bind on Public Self-Control -

The bargain entered into by Lenin's determined enforcement of the "democratic centralism" principle of his applied version of Marxism placed all genuine power and property in the hands of the authoritarian state, an arrangement enforced ever since Lenin's time by subsequent Soviet leaders. By executing this bargain, the dual objective involved in avoiding economic exploitation of the workers during rapid industrialization has, according to some 'neutral' sources, actually been achieved. In other essentially Marxist systems (notably China and several of the Soviets' Eastern European satellites), the rate of exploitation -- meaning the ratio between the commercial value of the average worker's production and what the worker is paid -- currently stands higher than in any of the countries of Western Europe or the United States. But, true to Lenin's promise and the fundamental purpose of Marxism, the Soviet Union by the late 1970s recorded the lowest annual rate of exploitation in manufacturing of any country in the world. The reported Soviet ratio was 1.3 to 1, compared to above 7.5 to 1 in mainland China, variously between 1.5 and 3.0 to 1 in the developed Western countries, and over 4.5 to 1 in Japan. Cuba, though mild in this regard for Latin America, recorded a rate almost identical to that of the United States,

124

presumably an improvement in this particular respect from its earlier, pre-revolutionary times.[1]

But, despite achieving outstanding rates of economic growth in the 1950s and early '60s, typically rising from a comparatively low level, no Communist system anywhere has ever managed to approach the level of either output or income per capita sustained by a large number of the Western market economies inside their home countries.[2]

So, Lenin's first and foremost objective might be said to have been largely achieved, at least in his own giant homeland. Yet, the three-generations-long comparative track record since his introduction of the new, experimental policy in his country simply cannot, for reasons of human nature doubtless more obvious in hindsight, give very much encouragement to orthodox ideologues of the Eastern Bloc.

In sum, Eastern Bloc GNP figures and comparative growth rates represent a rather dismal combination of circumstances, revealing roughly the economic fruits of the unimaginably expensive trade-off noted within the U.S.S.R. itself through seven brutal decades of history. Certainly, at least the gist of this situation is familiar to the leaders of the stormy and unpredictable present-day Third World, including those who have hardened into committed Communists in the crucibles of their struggles. Such facts, of course, are just as surely mostly *not* well-known by the resentful, unschooled masses who are seeing their already abysmal standards of living steadily deteriorate, and whom the revolutionary leaders claim to represent.

Thus, this chapter's first main point bears repeating: The spectacular failures and rigors of the Soviet Leninist system are sufficiently well-known. Hence, the opportunity for a more far-sighted and publicly accountable West to firmly recapture the ideological ground it has lost to its less resourceful natural world foe is certainly very great.

---

1. *UN Yearbook of Industrial Statistics*, 1980.
2. See *World Bank Atlas*, 1980 and 1983, and Kidron, Michael and Ronald Segal, *The New State of the World Atlas*, N.Y.: Simon & Schuster, 1984, Map 21.

The main features of the Soviet state are sometimes seen as sufficiently arbitrary to permit considerable constitutional flexibility within the present system. An important question, then, becomes, to what extent can it be documented that the long-familiar, up to now outwardly-rigid, centralized authoritarian cast of the modern Soviet state was deliberately established by the system's founder Lenin as a *necessary means* of achieving the desired economic consolidation of the Soviet empire? Is the form itself intractable? As we pursue this question, we must keep in mind that, at least for Lenin, any plan of economic development had to be kept consistent with the Marxist objective of excising capitalist power in order to permit a basic equality of rewards for the whole working public.

The doctrine of Marxism itself was devised as a here-and-now answer to real worldly woes and, fittingly, started its career as a 19th-century social gospel. It featured (interestingly, in common with 19th-century capitalist doctrine) a belief in an eventual "withering away of the state" in the millenarian fashion of that day.[3] Certainly, no interpretation of society could have been more typically Anglo-Saxon or Western than was early Marxism in its reference to hard-headed materialism as the single arbiter of value.

But the doctrine of Marxism was purposefully designed to directly benefit others besides the usual, more socially refined audience for 19th-century political tracts and essays, the leisure classes of the day. What this meant in practice was that those who first understood and accepted the Marxist message were not to be and were not, by and large, its first objects of mercy. Instead, its chief *advocates* were those who were non-workers themselves, but felt it their duty nonetheless to identify with and "represent" the interests of the depicted muddled masses of laborers being repressed by private, capitalist greed. Hence, the early Marxist partisans were arguing and acting *in the name of* the reputedly dull and helpless, albeit singularly numerous, "proletarians" they claimed to champion, in roughly the same fashion as the later Marxist-Leninist leaders in control of the purposefully repressed Soviet Union.

---

3. See Fromm, Erich, *Marx's Concept of Man*, N.Y.: Ungar, 1961, pp. 5, 18-19, for a sympathetic discussion.

It is notable that Marx, during his lifetime, declined to suggest any plan of government for the spontaneously revolutionary society he foretold, which, presumably, wouldn't long be needing one anyway. Thus, Lenin's genius was best applied to his devising of a system of government for the Soviet Union that could achieve and preserve the Marxian criterion of non-exploitation of labor, both by outside interests and by would-be capitalists surviving within the country. At the same time, Lenin's solution eventually brought about rapid, full-scale industrialization to completely transform the greater Russian Empire's vast but then still largely medieval economy.

The main principle Lenin applied, with thorough dedication if not certitude, from the first days following the November, 1917 Bolshevik coup d'etat, was the concept he had devised in basic form as early as 1904, which he referred to as "democratic centralism." He described the idea this way: "The main principle of democratic centralism is that of the higher cell being elected by the lower cell, the absolute binding force of all directions of the higher cell for a cell subordinate to it, and the existence of a commanding party centre [the Central Committee, with authority that is] indisputable for all leaders in party life, from one [Communist International] congress to the next."[4]

Despite its intriguing name, this principle quite obviously has not made the Soviet Union a majoritarian, or democratic, society, for two reasons. First, the actual right to vote that was to be applied in the leadership selection process was restricted to the Communist Party members who comprised the local "cells" (and who were in fact only a tiny, screened minority of the whole population). And second, the "higher cell" met in order to determine who the members of the "subordinate cells" would be; and, further, it could even execute ("purge") members at lower levels for unorthodoxy or perceived insolence.

When Lenin had urged his scheme for effective societal control at an earlier Comintern congress, even the notorious Polish-German Communist Rosa Luxemburg denounced it as "ultra-centralist." It would mean, she said, the dangerous institutionalization of a "sharp separation of the organized bodies of outspoken and active revolutionists from the unorganized though revolutionary active masses surrounding them." And it would impose, "on the other hand, strict discipline and direct, decisive

---

4. Lenin, "Resolution of the Second Congress of the Comintern", 1921, reproduced in Conquest, Robert, *V. I. Lenin*, N.Y.: Viking, 1972, p. 40.

and determining intervention of the central authorities in all expressions of life in the party's local organizations." Luxemburg complained further concerning the plan that "the central committee appears as the real, active nucleus of the party, and all other organizations merely as its executive organs." She thus noted the obvious: that the great and deep-rooted mass movement in convulsive, early 20th-century Russia had little or nothing to do with the activities of the Bolshevik party organization.[5] Hence, the real problem posed by Lenin's however well-meaning elitist approach to leadership, from a natural or national revolutionary standpoint, was that, while leadership is fundamentally necessary to avert disaster, whichever group wins a top-level power struggle, by whatever means, can *claim* to represent the general, public interest. (The very word "Bolshevik," of course, falsely denotes the representation of a majority.) And nearly all such groups everywhere in recent history, however empowered, "Marxist" or not, *do* so claim.

Then, why is it that *communist* regimes, in the Soviet Union and elsewhere, always desperately resist open, democratic means of actual control to benefit the large populations living under them? Lenin, confronting this issue early in the development of the Soviet Communist Party, explained that ruling party members had to be well-trained, "professional revolutionaries" and not run-of-the-mill workers or peasants, if they were to actually succeed in their purpose of overthrowing and replacing the state. He added that their leaders had to be chosen in secret in order to conceal their identity from the reigning "bourgeois" authorities.[6]

Even after the Bolsheviks had captured control of the state, the nature of their leadership selection process did not change insofar as the governed public was concerned. The rationale, obviously, was to avoid dilution or "reform" by the uninitiated of the ruling party's special secular revelation. Lenin also evidenced no intention of further changing the terms of rule in the Soviet Union after the new state was successfully launched. The purpose of the commendable early Soviet "liquidate illiteracy" campaign was, in his words, "only that every peasant should be

---

5. Rosa Luxemburg, Presentation at the Comintern Congress, 1904, quoted in Conquest, *ibid.*, pp. 40-41.
6. Lenin, sympathetically paraphrased in Hill, Christopher, *Lenin and the Russian Revolution*, Harmondworth, UK: Penguin, 1971, p. 56. The broad experience of collectivization under the Tsarist government after the emancipation of serfs in 1861 must also not be forgotten in this connection.

able to read for himself, without help, our decrees, orders, and proclamations. The aim is completely practical. No more."[7] Thus, actual, participatory citizenship for the masses of people was not contemplated. This meant no change at all in the significant respect of public authority from the earlier situation, when the last of the Tsars had manipulated and badgered the long-demanded constituent assemblies into a state of futility and nullity.

The long Russian revolutionary tradition, in fact, has hardly ever addressed and never emphasized the question of genuine popular government. It has been argued that the reason Marxist authoritarianism was widely if not universally accepted in the early years of its rule is that it made a new type of unearthly revelation the touchstone of public authority, reminding people of the harsh authority system of the monolithic Russian Orthodox Church, which had never undergone a refining reformation.[8] It has also often been suggested that the up-to-now final, lasting permutation of the sequential Russian Revolution was, after all, not revolutionary according to Western popular ideals, but instead was "revolutionary" in some radically new way, incomprehensible to outsiders. Yet, even if this is somehow true, it can hardly be said to cover for the tragic and extreme anti-public results this Revolution's ironic concepts of human nature and morality have entailed within the U.S.S.R. itself. But, still, the allure of freedom from the ravages of unbridled capitalist and foreign domination survives and thrives abroad in the world, and cannot be denied with impunity.

- The Simultaneous Bind on Creative Involvement -

It has often been pointed out that the Bolshevik program actually accomplished a *dual* "revolution" in Russian society. First, it accomplished the elimination of exploitation by capitalists, mainly by eliminating the capitalists. Its second qualified success involved a radical, at-all-costs program of fully industrializing the huge country's long-vegetating economy. For this, the new government conscripted all of the

---

7. Lenin, quoted in Conquest, *ibid.*, p. 23.
8. For instance, see Anderson, Thornton, *Russian Political Thought, An Introduction,* Ithaca, N.Y.: Cornell Univ. Press, 1967, pp. 361-62.

vast human and natural resources available within Russia and its attached dependent empire.[9]

In order to achieve these two objectives simultaneously, Lenin and the Bolsheviks, after they had grasped the mantle of power late in 1917, commandeered the services of large segments of the population, especially the small peasantry, which was by far the most numerous and tractable social class. Millions, of hapless peasants, along with numerous vilified larger farmers or *kulaks*, were compulsorily transplanted straightaway to the cities and mines to immediately and dramatically bolster the slow and painful work of industrial production and building then just underway.

Yet, opposition to such centralized high-handedness was, not unpredictably, considerable and widespread, and there was accordingly a very great deal of poorly coordinated armed resistance operating in Russia and adjacent repressed provinces for several years. This nearly-overwhelming internal resistance was led by members of the former nobility and the small middle class, whose socioeconomic status had been most obviously compromised. These were in turn joined by expeditionary units openly sent by the United States and a number of other Western countries, ostensibly to help with the job of "stabilizing" resource-rich Russia to participate in the new, post-War world economic order.[10]

The Soviet system's stringent centralization of production and planning was, nevertheless, achieved within a few years, under the authority and direction of an official oligarchy, the ruling Communist Party's Central Committee. Thus, both the *systolic* and the *diastolic* purposes of ordinary civilized society were coopted by the Central Committee and effectively sealed off from the natural functioning of the society, entailing consequences almost beyond imagining.

Totalitarian regimes in the past, while effectively cutting off the *systolic* (broad, popular nationalistic) function, had never succeeded in effectively monopolizing the direction of the *diastolic* (productive) power

---

9. See Von Laue, Theordore H., *Why Lenin? Why Stalin?*, second edition, Philadelphia: Lippincott, 1971, pp. 2-3.
10. McCauley, Martin, *The Soviet Union Since 1917*, London: Longman, 1981, pp. 28-33, highlights the Russian Civil War of 1917-22, in the context of the development of the state apparatus; Goldhurst, Richard, *The Midnight War*, N.Y.: McGraw-Hill, 1978, explores in detail the role and mission of the American expeditionary force sent to Russia at that time.

by radically centralizing productive authority and planning. The economic purposes of people in society were effectively frozen from top to bottom in the early Soviet Union, leaving no autonomy to the individual. Soviet society actually *is* revolutionary because its leaders have succeeded in doing this. It is properly seen as an "experiment" because its pervasive organizational pattern of negation and replacement was never achieved in any country before.

And the results, in terms of bringing about change and growth in the 1920s and after, starting from what are now called Third World conditions, were impressive. But the great spontaneous or induced enthusiasm necessary to keep a "revolution" going through generation after generation of continued economic sacrifice, coupled with the enormous social trade-off of individual growth, has, not too surprisingly, been lacking for a number of years now. Thus, the economy's revolutionary growth, once truly phenomenal, has since the end of the 1950s slid to a long, shuddering halt, still far short of the arguable goal of justifying the great trade-off of personal freedom by outpacing the capitalist West.

The still ongoing though muted East-West game is now one of continuing, drawn-out strategy to gain decisive world economic and political backing and access to the greatest population-based and resource-based trade and market shares in each continental area. And, amazingly at first glance, with the deep despair of much of the far-away, sinking Third World as a macabre backdrop, we in the West still appear to be no more than holding our own in a stark ebb-and-flow global nightmare of deception and trustless alliance. We are, in fact, presently more than holding our own on a sustained basis in only the fittest, richest, and most upwardly-mobile relative handful of world nations.[11]

The high human cost of enforcing Marxism in Russia via the Leninist strategy very clearly reveals that program's actual anti-popular nature, disillusioningly for some past and current believers. Before Lenin's death in 1922, during the period in which he and Trotsky held the decisive positions on the Central Committee, an estimated 12 million dissident and innocent Soviet citizens were lost fighting or as casual victims in a spate of counter-revolutionary civil wars. Many of these mostly unwilling

---

11. This assertion will be explored more fully in Chapter Six.

sacrifices to the time-extended Soviet Revolution occurred as a result of chaos that engulfed much of the country, as violent opposition to the abrupt curtailment of perceived individual rights involving occupation, place of residence, and property, spread and grew. The unprecedented uproar was caused as a side-effect of the arbitrary process by which the hallowed Russian industrial working class, or proletariat, which had scarcely existed before the 1917 Revolution, was actually being *created* by the Party out of spare, available human parts.[12] Altogether, since 1918, an estimated 60 million Soviet "citizens" have perished in opposition, or suspected opposition, to the Soviet regime, with untold millions more summarily incarcerated in state correctional facilities ranging from mental hospitals to Gulag prisons. A myriad of incidents of anguished opposition to state policies have, throughout Soviet history, been passed off both inside and outside the country merely as instances of "scattered banditry." As many as *three times* the tragic and justly-bewailed Soviet losses in all other wars in this century were thus caused internally as a direct result of the regime's very peculiar, hard morality turned against its own subjects.[13]

12. See Deutscher, Isaac, *The Unfinished Revolution, Russia, 1917-1967*, Oxford, U.K.: Oxford Univ. Press, 1967, pp. 47-48. The number is that arrived at by Aleksandr Solzhenitsyn from his researches into the shadowy Lenin era. See Solzhenitsyn, BBC interview with Janis Sapiets, February, 1979, in Solzhenitsyn, *East & West*, N.Y.: Harper & Row, 1980, pp. 152-53, 170; Andrew Cockburn, in *The Threat: Inside the Soviet Military Machine*, N.Y.: Vintage, 1984, p. 72, notes a spate of reports from the World War II ("Great Patriotic War") era to the effect "that the Wehrmacht was able to recruit as many as 700,000 Soviet non-Russians [Central Asians, Caucasians and others] to fight against their former fellow-citizens."

13. Solzhenitsyn, *ibid.*, pp. 170-72. Solzhenitsyn argues perceptively that many leading intellectuals in the West have tended to play down the viciousness of the Soviet regime due to what he views as a "common source of their ideological origins: materialism and atheism." The noted Russian dissident adds (p. 177) that he himself has "never advocated physical general revolution" in opposition to the regime because of the "demonstrated human destructiveness of that course." Instead, he has urged his people to simply "live not by lies. Cease supporting their ideology so that it crumbles and collapses."

- Economic and Social Results -

The Russian Revolution of 1917 can be seen as a general uprising to repudiate the antique, decrepit Tsarist regime's failure in two vital areas. First, in not bringing about industrialization rapidly enough to promote Russia's welfare, and second, in failing to sufficiently guard Russia's honor against foreign foes, including, intolerably, non-Western Japan. As such, the Revolution proper can hardly be viewed as anything but a negative mass movement, containing various and sundry factions, but lacking a positive consensus of any kind.

Yet, the Revolution itself was not betrayed by the aims of the triumphant if vaguely stated Marxism applied by Lenin and his regime to produce fundamental change. The widely-felt need in Russia to find a forward direction as the amorphous actual Revolution died down reached a point of crisis. Theodosius Dobshansky, a biologist and later emigre who was growing up in Moscow at that time, recalled how "the urgency of finding a meaning of life grew in the bloody tumult of the Russian Revolution, when life became most insecure and its sense least intelligible."[14]

The indirection of the revolution of 1917 in the midst of Russia's military disaster in World War I is reminiscent of the complexities of the French Revolution, which had also started as a surge of energy with little overall form, and the direction of which was also jerked precariously from hand to hand. And yet, the aim of the eventually-adopted Marxist movement, as expressed in *Das Kapital*, to bring the productive labor of the Russian majority "under their [the workers'] common control," was not in itself an unbecoming goal to espouse. Perhaps most Russians did espouse it.[15]

Word was spread throughout Russia that no over-all government would be needed in the new society, once the benefits of Marxian socialism had become obvious (ironically, the same thing Spencer had claimed for his doctrinaire *capitalist* system.) Indeed, the European Marxist ideologue Herbert Marcuse, representing a different shade of communism, still thought in the early 1960s that democratization within the Soviet state might eventually become practicable, once the rising standard of living had produced a high enough satisfaction quotient to insure against a free electorate's tampering with the sacred economic

---

14. Dobshansky, Theodosius, *The Biology of Ultimate Concern*, N.Y.: World, 1969, p. 1.
15. Marx, *Das Kapital*, III, transl. by Ernest Untermann, Chicago: Kerr & Company, 1909, p. 954; Fromm, *ibid.*, pp. 47-48, 107.

model.[16] Unfortunately for such predictions, the gap in living standards between Soviet and Western society has only widened since, with the economic satisfaction quotient within the "workers' paradise" remaining dismally low.

Modern Soviet society is, thus, still much more a function of control from above, by an autonomous ruling cartel, than the product of the irresistible movement from below that Marx had foretold. Viewed in terms of proportional changes among the society's functional classes under Lenin's directional legacy, the effect of Russia's "revolution" on its society over the decades has been extreme. The basic outward changes are summed up in the table below describing the composition of Soviet society as a whole. The statistics are taken from an article in the Soviet Communist Party newspaper *Pravda*:

(Percent of the Population)[17]

	1928	1937	1959	1962
Workers & Employees	17.6	45.7	68.3	73.6
Collective farm peasantry & artisans in cooperatives	2.9	48.8	31.4	26.3
Land owners, big & petty urban bourgeoisie, merchants & kulaks	4.6	-0-	-0-	-0-
Individual peasants & artisans not in cooperatives	74.9	5.5	0.3	0.1

16. See Ollman, Bertell, *Alienation, Marx's Concept of Man in Capitalist Society*, Cambridge, UK: University Press, 1971, p. 221; Marcuse, Herbert, *Soviet Marxism, A Critical Analysis*, N.Y.: Vintage, 1961, pp. 171-73.

17. *Pravda*, Dec. 6, 1964, pp. 2-4.

The society described by these figures cannot plausibly be said to have so *reordered itself* in the represented span of years. The class composition of the society did not *change*, but *was changed* violently and dramatically. So much, then, for the most basic stated Marxist objective, greater working public control over society, taken at face value.

Since the end of the Stalin period, the huge, official Soviet bureaucracy (presumably inconspicuously tucked into the broad "Workers & Employees" category) has increasingly jelled into an "electorate" of sorts within the state. It is a constituency which, although it has no say in the positive direction of Soviet state *policy*, the Central Committee, and particularly its presiding chairman, cannot afford to ignore or underestimate. Chairman Khrushchev ultimately learned this lesson, to his own undoing.[18] One arrangement this de facto Soviet "public" is reportedly not willing to tolerate for long, recalling the purges and terrors of Stalin's reign, is the unchecked concentration of hard authority in the hands of one individual at the top. Still, the multitudinous, overwhelming majority of the real Soviet public lies completely outside the system's real machinery of power, and hence remains for all intents at the mercy of its actions.

The normal Soviet structure of authority consists of the Central Committee and its most favored courtiers representing interests such as the military services at the top, with other high Party officials, commisars, and high-ranking military and para-military officers heading up a vast, subordinate civil service. Throughout the Soviet period, the official line has been that the top leaders, those few who monopolize the "rights of ownership" in Western terms, are legitimate representatives of the Soviet people because they are selected mainly from the ranks of the general working class. This principle allegedly insures that the opportunity to rise into the ruling class is at least open to all.

In the early 1970s, Soviet emigre Vladimir Andrle, under the aegis of the Centre for Russian and Eastern European Studies at the University of Birmingham, tested this so-called "dirty hands" claim of the origins of functioning officials. He was able to survey a reasonably broad though limited sample of Soviet industrial managers, functionally equivalent to CEOs and their immediate subordinates in the West, in order to determine the incidence of manual labor experience in Soviet management's background. Out of the fair number of managers on

---

18. See Cockburn, *ibid.*, pp. 115 ff; Deutcher, *ibid.*, pp. 56-58; Djilas, *New Class*, op. cit., pp. 38-40, ff; Marcuse, *ibid.*, p. 93.

whom information was obtainable who had started work in their present capacity before the outbreak of World War II, 29 had had manual employment experience previously and 20 had not, while for 4, the answer was unclear. For those whose managerial careers had begun after 1940, 11 had experienced prior manual employment, while 77 had not, with half a dozen cases indeterminable. Andrle's conclusion, based on the admittedly limited sample obtainable, was that even in this segment of the Soviet ruling elite nearest the status of most of the people, the claimed principle of representative recruitment was at the very least no longer being followed.

It is far from clear that such a principle was *ever* consistently followed. For instance, it is evident from other sources that throughout the critical 1920s and into the '30s, between 2,000 and 3,000 top plant managers employed in the Soviet Union were non-Communist specialists, who at least brought needed industrial experience to important industrial positions. Under Stalin during the 1930s, when these nonpartisan professionals finally seemed dispensable, they are reported to have been abruptly arrested and liquidated on Party orders. Even from the beginning, the claimed representativeness of the decision-making strata seems not to have been significant in the actual system.[19] The gap between Soviet officialdom and the artificial, though now very numerous class it was contrived to "represent," would seem to be extremely wide on all significant counts.

As we have already seen, a relatively tiny group of major financiers and multinational-scale business managers are now able to control with increasing firmness and confidence the course of American economic and even social decision-making, very largely for business and personal ends. Likewise, and equally destructively, the analogous bureaucratic elite in the Soviet Union normally guides that system resolutely in its own best financial interest (i.e., that of the elite), relatively unmoved by the desires and interests of the vast, effectively disfranchised political underclass. And the relative unproductiveness of such a monopolistic arrangement of effective authority has, there as well, now become clear.

---

19. Andrle, Vladimir, *Managerial Power in the Soviet Union*, Westmead, UK: D. C. Heath, 1976, pp. 2, 99; Dahrendorf, Ralf, *Class and Class Conflict in Industrial Society*, Palo Alto: Stanford Univ. Press, 1959 (transl. from 1957 German edition). Berle, A. A. and G. C. Means, *The Modern Corporation and Private Property*, N.Y.: Collier-Macmillan, 1967 (orig. publication 1932), and Anthony Giddens, *Sociology*, pp. 38-39, discuss the distinction between corporate ownership on one hand, and control, or so-called "ownership rights," on the other.

In Soviet society, where discretionary funds are far less available than in the United States or any of a number of Western societies, the necessary cohesion of the actual system of rule cannot be achieved solely through quantum salary differentials for the top echelon. The pay of Soviet managers and officials is generally much less as a proportion of their typical fellow countryman's pay than, for instance, is the case in the U.S. Instead, the essential incentives are provided mainly through the allocation of highly desired perquisites. Among the rewards are two, three, or reportedly up to four country homes in different environments to be used exclusively by the family of a high-ranking public official or commissar. The private use of state airplanes is common, along with the services of their attendant military personnel, plus the best of imported food, cars, and advanced technical gadgetry, exit visas for travel abroad, and boundless public adulation and social prestige.

Some observers have argued that the Soviets' bureaucratic leadership is more of an "accidental," therefore not really an entrenched, elite. They argue that its present power is not based on outright ownership per se, as is that of controlling elites in the West.[20] Such a conclusion overlooks two important points. First, there is no other organized group of sufficient size and cohesion in the U.S.S.R. to challenge the bureaucracy's real, permanent hold on power. The only possible exception is the armed forces, who, however, depend heavily on the rest of the massive, functional hierarchy to make their enormous, far-extended, day-to-day operations possible. It is well to remember that armed forces chiefs themselves have never held the top slots in the Soviet system, but have always been subordinate, even though signally influential.

Second, the ruling bureaucracy's iron web of survival is spun out of the need for protection and patronage of its individual members. This circumstance has demonstrably led to the proliferation throughout the system of "family circles," with virtually every senior official having himself risen through ranks of favoritism to gradually become the head and protector of a loyal "family" network of under-officials. All members of a particular "family" protect all others even to the death because of an evilly-ingenious rule for systemic preservation that has been in operation since at least the end of the Stalin era. In an instance of *reported* corruption or failure at any level in the chain of command, all heads roll,

---

20. For instance, see Marcuse, *loc. cit.*; Djilas, *ibid.*, p. 62; Cockburn, *loc. cit.*

from top to bottom. Hence, the privilege and license of the Soviet elite has been virtually limitless. Once in, one could, and probably can, as a rule, do almost anything at the nation's collective expense.

Thus, unless some calamity should befall, actually bringing down the Soviet state itself, the relative position of the system's rock-solid elite within it appears unassailable. Hence, the role of glaring, unequal privilege, extended as a social cost to members of the operative elite, will probably continue to infest this system that officially eschews all privilege. This set of circumstances accords the Soviet operating equivalent of the Hamiltonian "rich and well born" a powerful interest in the fortunes of the state, in order to secure vital support and acquiescence for the rulers' purposes. No president or general secretary can make operational changes in the prevailing system without this indispensable and costly interest group's permission.

Thus, in the case of *both* of the greatest modern officially egalitarian systems of rule, the result in the long run must be the subversion of the vastly underrepresented interest of the general public. In the U.S.S.R., the normal way to rise is through blind, but transparent, devotion to "egalitarian" Marxist-Leninist dogma. In the U.S., the new, artificial code word is "democracy," meaning, apparently, anti-socialism, but not democracy in the traditional Western sense of popular control.

Fortunately for us, the American system has not yet gone quite so far down the road to the common destination of total domination by a frozen elite as has the badly-ailing Soviet "workers'" system. Ultimately, though, unless there occurs an actual reversal in the common direction of the systemic trend, either in the United States or the Eastern Bloc, the result for the majority of the world of a definitive takeover internationally by one or the other competing superstructure would be virtually equal in effect. This is because the two systems have come to represent the interests of almost identically narrowed real constituencies.

The Yugoslav dissident Milovan Djilas reminded his readers several years ago of the course of events in the West after the original Industrial Revolution of the 1800s -- the most powerful *diastolic* thrust prior to the current one incorporating what are now called high tech capabilities. The dominant corporatists of that earlier time, he reported, were eventually compelled, "as a result of strikes and parliamentary action ...

to relinquish their other social powers so that workers may participate in sharing the profits of their work."[21]

There is today a prevalent multitude of "realist" politicians in the West, who would dismiss as remote the prospect of another very strong *systolic* resurgence still to come, capable of tipping the scales back in favor of a mixed balance of interests through positive governmental action forced by the sheer numbers and insistent demands of non-corporatist, as well as enlightened and socially responsible business-minded citizens. Such "realistic" politicians and pundits should note, however, that the second stroke of the full revolution has irresistibly followed the first in this country before, during the hard-knuckled first Industrial Revolution, and also the time before that, in the age of the American Revolution against callous, thoroughly investment-minded colonialism. And the greater public is bound by irradicable human nature to insist on its due, by one means or another, in the West again.

We in America still for now can act deliberately *through* the system to try to redress the balance in favor of the broad national interest; but to accomplish any sort of genuine reform at the real, permanent expense of the privileges of the ruling elite within the Soviet system, as Djilas notes, seems virtually impossible. The reason is because this "would be to abolish them as a class, ...being deprived of their monopoly over property, ideology, and government [meaning] the end of Communist monopolism and totalitarianism."[22] And, fairly obviously, no interest or sector is in a strong enough position to successfully and seriously challenge the equivalent of the strengthened American single-interest elite's continued hold on the Soviet social and political system, although certain other reforms, reflecting new management schemes and psychology without relinquishing genuine power, seem eminently possible. To understand what President Gorbachov is really doing in this regard at present, we would almost have to be in his shoes.

---

21. Djilas, *op. cit.*, pp. 45-46.
22. *Ibid.*; Michael Voslensky, in his book *Nomenklatura*, transl. by Eric Mosbacher, N.Y.: Doubleday, 1984, provides a revealing, inside view of this tiny minority class which normally dominates through delimitation Soviet policy and society for its own protection and benefit. See also Pipes, Richard, *Survival Is Not Enough*, N.Y.: Simon & Schuster, 1984, in this same connection.

In Russia, both before and after 1917, owing to the chill of despotism and the country's isolated location, the *diastolic* (wholesale economic) spark needed for revolutionary or even incremental improvement has always had to occur somewhere else. And the numerous answering *systolic* (popular) movements that have followed even in Russia have without a single exception been stifled in the cradle, following the ages-old habit of despotism. Hence, the medieval European age of subjection, dreaming, scheming, and wakeful resignation can be seen to continue there still. Only now is some of the recent accumulated steam of popular demand being vented without a firestorm of harsh, unseemly violence. And pragmatic but moderate Japan and West Germany may, as a result of the new Soviet moderation, be successfully persuaded to spark the necessary economic revitalization.

Meanwhile, the consequences of elite *diastolic* domination in the U.S.S.R. have quite likely been as important as the better-known costs of *systolic* repression. "The Soviet Union," American economist Jane Jacobs observed not long ago, "far from demonstrating the superiority of its planning and performance, continues unable to so much as feed itself, nor in other respects does it produce amply and diversely for its own people and producers. Indeed, as an economy the Soviet Union is eerily beginning to resemble a 'colonial' country, for it depends increasingly upon exporting natural resources to more highly developed countries and on importing sophisticated manufacturing goods, including even the machinery to exploit its natural resources for export."[23]

Even in the area of military prowess and production, the Soviet system's longtime first priority, an enormous amount of higher technological help has always entered the country from the outside. The needed help has come, since even before the dawn of atomic weaponry, from U.S. as well as German, French, British, and Japanese sources of development, both from openly available published information and through the well-documented and prodigious Soviet industrial espionage network.

"Importing Western technical ideas is an old Soviet practice," affirms Andrew Cockburn, a current student of the Soviet military structure. "The Klimov engines that powered most fighters during World War II were an adaptation of the French Hispano-Suiza design.

---

23. Jacobs, Jane, *Cities and the Wealth of Nations*, N.Y.: Random House, 1984, p. 5.

"The first post war Russian bomber, the TU-4. was an exact copy of an American B-29 bomber that landed in Siberia during the war. The story goes that the Soviet engineers found a small hole under the left wing with no ascertainable purpose. But since Stalin had ordered the plane to be copied perfectly, every single TU-4 had an identical hole drilled under the left wing. Unfortunately for the Russians, not all Western weapons concepts are good ones."[24]

The list of borrowings could most assuredly be quite long. Indeed, it is not easy to discover a first-line technological innovation, apart from Sputnik, that originated within the Soviet planning system. The Soviet state has, for instance, been completely dependent on Western sources for the design used in its computer technology since the advent of the high tech era, and modern Soviet Air Force planes reportedly tend to be modeled after American prototypes. Soviet planners, notoriously and embarrassingly, had to reach into Western Europe for help in constructing the massive Siberian gas pipeline in the early 1980s.

The technical gap, apparently widened by long-continued rigid, monolithic control, seems to be in no wise narrowing. Meanwhile, the GNP of the Soviet Union limps along at scarcely two-thirds that of the now competitively-faltering United States, a significantly smaller country in terms of population. The gap between the two rival power blocs in so many important phases of modern life remains not only considerable, but, just as important, very conspicuous.[25]

This is an important factor because the Bolshevik founders' October Revolution was never intended to stop with the capture of one imperial country, albeit a country that is a world in itself. The Soviets have leaned heavily on their founders' rhetoric in the process of helping to "liberate" since the Second World War a fair number of countries that had the misfortune of being their relatively small next-door neighbors.[26] But a bit more puzzlingly, a long procession of widely scattered emerging and low-income states have sided with Moscow in recent years and deliberately adhered to pro-Soviet principles in opposition to those of the more economically capable West.

---

24. Cockburn, *ibid.*, pp. 120-21, 146-47.

25. *Ibid.*, pp. 14, 218-46 ff.

26. See Deutscher, *ibid.*, pp. 57-58, 61. It is noteworthy that during the momentous post-War course of the Chinese Communist Revolution, the Soviet leaders backed Chiang Kai-shek's Nationalist forces, which they expected to emerge as winners. Hence, the Soviets, too, are demonstrably pragmatic in their own way and select their clients.

Such a seemingly paradoxical turn of events demands an explanation, and to say that each of these countries was simply subverted is neither sufficient nor totally accurate. America's continuing problem in attracting and holding friends among weaker Third World nations seems to stem, at least in large part, from changes in the values America has come to represent in the eyes of its beholders. As I suggested earlier, compulsion is really not popular, though it may partially work in the short run.

Further, it is not easy to see how a developing condition of monopolistic political and economic control subtly or blantantly tied to rather extreme, doctrinaire capitalism (i.e., *corporatism*) in America would work any better in the long run for a thoroughly dependent population than an analogous monopolistic political and economic control system under the banner of "communism" has worked out inside its rival, an almost equally well-endowed country naturally, up to now.

In either case, the loss of creative input and domestic market capacity entailed by the loss of genuine pluralism represented in the control mechanism is the unaffordable cost of highly concentrated political power, whether held by brute force and pragmatic untruths or bought with financial incentives and favors.

Also in either case, both the direct, as well as the indirect but much higher financial costs of maintaining the narrowed power system, are conveniently passed on by the self-interested group in control of the government, to be paid by the whole society. This enervating evasion of the costs of ruling group self-service through the mechanism of government is accomplished in ways already routinely familiar to the experienced power-elite on the Soviet side, but which the recently successful corporatist paralyzers of the representative political system in America are still learning.

At least for now, the United States and the West, especially if surging Japan is included, are far in the lead economically and productively and widening the gap. So much is obvious.

But, then again, it is obviously not the Soviet Union's relative lack of economic success, any more than the system's often-necessary repression of personal liberty, that has induced so many struggling, backward states on several continents to share much of its overall vision and system of aid.[27]

---

27. For a surprising, graphic view of ominous shifts of allegiance in the underdeveloped Third World since 1945, see Kidron, Michael and Dan Smith, *The War Atlas*, N.Y.: Simon & Schuster, 1983, Map 16.

Instead, its rather obvious appeal to numerous countries and powerful factions has been mainly owing to a combination of two things. First, this ponderous giant's relative lack of discretionary economic clout beyond its borders is, in effect, a reassuring aspect for nations distant from it. It *can't buy* controlling interest in their economies. Second, there is the thoroughly-redeeming prospect of military protection, or at least substantial aid, against a domineering American government acting in defense of that wealthier country's controlling corporate interests abroad. In some cases, particularly in Africa, the local bias (at times mixed with admiration) is instead against smaller Western European U.S. allies that fairly recently held colonies outright and continue to exert strong economic leverage. And again, the Soviets' own apparent triumph over foreign domination at home since the end of World War I is also still successfully touted as appropos. Like heroin, Soviet-brand Marxism is basically a bad product with horrific side effects; but, in desperately weakened nations, it still sells better than soap.

- Escaping the Soviet Time-Release Trap -

The American response to the long aftermath of disillusionment with our leadership overseas, if we really hope to finally win the world ideological argument and thereby secure peace and an opportunity for growth, must be to apply our vastly superior economic means not extravagantly, but deliberately in such a way as to actually help fulfill the aspirations of human populations in many countries for equitable opportunities and economic freedom. We could, simultaneously, expect to considerably enhance our own present and future overseas markets, but not necessarily to *immediately* maximize quarterly profits for all or any of our firms in the process. Though beguilingly resourceful in some other important ways, the establishment of Soviet Marxism lacks the financial means to compete with such a strategy, genuinely emphasizing the powerful economic development and self-realization dreams of our multitudinous potential allies and friends.

Such a new national policy emphasis on positive helping and healing rather than control schemes, widely applied, might appear to serve the long-term policy interests of the American nation as a whole at the expense of the necessarily cooperating American-based multinational business community. But, since a rising, world-wide economic tide could raise our ship at least as much as any by providing desperately sought new markets and increased buying power, initial impressions in this matter are apt to be mistaken. The problem involved might turn out instead to be one of balancing the strategic initial costs of a concerted trade/aid policy among the many firms involved, the American public, and participating allies following our new lead.

In the pages that follow, I will explore the appropriateness and merit of such a seemingly necessary change in U.S. international policy, permitting us to shift from a struggling, defensive position vis-à-vis our recuperating and reorganizing Marxist natural rival and our other, more active and obvious, economic competitors, to effective offense and positive problem-solving.

Chapter Six

THE INTERNATIONAL RELATIONS LEVEL

- The Constricted Constituency of Foreign Relations -

Most of the time over the past century, the determining logic of American foreign policy in specific situations has remained more or less a mystery to most Americans. Foreign policy is of the utmost actual importance to Americans, to be sure, since it contributes ultimately to war and peace, the state of the nation's economy, and our permanent quality of life. But the entire gamut of citizens routinely regarded as active, interested constituents in the course of foreign policy formation, whose views and direct interests are carefully considered by the policy establishment and the U.S. State Department, typically adds up to a small, very well-heeled group of special patrons practically all of whom are known to one another personally.

Situations infrequently arise in international affairs with sufficient clarity and immediate impact to produce broad public obstinance against the foreign policy establishment's prevailing view and firm insistence on unstinted representation of a different, broader public view in actual policy. One obvious example would be the slowly building, ultimately unyielding opposition that finally brought an unglorious end to the Vietnam War. Thus, in exceedingly rare and sharply focused instances, a public plurality has asserted its independently constituted perceived interests effectively, if but gradually, as was ultimately the case after many additional deaths and a rending struggle against institutionalized power at home over the U.S. role in Vietnam.

Yet, in the long run, the most capable, knowledgeable, and interested constituency -- and thus, the group most perfectly represented in actual policy -- remains the American-based majority of the multinational business community. Such has been more true for a longer time in foreign policy than in other areas of government because of widespread public ignorance of conditions overseas. Multinational businesses lobby heavily for policy outcomes they see as most favoring themselves, as just about anyone who could afford to, could do. In addition, because of their superior overseas experience and connections, they are most often able to fill crucial appointive positions, either with their own operatives, or with approved surrogates.[1]

Since the international business sector's claims of special knowledge (not necessarily the same as wisdom) can hardly be disputed, this quintessential case of policy domination by one sector of our national life must be judged according to its fruits over time. In this chapter, I will describe in general, and assess some aspects of, both the long-term *reality* of the domination of U.S. foreign policy by multinational business interests, and the *results* of this rather well-known circumstance for America's crucial international standing as well as for its domestic success. Finally, I will suggest a means of advantageously broadening the regular foreign policy constituency.

Perhaps the most important policy the active business constituency of U.S. foreign policy has been able to maintain or advance in recent decades has been the moderation, to the point of virtual insignificance, of direct, non-military U.S. governmental involvement overseas. The stage was set for this currently prevalent theme of federal non-involvement in regulation and standards for American-based international commerce (as opposed to *interstate* commerce, subsumed by design as a federal matter in the Constitution itself) early in the 19th century, when corporate licensing was conversely left up to individual states. Thus, direct national jurisdiction over American corporate activities overseas is still effectively prevented, even though the national and international, rather than the single licensing state's interest, is now involved on a incomparably grander scale.[2]

What this rather profound legal circumstance in fact means is that American companies are, in general, free of direct legal obligation to the United States in conducting their overseas operations. Hence, their de facto representation of America and its international interests is not normally conditioned by any sort of formal public accountability.

---

1. Domhoff, *ibid.*, pp. 85-88, 100-104 ff, quotes statistical evidence of this from a number of credible sources.

2. For instance, see the discussion of the landmark Dartmouth College case, decided under the tenure of the "lame duck" Federalist Marshall Supreme Court, in Chapter Two.

American government, thus, normally exercises little or no power on the larger public's behalf, either of guidance or restraint, over American companies operating overseas, even though they are by far the most influential representatives of American national interests and values in the world. Hence, our government's foreign policy, for the most part representing the wishes and thinking of its narrowed active foreign policy constituency, normally serves almost no direct purpose other than the extension and protection, through diplomacy and threat, of American business prerogatives. Informed foreign nationals in many less-developed, and hence vulnerable, countries of the world have long been more or less onto this open secret of American policy and its rather obvious meaning for them.

Since the close of the immediate post-War era of the late '40s, American direct foreign aid has increasingly been synonymous with military aid to regimes and contra-type rebels, sometimes, as it turned out, running *against* the tide of local democracy in the particular country. For the seldom-cited reasons stated in the preceding chapter, the menace of pandemic Marxism is still very real and needs to be dealt with. But overbearing, strictly self-serving, muscled policy stances favoring the severely narrowed U.S. foreign policy constituency, applied especially to resource-rich and strategic countries among the poorest and hence vulnerable, are generally counterproductive. This is true in part because they tend to betray the traditional democratic values that are still held by most run-of-the-mill American citizens. Such unequal, one-sided policies inevitably win us countless more bitterly disillusioned enemies than friends among the rapidly growing and increasingly deprived mass populations of the Third World.

A more representative U.S. foreign policy that would better serve the American national interest in steady overseas progress, partnership, and stability is by no means the practical impossibility that many critics of such a suggestion would doubtless claim it to be. In fact, such a policy could very probably serve the long-term interests of the large corporate business community itself much more effectively by producing a new national commitment of citizen support and active involvement in the United States. A desirable degree of broad, interested-party coordination in planning could be integrated into the process, as well as an enforceable and convincing curb on unrepresentative and reprehensible American (literally, *un-American*) business activities abroad. I will restate these criteria of a truly *national* U.S. foreign policy more specifically ahead.

On the opposite side, to refuse to seriously address the apparent failure of our present, fragmented international stance in some coordinated way is no longer a realistic choice. To continue to operate in the piecemeal and reactive manner that we have overseas can only assure the specter of the mounting disaster, slowly re-materialing after a termporary, post-Reagan period of readjustment, of an unprecedented, *systolic* surge, both active and non-associative, against strongly-pushed corporatist and other exclusively elitist interests in the world. Our own powerful multinational operatives could, in fact, by their obstinate resistance to working and planning effectively in concert with other American interests, put Marx's well-reasoned scenario of mass desperation, repulsion, and spontaneous reorganization on target within the next one to two decades. Ample evidence, to be sampled just ahead, suggests that Eastern Bloc ideologues are, in fact, counting heavily on continued Western irrationality in the world economic crisis now well underway to gradually deliver to their side a growing number of desperate new clients strategically located throughout the world. Out-and-out war may be neither an inevitable nor even a very likely result; but continued struggle for influence and leverage is probably inevitable between the world corporatists locally represented in all countries and their multitude of potential foes among the teeming billions economically left out. Having no taste for failure, the ever-ambitious Soviets are currently concerned with renewing their latent capacity to compete in defense of one of these major parties in the world arena. Must it, then, fall to us to press the claims of the narrowed world elite?

- Results of the Current U.S. Bi-Polar Policy -

Though its credo is unqualified competition and freedom, mega-scale American business has accepted neither the implications of serious international competition nor arrangements viewed as roadblocks imposed by legally sovereign host countries with grace.

And the large business sector's disdain for the new level of foreign competition has, due to that sector's domination of the policy process, affected the policy arm of the government as well. It has lent at least an undertone of desperation and heightened militancy to American dealings with a host of allies and disaffected countries alike, including Nicaragua and Japan, Guyana and Guatemala. In practice, the American foreign relations establishment has long tended, after a period of analysis and "fact-finding" on a subject, to accede, almost as a matter of course, to the operating requirements or preferences of a dominant part of the American international business community. The common underlying goal seems to be to preserve or restore a remembered status quo level of power -- reflecting the extended period after World War II when U.S.

business was truly unchallenged -- conducive to corporate expansion and profitability within areas of actual and potential U.S. influence.

Results in specific countries, in the past generally unknown to the American public until reported much later, often fly directly in the face of such American public values as national and individual self-determination, improvement of conditions and opportunities for oppressed and impoverished people trying to advance, and a decent respect for the bona fide majority interpretation of international law.

To cite a high-profile regional example lending particular substance to these allegations of distinctively partial policy abuse: during the past century in the countries of Central America, much of the food-producing land that the non-landowning peasant majority once depended on for sustenance, has been diverted from that purpose to produce bananas or coffee for export by local *caudillos* (large landlords) and American and European companies, with American (earlier, British) government support. The business status quo in Central America was openly sustained on half a dozen occasions, long before the threat of Marxist doctrine and Soviet alliance entered the scene, by American troops and arms sent to quash popular reform efforts, including those established by specific popular mandate. It is only now becoming well-known in this country that the policy of the United States has long been to support military and civilian strongmen in the region expediently willing to favor American business interests over the aspirations of their own people for economic growth produced by more beneficial use of some of the local resources.[3] Unfortunately, even widely-supported nationalist leaders, such as the currently prevailing faction of anti-Somoza forces in Nicaragua, sometimes find it necessary to embrace Marxist strategy and appeal for

---

3. For instance, see LaFeber, Walter, *Inevitable Revolutions*, N.Y.: Norton, 1983, pp. 8-11 ff; Schlesinger, Stephen and Stephen Kinzer, *Bitter Fruit*, Garden City, N.Y.: Doubleday, 1982; Maira, Luis, "The American National Interest and Interpretations of Crisis in Central America," in Diskin, Martin, ed., *Trouble in Our Back Yard*, N.Y.: Pantheon, 1983, pp. 36-42. Valenta, Jiri and Virginia Valenta, in an article entitled "Soviet Strategy and Policies in the Caribbean Basin," in Wiarda, Howard J., ed., *Rift and Revolution, the Central American Imbroglio*, Washington: American Enterprise Institute, 1984, p. 249, conclude: "It would be a tragedy and failure of the Western democracies to allow the Soviets ostensibly to champion the cause of political and economic justice, the traditional undertaking of democracies, while in the long run furthering the political, military, and social objectives of totalitarianism. ...If unresolved, the socioeconomic problems in the Central American isthmus, exacerbated by current U.S. economic difficulties, might sooner or later engulf the United States in a conflict of overwhelming dimensions."

the Soviet Union's protection in order to keep the direction of their country's affairs in local rather than U.S. hands. The strong instinct of the corporatist American policy establishment is, then, inevitably, to militarily or economically undercut and remove the new, unwelcome regime, in order to restore something resembling the former pro-foreign, pro-corporatist, anti-popular arrangement, which was the direct cause of anguished, grass roots rebellion in the first place.

Farther south, the oppressive Pinochet military regime in Chile is the still-surviving result of such a restoration, after covert American intervention against the last popularly-elected administration of the country in the early 1970s at the insistence of well-connected American copper and nitrate interests. Nor should it be quickly forgotten that Manuel Noriega, the now-vilified Panamanian millitary strongman, ruled with U.S. support until he stopped following Reagan administration suggestions in secretly supporting the Nicaraguan Contras.

In the case of several of the sometimes-wayward Central American countries (Nicaragua, El Salvador, Guatamala, and by recent accounts Honduras), it is significant that little or nothing has been said publicly by U.S. officials about the far-reaching institutional and technical assistance actually needed to reduce the age-long economic growth lag behind prodigious population growth and patiently instill a general acceptance of benevolent hemispheric leadership, though not domination, from Washington with its technically advanced means to assist.

The current regional drama, involving rebellion against local and perceived foreign-based oppression and Washington's predictable and usually successful attempt to restore its corporatist constituents' private supporters in local power, has been more-or-less repeated many times, but in less limelight. In addition to the instances of the above-named countries, the familiar pattern has also been repeated in the still-memorable past, in cooperation with local business clients, in such other "developing" western hemisphere countries as Cuba, the Dominican Republic, and Brazil.

But never before has a U.S. administration attempted to enforce the multinational business mandate in the region with the more-or-less full knowledge of the American public, which now, interestingly, bodes likely to permanently short-circuit, pending public re-education, the implementation of preferred administration policy goals by its overwhelming, steadfast opposition. A corporatist-dominated U.S. administration may yet find a pretext to literally march on Managua. But television news and the proliferation of non-business international travel seem for now to have brought the separation between what are in fact

American corporate goals and public goals and interests into sharp relief for a critical mass of Americans still imbued with the pain of unsuccessfully invading Vietnam, Laos, and Cambodia to try to force American solutions on determined Third World nationals.

For similar, primarily long-range business-related reasons, the last American administration relinquished the much needed active encouragement of popular groups in South Africa trying to bring an end to race-sanctioned political domination, to interested Marxist governments. The Soviet Union and other Marxist regimes may, as a consequence, reap the inestimable, far-reaching benefits of future black-majority or interracial South African economic and strategic support at "democratic" America's expense. Such, indeed, might eventually be the heavy, long-term material and moral cost to the entire American nation of eking out just another year or two's expedient business with a floundering, reactionary regime whose goals and methods are uniformly rejected by the American mainstream, instead of supporting its overwhelming majority, harshly oppressed internal opposition.

Nor is the taint of this narrow drift of thinking a new feature of our foreign policy. By similarly slanted, single-criterion corporatist logic, the U.S. government earlier failed for over a decade to offer meaningful support for the aspirations of large, impoverished African nations painfully wriggling free after four centuries of rule by the decrepit Portuguese Empire. Then, in 1974, the U.S. State Department announced its fears for "the future of democracy in Portugal," when that antique country's longtime, fascist-style dictatorship was being overthrown by the popular revolution that in fact *led to* democracy as well as the freeing of the inhumanly oppressed Portuguese African colonies.[4] We repeatedly seem to expect our "principled" lack of support for and opposition to emerging and struggling African, Asian, and Latin American peoples to be somehow repaid by their later gratitude and acceptance of our commercial overlordship. The present pro-Marxist stance of long-besieged governments in Mozambique and Angola in former Portuguese Africa remains as another bitter living monument to earlier, perhaps still-deepening Western official indifference to suffering.

Whether we can withstand the degree of honest internal examination required for redressment and adjustment to little-discussed, rapidly

---

4. Official U.S. State Department public statement, quoted in Green, Gil, *Portugal's Revolution*, N.Y.: International, 1976, p. 80.

deteriorating larger world realities remains an open question. Yet, the time seems nearly ripe, given increased public awareness of some of our current less-than-creditable foreign policy objectives, for our government's ironic, democratic rhetoric to be redeemed, especially in our actions toward numerous smaller, justly fearful nations. The vehicle of replacement or redemption of our relations needs very much to be our own genuine and still-challenging revolutionary values, even when these values might actually involve temporary and heartfelt sacrifices in others' behalf. Such values include the right of national self-determination and the essential equality of the value of human beings everywhere. I think that *our own* immediate future world position demands as much, and, of equal importance, that such a practical about-face in our external policy is eminently possible both in economic and political terms, *if* the corporatist stranglehold on the formulation of this country's national policy can be loosened.

- Our Fragmented Business Sector's Inability to Compete -

The Soviet Union, though it lacks the financial strength to even begin to effectivelycapitalize the enormous Third World -- a role reserved at present for an essentially democratic West -- conducts its external relations ruthlessly and pragmatically and with some skill. So much is perfectly well-known worldwide.

Americans, meanwhile, although their earlier, not wholly undeserved reputation for democratic earnestness and fairness still survives at least in a sort of wistful twilight, are increasingly well-known abroad these days for intransigent misunderstanding and disregard for local sentiments and priorities. Our insistences upon local compliance with our plans, backed by intimidating military and market strength and the self-serving control by our corporations over what still amounts to almost half of the entire world's craved financial power, are deeply, even if irrationally, resented in many quarters of the world. Such righteous resentment in the face of widespread ruin is surely not beyond our ability to comprehend.[5]

We, together with Japan and a handful of somewhat lesser but important powers now uniting in Western Europe, thus control the main

---

5. See *New State of the World Atlas,* maps 21, 30, 31 and accompanying text.

152

hope of global regeneration and development in the crucial economic sense. Yet our system's built-in insistence upon investing abroad only where to do so means large and immediate profits for American companies, and our insistence upon compliance with our agenda by weaker nations, have sporadically served to drive beleaguered, independence-minded countries into the protecting arms of rival Soviet power, often providing the lone credible alternative to Western domination.

Up to now, we simply have not permitted ourselves to see our powerful, purely capital-serving private and public actions as contributing *causes* of much unrest abroad. Yet, it is Americans whose government has secretly mined harbors in pursuit of "peacetime" objectives, and it is, lamentably, our government which, while complaining loudly the whole time of Arab terrorists, proceeded in the early 1980s to fire 900-pound explosive shells blindly into the village-strewn Lebanese countryside from offshore. And it is we who now still find ourselves almost uniquely in danger when we work and travel in certain, wide areas abroad. In other areas, such as much of Latin America, the welcome mat for us has grown increasingly threadbare of late.

Paul Theroux, the American traveler and writer, remarks that even Western Europeans are bewildered and a bit frightened at times by our government's actions in the world. He notes that there are "parts of the world that are bankrupt and will never be able to repay their loans without help from the United States or other countries.... There are some people who are angry at the United States for making them stay in their own countries. Their nations became Americanized and then failed economically and industrially, [while] in the 1960s they thought something positive might happen in their land."[6] What promise there was appears today in a great many reasonably well-endowed countries to be slipping ever farther away. The only *visible* Americans in some parts of the world show interest only in profit from exporting the countries' raw resources, insuring submissive control over their source, and maintaining the supply of low-priced labor and commodities.

The late Forbes Burnham, the first President of Guyana, led his English-speaking northern South American nation to independence in 1964 and steered it on a carefully non-aligned international course for 20

---

6. Paul Theroux, interviewed in *U.S. News & World Report*, July 15, 1985, p. 34.

years. He held out in the early years of his tenure against rival Cheddi Jagan's strong leftist political forces, while refusing to let American advisors dictate the country's policies. In his later years, he complained that the U.S. spurned him for his genuine independence. "With a significant part of the West," he concluded, "there is the feeling that if you're not with me, you must be against me." In the 1980s, the United States cut off its loan programs with Guyana and managed to block a low-interest World Bank loan of $40 million. Guyana, needing funds for development, but not willing to pay the American political price, responded by signing last-ditch trade agreements with China, Bulgaria, and North Korea, while continuing to condemn the Soviet Union in the UN for occupying Afghanistan.[7]

And Guyana's experience is not entirely unique, as Brazil, Japan, New Zealand, and the European Community have all been reminded of late. National independence appears to mean something different to the American government now than in 1776, when "a decent respect for the opinions of mankind" was first coming into vogue as a new, revolutionary idea.[8] In fact, the U.S. administration's immediate concern about Nicaragua seems to be that the thus-far fairly limited involvement of two rival powers (the Soviets and Cuba) necessarily present to help guard the regime in Nicaragua, has the effect of rendering the "crisis" of an independent-minded government in the Central America region for once unresolvable by unilateral interventionist action of the U.S. The existence within the Central American isthmus of "a long train of abuses" that have led to popular rebellion in the number of economically deteriorating countries that the interested American business community and the U.S. State Department have come to regard as U.S. satellites has, meanwhile, been disregarded as even a contributing factor by single-minded U.S. corporatist partisans.[9]

Hence, the more the aspirations of masses of people in the Third World are frustrated and ignored due to Western and particularly American business callousness, stinginess, and an overpowering need to show maximum immediate profits at whatever cost, the more ground the newly media-wise Soviets and their entrenched allies may stand to gain as latent protectors and ideological mentors of radicalized popular revolts.

7. *Des Moines Register,* August 7, 1985, p. 6A.
8. Thomas Jefferson, *Declaration of Independence.*
9. See Valenta, *ibid.,* pp. 198-99.

The already unsupportably large populations in numerous raw material source countries in Latin America and Africa that have not been able to adequately industrialize due to a lack of funds, continue to double every 20 to 25 years, whether or not they have a spectacularly ballooning foreign debt facing them. Situations are, thus, being produced that, without substantial and determined capital and material assistance, can *only* become much more grim. Thus, ominously, most poor and underdeveloped nations face the certain immediate prospect of falling yet farther behind in struggling to meet their basic needs, making them more, rather than less, vulnerable to popular rebellions as rightful and essential as our own Revolution. Yet, such inevitable movements for change themselves continue to be viewed as calamitous from the standpoint of long-standing and emphatically unrepresentative U.S. foreign policy interests. We cannot possibly force down the lids on very many boiling pots at once. An American change of perspective has thus gradually become, for ourselves even more than for others, an absolute necessity. If the U.S. cannot accept the challenge of offering the needed kind of leadership abroad, the baton will surely be passed. Such may be the next important illustration of the law of supply and demand.

In spite of long-standing claims, money is not everything in America. It may have indeed become "the sex of the '80s" as widely advertised. But if so, its chaser, though not serious competitor, in America in the '80s has been sports, most notably the jarring, uniquely American power game of football, with the likewise home-grown speed and coordination contest we call baseball still tremendously popular as well. Perhaps neither of these two traditional American pastimes is well-understood intuitively or cross-culturally. American football, in particular, seems as incomprehensible to people overseas as cricket is to us. Yet all of our great games are plainly goal-oriented, with each conforming to its own complex rules and rites.

Still, our most serious current pastime, more popular in recent years than at any time since the 1920s, is financial investment. This is not surprising. Two-thirds of the world's multinational companies are, after all, basically American firms even today. And, differing from the other two popular games mentioned, one need not be blessed with heroic size, strength, or fleetness of foot to play. Being American or otherwise accessible, and average or above for an American economically, is qualification enough to participate at least to a modest degree; and the financial rewards in a basically robust economic environment with good advice over time make it eminently worthwhile for at least a fair portion of these so favored.

Like television, the computer, and the automobile, Americans practically invented this wondrous financial mania in its present form. And, generally speaking, many basically well-off Americans have, at least up until recently, profited handsomely as individuals. Yet, paradoxically, we were somehow all the while in the process of losing our collective shirts to overseas competitors here, too, just as with the fore mentioned trio of other once basic American products.

American business leaders lavishly praised wide-open international competition back when we were the only surviving world-class economy in the 1940s and '50s. But now, many suspect some enormity of foul play, or at least un-American collusion by foreign firms under foreign government auspices, as probable cause for our recent inability to control even our own domestic share of the world market in our current, declared strong suit, now narrowed to highly sophisticated consumer and capital goods and arms. Here, we are steadily losing our prospective world market share and research lead to Japanese firms and new Korean producers, as well as to other Asians and Europeans.

It gives a sort of cold comfort to learn that, in contrast with our own seemingly more-virile perferences, the traditional national pastime of Japan is a gentile and venerable oriental boardgame called "Go". The idea of Go is for two opponents to place little stones in turn on a square grid so as to eventually occupy, hold, surround, or capture as much of the entire board as possible. By the end, one player has clearly dominated the other.

In the Japanese game, several patterns may (indeed, *must*) be in the process of being built simultaneously by the successful player. To survive long and succeed in bringing triumph, one's simultaneously growing patterns must be carefully planned, coordinated, and executed. Either lack of coordination, or simply building onto one single, highly successful regional pattern, will inevitably lead not to diminished success, but to total defeat, which is ignominious to the Japanese.

And, just as obviously now, our accustomed American style of forceful, linear, single-goal play, pursued independently and vigorously by self-maximizing players loudly extolling their membership on the same "team", will not cut it in a global version of play with geographic proportions. Our most dangerous rhetorical and military adversaries may, indeed, still be the Soviets, quite likely to continue playing a subtle, slowed, long-term game of their own. But our best friends, in that they

156

may force us by their far more refined strategy, as a last, seemingly agonizing resort, into a winning, coordinated strategy of our own, are the wonderfully successful but far less well-endowed capitalists, resource-wise, of Japan. We may, following their compelling lead, be forced to adopt an international strategy that can put us, too, in sync with a restless real-world majority who would be glad to follow us with our technology, capital, and reasserted underlying respect for the opinions of mankind, into a mutually brighter day.

Of course, powerful Americans -- indeed, powerful people everywhere, and especially those outside of government and other humbling institutions -- tend to regard even the suggestion of interdependent, coordinated activity entailed by participation as part of an organized society, as, to quote one observer, "a kind of decline in sovereignty."[10] Certainly, history shows that the strongest of America's private enterprises have seldom been eager to compromise their sovereignty, even in times of national emergency. To solicit public sympathy for their highly prized independence of action, corporatists in America have tried to convince the public (and surprisingly often with success) that a type of society including them as mere co-members under the law would be in some fashion "un-American," or "socialistic."

Applying the same criteria, a private citizen's service on a jury, political participation along with others, and tax support of law enforcement agencies, roads, and schools would be enough to make her or him a "socialist." In actual fact, our many independent, uncoordinated, and mutually competing companies overseas are left virtually unhampered, to pursue, in effect, each a sovereign foreign policy of its own in relating to foreign governments. This fragmented mode of national policy, with our theoretically representative federal government reduced to posturing, protecting, and issuing policy pronouncements, is proving about as successful today at meeting tightly organized foreign competition in applied technology and trade, as the disorganized Barbary Pirates were in taking on the early U.S. Navy.

Hence, some form of mutually binding national industrial strategy needs to be devised and applied by the U.S. community, and very soon, if we seriously hope to retain any part of the great measure of economic security and advantages in rapidly expanding commerce that accrue to

---

10. See Stanley Hoffman, "The American Style: Our Past and Our Principles," *Foreign Affairs*, January, 1968, p. 367.

the leading nation. And, while we're involved with this particular problem, as we soon must be, the blueprint for national unity we settle on in devising workable policy tools can be tremendously strengthened by including credible representation from the public, or broad, non-enterpreneurial national interest. This purpose could be accomplished by including actual participants solicited from all impacted segments of society, and not just owners of industry and finance, in the specially designed ongoing policy formation mechanism that must emerge.

And, taking this a step further, we could resolve at least one additional serious problem through regular, collaborative planning that our companies, acting entirely independently, could never overcome because of their singular purpose and their mutual competition. We could specify that the new policy that emerged be directed specifically toward the nurture of healthy and friendly market economies throughout the underdeveloped world. We could, thus, if we would, compete by fostering mutual growth and healing in the resource-filled world around us.

Or, without the effort and initial discomfort involved in turning our policy around in this way, we can probably expect to reap a rising *systolic* whirlwind of terror and intransigence, to be followed perhaps by nuclear ransom eminating from the most bitterly exploited and derelict outcasts among nations. We still have a choice: we can all collaborate, or our collective tombstone will likely read, "They stood alone."

In his book *Trade War*, Steven Schlossstein, a rare combination trade and investment analyst and Japan scholar, highlights the distinction between Japanese and American industrial policies with his observation that during one recent period of tight competition, "American steelmakers were in business to make money. Japanese were in business to make steel." He adds that "the [American] steel companies also had an ideological fixation with paper profits that prevented them from pricing more aggressively in down markets and from spending more rationally to upgrade plant and equipment."[11] He cites other crucial differences in the book as well.

---

11. Schlossstein, Steven, *Trade War: Greed, Power, and Industrial Policy on Opposite Sides of the Pacific*, N.Y.: Congdon & Weed, 1984, pp. 44-45, 47.

Business futurist Marvin Cetron states the main, core problem of American firms trying to compete every bit as succinctly: "Why can't American business be as adept, as fleet-footed as the Japanese at turning its technology into [better] products? One reason, of course, is management's preoccupation with short-term results -- the Harvard MBA syndrome that measures performance on the basis of profitability in this quarter and next."[12]

Schlossstein judiciously observes that the American steel industry that was hard-pressed to compete "was characterized by ... high union wages, escalating to 70 percent over the American industrial average by the late 1970s."[13] The results of the steel competition are already in. The focus is now on the field tentatively considered America's strong suit and our fondest hope for technostructural leadership through at least the rising generation: microcomputerization. Thus far, the respective development and marketing strategies on the two sides of the Pacific have remained essentially the same as with the respective steel industries earlier, with talk of the need of change, but with a number of robust U.S. firms individually facing the experienced, fully united, societally integrated trade strategy of the Japanese in mismatched competition.

The method by which the Japanese achieve their virtually invincible united front, which is, needless to say, in their national interest, meriting across-the-board public support while retaining the indispensable incentives and financial choice of vigorous venture capitalism, will be discussed in more detail ahead.

An obvious common problem looms over the numerous segments of American business now facing heavy foreign competition from Japan, her rising Asian spawn, and the European Community. The great problem is: how to defer a considerably larger slice of earnings into product oriented research and development without occasioning massive pullouts on the part of disenchanted investors acting on their brokers' best advice?

---

12. Cetron, Marvin, et al, *The Future of American Business, The U.S. in World Competition*, N.Y.: McGraw-Hill, 1985, p. 12.
13. Schlossstein, *ibid.*, p. 44.

Marvin Cetron's answer to this perennial dilemma, that of offering new and greater tax incentives to generate more research and development aid for qualifying firms from the public purse, perhaps once again merits consideration. But only if the appropriate exemptions earmarked for R & D are this time *enforced* as such in their implementation, something that was notoriously *not* done when major fiscal incentives were extended for plant modernization last time, in the early 1980s.[14]

Yet, the merit of Cetron's not-so-new suggestion is still limited by the fact that, while there is already more total potential capital available in the U.S. than virtually anywhere else on earth, our R & D budget in industry as a percentage of income still remains relatively very low. If we are to actually overcome our system's most serious barrier to reaching required levels of reinvestment, the discretionary authority of salaried top managers who, as I explained in Chapter 3, exercise most of the crucial "rights of ownership" in the American system most of the time, must be partially set aside.

Instead, negotiated, across-the-board mutual deductions from profit ledgers in order to neutralize the competitive disadvantage entailed in R & D investment for the large, basically American firms still comprising the majority of the world's multinationals, could achieve the necessary purpose non-prejudicially, to benefit the entire system. (Japanese firms, to cite a leading example, are signed into such a mutually beneficial pact under government aegis, a concession to which they seem to owe much of their competitive success.)

As novel as moderated industry-wide cooperation may at first be for competing firms, the often-pleaded strategy of total voluntarism simply would not work in this instance, because it would reward dissenters in the short run and send most cooperating firms spinning off toward liquidation. To regain the edge in competition for the eminently marketable products that our overall financial and resource strength should permit us to produce, our firms must either be required or all agree to act in concert. For this purpose, our participating firms simply cannot avoid mutually consigning a fair-sized, competitive share of their earnings for development of better products and wider markets, as the Japanese learned to do a generation ago. On the other side of the coin, the view that multinationals, by nature, owe allegiance to absolutely no

---

14. See Cetron, *ibid.*, pp. 18 ff, for specifics.

one for any purpose is intolerable, because the public simply cannot expect to receive what it is not owed.

The only slightly less-extreme view that American companies cannot cooperate because they must be given their head by society to successfully compete with their foreign competitors in an all-out, twilight donnybrook, has shown itself to be absurd. Because, a great deal has already been tried in that direction from the later Carter administration's sudden and perhaps laudable early beginnings of de-regulation on. But the more the unbounded approach has been tried, the more the dominantly American, yet sovereign multinationals, as powerful as they generally are compared with *individual* overseas firms, have continued to steadily lose ground to such national constructs as the juggernaut respectfully known as "Japan, Inc.", the unified representation of a highly-successful industrial strategy.

The new real life nightmare of dangerous, economy wrecking foreign competition is precisely the "crisis" adopted by America's active small minority class of suddenly dominant corporatists as a rationalization for their efforts to "streamline" their nation's once-lionized system of governance. At gravest risk, as we have seen, are a number of so-called "archaic" power-balancing safeguards molded into our Constitutional machinery of government to prevent narrow concentrations of power, from whatever side, from exercising control.

The nearly quarter of a billion people who are American citizens cannot afford the folly of staking our intertwined fortunes and future on a few hundred ardently corporatist business leaders permitted to go on an unbridled, uncoordinated, all-out crusade against powerfully integrated world-scale economic powers. The mechanism and authority of our open, representative system of government need not be further impaired or sacrificed for such an ill-advised purpose, because the effort has already shown itself to be, to put it mildly, counterproductive.

Instead, to employ the current idiom of the street, we must now begin to substitute the leveraged strength of pooled brain power for the assertion of raw buying power we have long been accustomed to, and which has of late become rightly stigmatized in *public* sector contexts as "throwing money at the problem."

The currently dominant political objective on the national scene is still to loosen the essential and restrictive safeguards or "fetters" built into our public institutions by dramatically strengthening the hand of the more easily manageable executive branch and gutting the remaining authority of public law accordingly, in order to soup up the failing international strategy of fragmented autonomy. This is the essence of

161

the plan of the still *politically* well-integrated though small true corporatist minority. And such an approach is utter, rejectable nonsense from the point of view of an informed public. No plan could be a more irresponsible answer to the present economic and social crisis we are in.[15]

- American Strength -

So it is that we are now faced with three great, intrinsically related international problems. One is, inescapably, the maintenance of America's economic leadership role in order to yet retain, against all odds, the vitality and choice that technostructural leadership entails, and in order to support the development of truly open societies elsewhere. The second is that of turning back the Soviet Marxists' continuing, although presently scaled back, recently more refined and soon-to-be redefined challenge for world ideological leadership and reorganization. The neglected and often negated third problem involves our necessary front-line participation in developing the potential of the currently less-developed countries as an enormous group of truly friendly, upwardly mobile, self-governing producers and markets, contributing maximally in the process to both human welfare and freedom.

No doubt, relatively few Americans would disagree on principle with any of these three basic objectives. But some would argue that the three objectives are incompatible and financially unrealistic in our a brutally competitive "post-modern" world. The opposite notion, that the three purposes listed are *inextricably* linked, however, is not new, and is demonstrably yet more plausible.

A summary entitled "What the U.S. Hopes For," compiled at the request of the U.S. Senate Foreign Relations Committee by the Center for International Studies at M.I.T. back in the early 1960s, recommended among its five cardinal objectives the following: "1) Maintain their [i.e., Third World countries'] independence of powers hostile or potentially hostile to the United States. ... 3) Progressively meet the aspirations of a majority of their people without resort to totalitarian controls. ... 4) Move

---

15. Introducing the repeatedly requested Presidential line item veto at this point would, for example, tend to de-fang the far less-controllable legislative branch of the national government, pulling us a giant step closer to government by executive committee -- i.e., by a sort of publicly-unaccountable American Central Committee.

162

toward increasingly wide and responsible participation [in countries abroad] by all groups in political, social and economic processes under stable rules of law, that is, toward their own version of working democracy."[16]

A 1959 report commissioned by the Rockefeller Brothers Fund noted, similarly, that "the United States..., by acting according to its own best instincts and traditions ... is meeting the deep necessities of the cold war. [Because] the development of free institutions, democratic progress and advancing well-being will, if consistently and imaginatively furthered, prove not only desirable in themselves but the best over-all strategy for warding off the expansion of the Communist empires."[17]

The laudable triad of basic U.S. policy interests that emerged from both of these key reports -- i.e., fostering the competitive advantage of the United States, minimizing prospects for the spread of Soviet influence, and helping realize the aspirations of citizens of emerging nations to a free, fair, and full life -- is also much in evidence in the rhetoric that has typified most American administrations since.

But many foreign observers have concluded, after long observation, that the U.S. government itself, regardless of our *national* intent, basically lacks independence of and authority over the powerful American companies operating in their countries. Hence, specific policies favoring development in and for weaker and newer countries are never, or almost never, implemented. What observers overseas have witnessed in practice in their countries in recent years is overwhelmingly a fragmented *private-sector* American policy forwarding the sole, all-encompassing criterion of maximizing American corporate income opportunities, with either the outright approval or acquiescence of a completely perfunctory U.S. government.

Scornfully independent, basically unaccountable to their own nation, its sanctions, or its norms, America's multinational corporations often operate like wealthy, third-class potentates in their relations with governments and political factions abroad, their financial strength in fact

---

16. Foreign Policy Association - World Affairs Center, *U.S. Foreign Policy Goals: What Experts Propose*, N.Y.: Headline Series, No. 142, July-August, 1960, quoting an M.I.T. International Studies Center report, *United States Foreign Policy: Economic, Social, and Political Change in the Underdeveloped Countries*, Washington: USGPO, March 30, 1960, p. 3.

17. *Special Studies Project Report I*, Rockefeller Brothers Fund, N.Y.: Doubleday, 1959.

dwarfing that of *most* struggling Third World governments. Barnet and Muller, in their book *Global Reach*, observed a few years ago that multinational companies' corporate diplomats consistently "try to persuade host foreign governments, local businessmen, or anyone who will listen that there is no conflict between corporate goals and national goals." To skilled and unskilled workers hired in the countries, the well-financed corporations are always able to offer a few dollars or a few cents a day above the consistently-miserable going wage rate. To educated local elites, the multinationals offer job and investment opportunities considerably beyond the means of relatively poorly-financed local competitors. Local financial and natural resources thus continue to funnel freely and rapidly to developed world rather than impoverished local destinations.

Barnet and Muller reported that those foreign government officials who continued, nevertheless, to perceive a conflict between their nation's interests and those of the multinational company, were said to "have succumbed to 'irrational nationalism'." At the same time, the companies would characteristically attempt to drive well-financed wedges where necessary to attain their goals by "bidding for the loyalties of several different constituencies."[18]

The duality of interests spawned by *official* American devotion to freedom and improvement of the quality of life in the world and the simultaneous self-serving independence of unrestrained American business overseas assuredly runs counter to the sincere hopes of most Americans for well-meaning relations abroad. It also appears to run contrary, even in the short run, to our own national best interests. The disparity of American words and deeds leads in the longer run not to confusion, but to a certain deafness throughout the varied and enormous Third World to all of American's appeals to democratic values. This quality of indifference is often followed, unfortunately but not mysteriously, by a deeply ingrained image of unhesitating American duplicity with the worst political elements, and eventually, in the hardest pressed countries, by violent revolt against overwhelming U.S. (in some

---

18. Barnet and Muller, *ibid.*, p. 89. To cite an instance of rather extreme conflict, two large, representative American companies (Johnson & Johnson and Esso) operating in Brazil in the mid-1970s were reported to have taken out of that country respectively 32 and 25 times the amount of capital they had invested in it, resulting cumulatively in serious "decapitalization" of the country's fragile economy. See *Los Angeles Times*, December 1, 1975.

places European) economic and seemingly attendant military power. Yet, the hostility and resentment so often evident would very likely be mostly avoidable through a crafted policy of industrial development assistance and seriously-sanctioned accountability to American public standards of practice and intent.

It seems no more defensible for a U.S. company to be permitted to act in opposition to official, publicly endorsed U.S. policy goals overseas, than for an American academic to be protected in instructing his college class in blowing up buildings or giving away classified defense secrets under the mantle of freedom of speech or academic freedom. In either case, the offense is not comprised of practicing the essential freedom, but in committing an act of virulence against the interests of the larger community.

Clearly, there is a place for the assertion of public authority against abusers of freedom in defense of more general freedom within American society. Likewise, the federal government's refusal to judge American economic behavior abroad is unlikely to forward any of the oft-echoed triad of essential, long-term American overseas objectives. It is plain that the two levels of our overseas involvement -- public and private -- ought to be brought into sync, in order for the *national* interest of the United States to be served.

The result of our policy of permissiveness in this regard in a world at large that is neither stupid not willingly servile to American corporate interests has already become apparent. The now-intermittent evaporation (in parts of the Middle East, Central America, former Portuguese Africa and still-minority-ruled South Africa, perhaps Central or Southeastern Europe next, etc.) of America's potential investment opportunities, markets, and finally its very means of reasonably affluent survival, must certainly continue without a policy turnaround. The competition, it must be recognized, is prepared to best our unworthy performance here as well.

Meanwhile, the scantly-camouflaged corporate dominance of the '80s over the nerve center of the American political system has led, for the first time in more than half a century, to an *official* administration policy fully embracing the principle of government economic non-participation abroad, with the enormous exception of military trafficking at public expense. I am referring to the founding corporatist Reagan administration's so-called "program for developing countries," unveiled in a major speech by the still-new President at the height of his personal popularity and power, on October 15, 1981.

At the heart of America's new official stance, the recently-wounded President's speech announced, are three features closely related to the activities of multinational corporations. These include: "1) reliance on markets to stimulate growth and development," repudiating direct involvement; "2) reliance on the private sector to lead development; and 3) minimizing government 'interference' in the market."[19]

It is hard to see how such an official policy could be called a program *for developing countries*, when the easily predictable effect is to insure American-based companies free rein to pursue their own interest unilaterally, for the singular benefit of their controlling owners, managers, and company investors. Also worthy of note is the fact that the giant collectives thus guaranteed the corporatist administration's exclusive support in pursuing objectives, are almost always in direct competition for resources and markets with vastly overmatched, far less financially able local companies within the developing countries in the same sorts of industries, making it very difficult for local development to occur. Hence, the Reagan administration's real objective in departing from earlier, mixed-means guidelines must again be seen as something completely different from its stated objective.

Policy analyst Richard Newfarmer foresees continued and increased opposition to actions of our independent multinationals in many countries in answer to the now officially-established American approach. This increasing backlash, he has predicted, will lead to the justification of a new rash of covert, as well as loud rhetorical and if necessary violent attempts by the U.S. to de-stabilize uncooperative popular and unpopular local regimes.[20] Announced by President Reagan as a more "useful" substitute for the direct aid programs launched occasionally by the American government in the past, the new official policy strikingly reveals the corporatist administration's narrow base of actual power, for it appears to serve no one else.[21]

---

19. See Newfarmer, Richard S., "Multinationals and Marketplace Magic in the 1980s", in Kindleberger, Charles P. and David B. Anderson, eds., *The Multinational Corporation in the 1980s*, Cambridge, MA: M.I.T. Press., 1983, pp. 162 ff.

20. Newfarmer, *loc. cit.*

21. *Ibid.* The Reagan administration's "Caribbean Basin Initiative," despite its public billing as a regional economic aid initiative, actually encourages and subsidizes relocation of American industrial jobs to a convenient, super low-cost foreign labor market. An instructive comparison can be made between the recent developmental progress recorded by Japan's economic progenies in Asia and the western Pacific and ours in Latin American and elsewhere.

In the meantime, within the U.S., numerous companies have strained their available resources well beyond the limit of reasonable safety and contributed to their and our uncompetitiveness on the world scene by aggressively gobbling up one another. Very frequently, they used their specially orchestrated major tax breaks, approved initially in 1981 to stimulate new plant construction and modernization, for this mainly non-productive and extraordinarily draining activity instead, often carrying them far outside their known productive baliwicks. By so doing, many companies were able to quietly pass on major portions of the additional incurred costs to the public, while scornfully defeating the stated purpose of the in fact economically and socially scandalous legislation. Such was commonly its outcome because compliance with the express purpose was never mandated in the corporatist-sponsored measure.

Largely as a result of such unfortunately typical cavalier large corporate and corporatist attitudes and behavior, American consumers have increasingly found themselves looking to the foreign competition for savings and also for quality, an aspect of production falling outside the purview of the typical large American firm's ruling *financial* managers.

As a nation, America today re-invests about half as much of its gross income into research and development as do, for example, a number of the now-combining Western European economies. This is apparently due largely to the fact that channeling money in that critical direction (i.e., into R & D) reduces the quotable profits and dividends that get managers raises and tenure now and attract new investment for the next quarter. According to *Mergerstat Review*, the standard digest of its subject, a total of 2,395 mergers and acquisitions were completed back in 1981 alone, running the American economy $82.6 billion in direct costs, or 3 percent of our GNP and almost half the amount of the often-decried subsequently annual federal deficit. Not surprisingly, then, the results are economically destabilizing as well as unproductive. And the totals have risen steadily nearly every year since (4,042, for instance, were recorded in 1986), under the indulgent eye of a purely corporatist federal administration.[22]

America's foreign policy of recent years, its excesses in part reflecting American large business' realistic fears of losing access to more material sources and markets long taken for granted, has come to exhibit an air of

---

22. See discussion in Schlossstein, *ibid.*, pp. 147 ff.

outright possessiveness of economic privileges abroad. Such overweeningness has been routinely enforced by the military threat to "protect" or "free" errant countries found to lie within our preferred sphere of interest, and thus beyond tolerable competition or choice. Local public preferences abroad have thus come to be characterized as mere "political considerations," and confidentially to be viewed as unaffordable luxuries. If immediate and local reaction to American intervention appears favorable, it's seen as a plumb and exploited for propaganda. If not, realities can be obscured, and the press can even be excluded, if necessary, on security grounds. Independent actions disfavoring American business by governments in weaker countries are, accordingly, then, denounced summarily as "undemocratic".

Our uncoordinated international trading sector is, nevertheless, hard pressed now by serious global competition, perversely stemming from important and prosperous allies like Japan and West Germany, against whom we are *so far* reluctant to retaliate in a truly hostile manner. Our first true modern-day corporatist administration hence became understandably obsessed with aggressively defending all of our accustomed overseas strategic and supply zones, by force where necessary, from either outside geopolitical competition or takeover by uncooperative locals. We might well ask ourselves why it is that the major "rebellions" against corporatist authority and order have occurred in the particular perennially-impoverished countries where they have, instead of, for instance, in Switzerland or Canada, and then strive to help alleviate the outstanding direct causes of discontent, instead of simply condemning the form of the reactions.

In the words of one long-time American resident analyst of trends in Europe, our foreign policy [under then-President Reagan] was no longer subject to being criticized as "moral and naive," as was, for instance, arguably the case earlier. Instead, under the pressure of unnerving defections and rebellions and faced with steadily-escalating competition, our policy quickly froze into "too simplistic a view," one of good vs. evil. "We continue," journalist James Goldsborough explained at the time, "to try to force a complex world of multiplying power centers, regional cartels, and crumbling alliances back into a neat East-West box."[23] And

---

23. See Goldsborough, James Oliver, *Rebel Europe*, N.Y.: Macmillan, 1982, p. 179, ff. Goldsborough would surely argue that the traditional Wilsonian Containment doctrine held little relevance beyond the reach of the Soviets' ability to control and dictate key events, as opposed to responding to them.

the terms we can now offer to those nations that are disposed to find favor with us, increasingly since we have been hard put to compete even in our own national market, characteristically narrow down to a single, all-too-familiar criterion. That criterion is, unfortunately, the maximization of immediate and near-term profit opportunities for American enterprise, with any significant diversions of wealth toward other purposes, up to and including the basic needs and protective rights of an ally, routinely viewed as unacceptable losses. Even Poland now understands that. Movement along any other policy course but ours, designed to gratify sponsoring American large business, invites intractable, overt or covert U.S. opposition. Such, it has been judged, must be our survivalist policy.

On the other hand, Japan's foreign economic presence has somehow managed to grow quietly far broader and more secure in the world than our own. Japan's dependence on overseas markets and sources of commodities and materials is, indeed, far greater than ours, or than we would probably want; and yet, it is, by all indications, accommodated without unseemly rancor.

This would seem to be mostly not because of some peccadillo of cultural strangeness, but because Japan successfully interweaves a policy of prodigious foreign technological and economic assistance with its mainly self-serving and highly-skilled worldwide private trading ventures. Provided in the process are a public forum for Japanese inter-company cooperation, a satisfactory degree of coordinated trade planning, and critical industrial input into a comparatively active central foreign policy. In turn, much public overseas investment is funneled through privately managed overseas ventures to carry out generous, and yet calculated, foreign technological assistance programs. Such programs as these, the less-advanced trading partners of the Japanese naturally welcome on the extremely perilous and lonely latter-day road to becoming significant advanced goods markets and exporters themselves. Japan has recently announced an intended *step-up* in this activity, as well as in Third World debt assistance, despite U.S. misgivings and warnings.

As noted Japan scholar Chalmers Johnson has pointed out, Japan's experience at honing its united front industrial policy, resulting in the present-day "binary" (dual purpose) foreign policy that has brought unmatched success to its firms and its still-burgeoning economy, is far from new. The policy dates in some measure back to at least 1932, when the Great Depression threatened the Japanese with economic collapse.[24]

This tremendously successful policy has required much patience and restraint on the part of its many now-powerful private sector participants. Japan, meanwhile, has advanced since World War II from producing and marketing trinkets in the early 1950s, all the time re-investing a common share of company profits and learning from American companies and others. Its climb has continued, step-by-step, through eventual primacy in bicycles, steel, and custom-built cars for the world's roads, to the threshold of an equally commanding position in computer technology and bionics in the early 1990s and beyond.

It is not particularly surprising, if we will but stop and think about it, that our individual firms, although giants in their own genre of organization, are usually not able to compete successfully. Because, they are striving to compete, one by one, with individual Japanese firms that are welded for their own advantage, with the necessary participation and backing of the rest of the society, into a solid but flexible, highly special force. We must recognize that the Japanese, like ourselves, possess what we would call an inalienable right to organize their society internally as they wish. And we must also come to realize that coordinated national defense forces, albeit economic ones, usually have little difficulty in routing uncoordinated, willfully separate platoons such as ours.

Despite its seemingly unchallengable economic primacy of late, Japan is really a very much smaller nation, occupying a small, isolated island country, with an immeasurably inferior natural resource base compared to that of the United States; indeed, even to that of Texas! And just as Japan's economic deliverance (i.e., its emergence as a routinely effective, though still problem-plagued society) was born of crisis and relentless necessity, so must ours be. It must be noted that this currently more-successful economic rival is neither a totalitarian nor a socialist society, but a *democracy* -- putting into practice a form of governance the Japanese admired and willingly adopted from America and the West.

---

24. Johnson, Chalmers, *MITI and the Japanese Miracle: The Growth of Industrial Policy, 1925-1975,* Stanford, CA: Stanford Univ. Press, 1982; the point is discussed in Schlossstein, *ibid.,* p. 211. Also see Gibney, Frank, *Japan, The Fragile Superpower,* N.Y.: New American Library, 1980, p. 271.

There *are* features of Japanese society that run contrary to the predominant grain of American culture, to be sure. But it is not necessary to mention any of them to account for Japan's super-successfully integrated foreign aid-trade policy. An almost forgotten, related fact is that our own system's success has also been based up until now as much on well-conceived collective or cooperative action as on individual action. The corporate form of financial organization itself is Exhibit Number One of that.

Rugged "individualism" for American multinationals simply is not working as an active policy in straight-up competition with others, and we need to recognize as much. It may actually be that the extraordinary "windfall" investment opportunities created by the planned early Reagan budget deficits and their accompanying, unheralded transfer funding at compound interest billed to taxpayers have alone provided the edge needed to maintain the uncoordinated, massive units now dominant in the American political economy in an apparent "boom" situation for several years. Nothing else seems to account for it, with so many of our basic industries having simultaneously fallen on extremely hard times in competition with prosperous rivals overseas.

But, in the interim, relative success against our international competitors is steadily becoming more, and not less, important for the survival of our whole economy and culture. Barring economic exhaustion -- at least a possibility, given the amount of debt we now owe and superintend on all sides -- we will perhaps after all, belatedly and reluctantly, undertake a sufficiently unified national industrial strategy, simply because we *must* in order to survive competitively.

The more the broader public interest is represented in the formation and guidance of this badly-needed industrial strategy, the better integrated the changed policy, and our own system of self-government, will be, with such a world-orienting instrument as a central feature.

A related, mutually advantageous market development policy to at least moderately assist our less-advantaged Third World trading partners in their development efforts, emulating and coordinating with Japan's highly-successful example, could very well become even more successful and important globally than is Japan's. We simply would be able, if we were willing, to bring a much greater stock of domestic resources and financing to bear to the task of gaining markets, hearts, minds, and futures.

To repeat one crucial point: the now re-charging and reorganizing Soviet clientage system possesses neither the material means nor the majoritarian, democratic example to effectively counter a true revolutionary program of this kind. Thus, by integrating our efforts and our objectives, as do the wisely ecclectic and *successful* Japanese, we could, in like manner, "kill three birds with one stone" (old American proverb).

- *Unite or Die*[*] -

[*] (Slogan from an early American Revolutionary banner featuring a dismembered serpant, its segments bearing the names of thirteen divided colonies. This rubric's message may seem a bit harsh for now; but is the socio-economic crisis facing us now really any less profound than that faced by our 18th-century predecessors? At root, in both cases, is a crisis of accountability of leadership.)

Business interests are forever complaining of government's "interference" in their affairs. They may, at times, have a point and are certainly entitled to pursue redress. (Although, in the virtual absence of any effective, substantive authority over the actions of major-scale corporations, it is notable that their complaints now frequently seem to center around having to fill out virtually useless bureaucratic forms.) But when large businesses work successfully through political means to gain exemption from or nullify laws and judicious measures protective of the larger society, they are flaunting their concentrations of power. And insofar as they succeed, through contributions to politics, illegal or legal, in shaping the behavior of society while freeing themselves from the society's normal power of consent and review, they are acting illegitimately and throwing the society's self-regulatory system out of whack.

There has long been resistance by American business against the idea of active peacetime public sector participation overseas. Even the post-World War II programs that ultimately prompted Western Europe's impressive recovery, sparked its continuing economic integration, and restored it as a viable and growing market, were widely opposed by major business interests because they obviously spelled a rapid decrease in the need for emergency American exports.[25]

---

25. See Vernon, Raymond, *Sovereignty at Bay, The Multinational Spread of U.S. Enterprises*, N.Y.: Basic Books, 1971, pp. 211-12.

But a publicly accountable American government necessarily assumed the lead in defining and organizing America's proper response to a remediable economic crisis involving countries we needed to continue to count among our international allies at that time. Just so, government must play the leading role, at least as moderator and facilitator, in an offensive, perhaps alongside our European allies and already-involved Japan, to help reverse the worsening and increasingly volatile economic stagnation crisis facing a clear majority of the world's nations now, mega-debtors and not. Because, as international relations specialist Kenneth Thompson once put it, "No one is served while men prate about values and ignore man's terrible predicament."[26] The United States simply *cannot* long prosper in these days of spontaneous tumult and terror from many sources, by lipping freedom and simultaneously acting to freeze the oppressive status quo in the numerous countries where practicing its single-goal policy has, in an unbelievably powerful way, contributed to rapidly escalating economic and social problems.

Certainly, an undreamed of wealth of new technical means have become available to facilitate resource development in the last few years. But for all that, the enormous, less-developed and poverty-ridden southern 70 percent, in rough terms, of the world continues to lag increasingly and ominously behind the affluent and advanced-industrial "North." The so-called "South", including virtually all of fast-multiplying Africa, Latin America, and teeming southern Asia, now contains some four-fifths of the world's population and currently contributes over 90 percent of its population increase. Without special, targeted help from the much more affluent portion of the world, the prospects of most of the South's beleaguered and fractured societies already loom as all but hopeless. This is in large part because the needed level of technical research and development aid to at least partially replenish the conditions of life for the vast and growing world majority in the South is literally the North's alone to impart.

The provocative Brandt Commission report on world development, published in 1980, was appropriately subtitled "A Program for Survival." This concise, decidedly grim digest report concluded a two-year investigation by an international team of eminent scholars and statesmen organized and led by former West German Chancellor Willy Brandt. It

---

26. Thompson, Kenneth W., "American Democracy and the Third World, Convergence and Contradictions", in Halle, Louis, J., and Kenneth W. Thompson, eds., *Foreign Policy and the Democratic Process: The Geneva Papers*, Washington: University Press of America, 1978, p. 74.

pointed out, for openers, that "over 90 percent of the world's manufacturing industry is in the North. Most patents and new technology are the property of multinational corporations of the North, which conduct a large share of world investment and world trade in raw materials and manufactures. Because of this economic power northern countries dominate the international economic system. ... Most of [the less-developed countries] find the currents too strong for them."[27] Indeed, playing on the "level playing field" now being urged is one thing; but veteran professionals insisting on matched competition against even the significantly malnourished and the underdeveloped, with and for their resources, seems symptomatic of something else again. To avoid total catastrophe, the Third World must be nurtured back to health as part of the world, rather than beaten, pillaged and excluded. Perhaps fortunately and perhaps not, the choice is ours.

An absolutely critical result of the disbalance of means, according to the Brandt report, is that "the North accounts for about 96 percent of the world's spending on research and development. The scientists and engineers, the advanced institutions of education and research, the modern plants, the consumer demand and finance are all found mainly in the richest countries."[28]

Many of our reactions in America these days, under the influence of the single-criterion government policy described here, are exactly the *opposite* of what our policies will need to be if we are much longer to play any kind of a leading role in a viable worldwide economic system. For instance, the once lamented "brain drain" of talent from poverty-ridden countries by way of migrant students in American and European universities staying to enhance the richer countries' share, would seem to be enough of a price for disadvantaged nations to pay for a returning trickle of technology and leadership. But now, there is growing sentiment in much of the advanced world that the skills and resource-transforming secrets imparted in this way are too valuable to be given away without cost. Thus, even this frail lifeline now seems likely to be retracted or priced pratically beyond reach.[29]

---

27. Brandt, Willy, et al, (The Independent Commission on International Development Issues), *North-South, A Program for Survival*, Cambridge, MA: M.I.T. Press, 1980, p. 32.

28. *Ibid.*, p. 194.

29. For instance, see Cetron, *ibid.*, pp. 3-4, 7. Another dimension of this issue is the alleged ease with which research secrets reach Soviet and other potentially-hostile hands via this open route. Conversely, international students have recently been actively recruited and predominate in many U.S. colleges -- in selected fields -- as never before. See "Colleges Turn Abroad to Find More Students", *U.S. News & World Report*, March 11, 1985, p. 72.

The Brandt Commission report points out that infusions of technology and financing into the now least-developed of the so-called Third World countries are needed to support more wage earners and inflate miniscule market economies in order to make possible more equitable internal distributions of income.[30] From the affluent North's standpoint, promoting potential trade and economic partners beyond the pale would surely make more sense than promoting a generation of intractable foes, terrorists, and bitter Soviet Bloc or, at best, Japanese clients, through sheer greed and indifference to pain we could advantageously help alleviate.

Futurist business writer Marvin Cetron breezily forecasts, in this connection, that "advances in bio-engineering by the turn of the century will make it possible to farm both the oceans and the deserts, putting an end to hunger and famine within sight."[31] But, unfortunately, he fails to pursue the equally important question in his recent book of who will pioneer and finance the necessary but costly application of the vital technical advances he foresees, and for whose benefit. On this point, the corporatist approach has no satisfactory answer. The immediate-maximization fixation of the so-called North, especially in paradoxically beleaguered America, still for now its richest member, promises to very severely limit the value of the technological breakthroughs on the horizon for world peace, political and economic freedom, and the expansion of life-saving world commerce.

Hence, a vital question, both morally and in a self-interest sense, arises for those of us fortunate enough to be living in the advanced countries: Will our top-heavy political economy permit us to look far enough beyond its current leaders' short-term visions of portfolio enhancement to actually help the weaker nations we now either manipulate to our own illusory advantage or, in some resource-poor cases, simply ignore, to gain a last-ditch foothold on planet earth?

America's rate of official, direct, peaceful foreign aid has hovered in recent years in the neighborhood of one-fifth of one percent of our gross national product. Unbeknownst to most American citizens, the U.S. ranks at or near the bottom among the affluent nations of the North in this category. Such countries as the Netherlands, Norway, and Sweden regularly contribute approximately five times as much developmental aid proportionately, or nearly one percent of GNP.[32]

---

30. Brandt et al, *ibid.*, p. 95.
31. Cetron, *ibid.*, p. xviii.
32. Mosley, Paul, "The Political Economy of Foreign Aid: A Model of the Market for a Public Good", *Economic Development and Cultural Change*, 33:2, January 1985, p. 391, cites the rate of direct foreign aid imparted by these three smaller developed

There is no indication that the higher rate of direct assistance rendered by these three particular affluent economies -- still under one-tenth of the biblical tithe -- is in any sense either breaking them or crippling their competitive industries.

The United States still has, at least at present, the most productive economy in the world overall. We could almost certainly enhance our present world leadership position and future economic prospects quite dramatically by directly subsidizing or handicapping carefully selected and assigned projects by our companies abroad up to even Holland's or Norway's foreign aid rate. We need apply only the sole criterion of bringing the greatest return in terms of increased capital goods production to the country in question by introducing critical skills and equipment. The only objective needed would be that of helping nations pull themselves up from wrenching poverty and debt. And we could, by following this formula, make a critical difference, while recovering our own much-eroded stature.

We could easily justify the expenditure of the basic, minimal amount of $45 to $50 billion annually, over five times our abstemious contribution in non-military aid now, in terms of the value of the friendly links that would result for national defense alone. (For purposes of comparison, the recent cost of maintaining American troops and military hardware in Europe alone has amounted to about $90 billion annually.) The immediate and long-term tangible and intangible return we could expect to realize, in terms of crucial overseas support and new market growth, could, in fact, enormously exceed this expenditure. The expanded markets we could secure would accrue to our international business sector. And a direct link, now virtually non-existent, would be forged as an added benefit between the unrealistically sheltered and insulated mass of the American people and the growing majority of our fellow human beings in areas out beyond Europe, Japan, and Tijuana.

---

nations as 0.93% and 0.94% of their respective GNPs in 1979, and the rate for the U.S. as 0.20%. Kidron and Smith, *ibid.*, introduction to Part Four, point out that "rich states spend on official development aid to poor states less than half of one percent of [the amount of] annual military spending worldwide. The contrast between the wealth devoted to military purposes and the poverty of much of humanity ... is a standing indictment of utterly distorted priorities."

Indeed, the value of the much-needed good will, protection of vital trade connections, and increased market share presently availed to Japan by a so far less-daring program of this kind, is beyond calculation. It spells the difference for them between their enviable and envied success and disaster. Our own partially self-serving participation, along with Japan and other industrialized nations who might be convinced to follow our lead, could make a considerable difference both in Third World developmental prospects and morale, and in the long-term global geopolitical outlook. And, again, if escalation under such a policy should become necessary to attain our longtime rhetorical three-fold objective, we could rest secure in the knowledge that no intriguing authoritarian Eastern Bloc could, at least for now, begin to match our efforts to gain and hold world influence for those among our values that are both benevolent and cherished by a clear, solid majority of us.[33]

Ironically, then, perhaps we can actually win our international struggle over the long haul only by deserving to. That is, by exploiting our own potential strength rather than the weaknesses of smaller and poorer nations, unfortunately too often viewed by foreign policy strategists now as a network of strategic bases and bargain basements of commodities and labor to be preserved from national self-government and change.

The greatest value for us of switching from a protective to an apparently altruistic, comprehensive policy would, almost certainly, be that of finally confounding the long-standing, plausible Marxist prediction concerning the irrationality leading to ruin of the capitalist world's insistence upon self-maximization. We have it on credible, inside

---

33. The GNP per capita of the U.S.S.R. is currently less than half that of the United States. Put another way, its *absolute* GNP is approximately two-thirds the size of ours, but must be stretched to support a population one-fifth larger, leaving less flexibility and far fewer policy options than we possess.

authority that our present policy of domineering and coercing is applauded by Soviet long-term strategists, precisely because it neatly dovetails with, and promises to make successful, their future efforts to sway the loyalties of all increasingly-impoverished nations around the globe.[34]

America's basic international policy options, in addition to that of going down struggling with our current, naive, corporatist-dominated anti-policy, are three in number. One long-resisted alternative, that of resorting to stringent government control of American trade and foreign investment, would, or should, be unthinkable. Such would be to unleash bureaucratic ineptitude, curtail initiative, and practically invite major businesses to relocate outside the country. On the other hand, to permit multinationals to unite on their own in forging a stronger collective trade "policy" representing the multinational business sector alone, would still leave other portions of American society effectively unrepresented and truly hapless and vulnerable in the larger world. In addition, by reinforcing the single-criterion emphasis on corporate profit without wider community input, this second alternative could be expected to alienate vulnerable potential friends and allies even more than at present.

The third alternative is to forge a more open, unified national policy integrating foreign trade and aid, with effective leadership from industry modulated by public input and review. By adopting this sort of policy, our broad, permanent national interests could be served and international cooperation and mutual respect nurtured, both legitimizing and restoring the prospects and value of American world leadership. And, additional and expanded markets would result for American investment and trade.

The opportunities for positive international leadership and influence today are many, extending even as far as the financially-leveled Hanoi regime now ruling Vietnam, whose leaders are actively seeking U.S. domestic technical assistance. The misguidedly Marxist Vietnamese

---

34. For a perceptive and enlightening former insider's view of long-term Soviet policy objectives, see Sejna, Jan, *We Will Bury You*, London: Sidgwick & Jackson, 1982. Also see Luttwak, Edward N., *The Grand Strategy of the Soviet Union*, N.Y.: St. Martin's Press, 1983, pp. 162-63, for a more traditional, militarist view of the Soviets' destabilization efforts.

reportedly refer to the now-rare American official representatives who occasionally visit as "Russians with money."[35] Our potential for long-term influence in many quarters seems to be limited only by our current lack of will to lead and heal rather than exploit and control. Marx reasoned rather simplistically that the highly-developed West would eventually dig its own grave by refusing to share the benefits of its then-beginning locational and resource advantages. Over the next several years, we can either make him a true prophet, or confound him forever.

Should our leaders persevere in guiding us on our present course internationally, they (and we) will no doubt find high costs of various sorts incurred in the process of integrating and preserving an extended, quasi-independent empire of trade and alliance essentially by force.

But such an effort would almost certainly not be unprecedented. Twenty-five hundred years ago, in his account of the Peloponnesian Wars, Thucydides, an Athenian, explained how it happened that most of Athens' one-time close allies against the terrifying, alien threat of the Persians defected from her leadership and forcefully united against her in the next generation, permanently ending her supremacy. "Of all the causes of defection," Thucydides wrote, "that connected with arrears of tribute and [naval] vessels, and with failure of service, was the chief; the Athenians were very severe and exacting, and made themselves offensive by applying the screw of neccessity. ...In other aspects the Athenians were not the old popular rulers they had been at first; ...It [became] easy for them to reduce any that tried to leave the confederacy."[36] Feeling exploited and badly used, Athens' former allies, most of them much smaller, resorted to the leadership of totalitarian Sparta for refuge against her, due, in retrospect, to Athens' unwillingness to translate her heralded ideology of democracy into principled, persuasive action beyond her shores.

---

35. Reported by Bryant Gumbel, NBC-TV *Today*, from Hanoi, spring, 1985.
36. Thucydides (5th century B.C.), *History of the Peloponnesian War*, transl. by Sir Richard Livingstone, London: Oxford Univ. Press, 1959, pp. 52-53.

Some four centuries later, the renowned Roman statesman Cicero was forced to conclude, just before the dawn of the age of the tyrannical Caesars, that it was "due to our own moral failure and not to any accident of chance that, while retaining the name, we have lost the reality of a republic."[37] Historian Moses Hadas writes that during this period of Roman expansion and increasing extension of hardening Roman authority to other nations, mindless of their preferences or welfare, Mithradates IV, a local chieftain and guerrilla leader in northern Asia Minor, had 80,000 overseas Italian residents of an area near the Black Sea slaughtered in a single day. "A sufficient indication of the esteem in which Roman publicans were held," Hadas concludes, perhaps ominously for us.[38]

More recently, some 230 separate wars and major military actions were engaged in around the world by the British and colonial loyalist troops during the 63 years of Queen Victoria's reign in the 19th century in order to preserve and defend the British Empire from its parochial "enemies." Though the costs in blood and nerves of imposing the imperial imperative were high, it could still be argued that Britain herself was relatively better off economically at the time for maintaining a world empire of trade and supply, albeit by force when necessary. But then, it must be conceded that the ultimate independence of Britain's numerous subject nations was both as rightful as slavery is unrightful, and also inevitable, given the differences of culture and interest involved.[39]

If we really want to perceive ourselves as inheritors of Britain's 19th-century mantle of imposed leadership on the world scene, as many policy specialists and scholars of history suggest, then we need to examine all of the implications of that particular role carefully. As long as we persist in maintaining world order according to our own lights by main force and threat of self-serving sanction, we can expect to become increasingly isolated by the tide of world opinion and to find our protestations of guarding freedom ignored by thoughtful realists, patriots, and scoundrels the world over. Almost certainly, we could do better these days by

---

37. Cicero (1st century B.C.), quoted in Barrows, R.H., *The Romans*, Harmondsworth, UK: Penguin, 1967, p. 43.
38. Hadas, Moses, *A History of Rome*, Garden City, N.Y.: Doubleday, 1956, pp. 55-56.
39. See Farwell, Byron, *Queen Victoria's Little Wars*, N.Y.: Norton, 1985.

adapting to the task of world economic and moral leadership something close to Japan's far more successful latter-day trade/aid style of policy, which, incidently, was developed in its finished form only after Japan had been deprived of imperial force as an option.

Then, what has kept us from practicing the better part of valor, if the lessons are all around us? I will try to explain by example. Barnet and Muller described the self-styled "Council of the Americas" in their book *Global Reach* over a decade ago as "a mutual-support association of the 200 principal U.S.-based corporations operating in Latin America." This arch-corporatist "Council," the book reported, suggested as a slogan for its members in their dealings within the separate, mostly small countries in this region where we have since become embroiled, the phrase "Consumer democracy is more important than political democracy," in order to urge the pleasures of consumption as the new national interest.[40] One basic problem with this notion, understandably close to the hearts of company boards, is that most of the residents of Central America and elsewhere throughout much of the world, are hardly consumers of any sort, and are scarcely able to make their way any closer to becoming consumer participants in any kind of democracy of the marketplace. They can at best, as a rule, scrape by on marginal land or as poverty-scale rural and urban labor. Foreign profiteering, making distant and thus naively innocent financial managers and company investors happy, necessarily excludes them from its benefits.

French sociologist Armand Mattelart, more of a realist in the literal sense, saw the beginning of deepest trouble for current U.S. policy in the fact that the way to power for a growing politically conscious plurality in Third World countries is "to subvert the outside development model that corresponds to the logic of expansion of transnational capital."[41] He predicted that a growing number of malcontents shut out of the present system by its monopolization of profitable opportunities would strive

---

40. Barnet and Muller, *ibid.*, p. 89.
41. Mattelart, Armand, *Transnationals & The Third World*, transl. by David Buxton, South Hadley, MA: Garvey, 1983, p. 151.

relentlessly to end "consumer democracy," the province of the heavily armed and protected U.S.-backed small minority of loyal well-heeled consumers. The malcontented majority or near-majority, with ever-growing families to feed, would support virtually any self-governing arrangement with new (still, for now, necessarily Soviet Bloc) backing. In other words, increasingly oppressed majorities or very large minorities should be expected to react *systolically*, because, at some point, it becomes necessary. There is simply nothing for them to lose by trying. This has nothing to do with either ideology or free choice. In a small but gradually growing number of Third World countries, the end of quiescence has already passed, producing what looks like permanent upheaval.

Central America specialist Philip Berryman notes a steadfast refusal in the developed world to *consider* this simple logic of necessity. He notes that "currently it is out of fashion to speak of 'North-South' issues, much less to use terms like interdependence or New International Economic Order. [But] despite the shift in the public mood, ... the reality remains: most of the world's human beings live in dire poverty while a small circle of nations, primarily those around the North Atlantic, dominate the world economy."[42] Recent corporate domination over international decision-making is failing to produce àn acceptable world order mainly because it fails to realistically address the most pressing world problems. As a form of coopted governance, it undoubtedly will either have to face the world's voters in one way or another, or else freely read the signs and relinquish much of its co-opted and ill-suited power to allocate.

We Americans need but open our eyes to realize, as a concerned, democratic nation in our own right, that excessive, neo-Darwinian corporatism is working against our true international interests on virtually every front. By our system's absurd anarchical approach to economic relations and its active single-criterion concern with unshared institutional profit, we have been *losing* ground in the world in the most literal sense. We have been losing to product-minded Japan, Europe, and recently, at least in certain advanced product areas, to South Korea, the leader among the new "four dragons" of Asian high technology, as well.

---

42. Berryman, Philip, *Inside Central America*, N.Y.: Pantheon, 1985, p. 127.

By defending with violence and retaliatory threats the status quo of our economically flattened and increasingly uncertain sources of supply, we are trading our potential for positive leadership for the role of a self-justified enforcer. And by our miserly technical aid non-response to pandemic economic tragedy, we are losing our current, priceless opportunity to recover from the presently capital-poor Marxian systems of the world the role of true friend and ally to the hard-hit nations on the margins who are genuinely desperate for economic and social change.

With an ounce of insight, we could yet confound the unbelieving wise of the world and rejuvenate the motive force of our once-vaunted democracy, to our own great benefit, by dint of our international actions. Until such time, our government's hypocrisy in employing that once-revolutionary word will continue to disillusion and drive away emerging, large, small and poor nations, just as ancient Athens' eventually drove her despised allies into the unquenchable opposition of the damned.

Former Chancellor Brandt, in the introduction to his commission's little-noted report, notes that it is "chaos -- as a result of mass hunger, economic disaster, environmental catastrophes, and terrorism," that presents the greatest barrier to an age of peace in the world.[43] In a curiously-related fashion, Karl Von Clausewitz, the renowned 19th-century military strategist, and an authentic genius of the West, noted that war itself can be compared most closely to "commerce, which is also a conflict of interest and human activity." In fact, the distance separating them, since they involve competition for the control of resources necessary to both sustain and outwardly enrich life, is really negligible when the specter of material threat prevails over higher and more lasting human values and people find themselves fighting like animals.[44]

A generation earlier, philosopher Honda Rimei (1744-1821) had managed to convince the reticent Japanese that "foreign trade is a war in which each party seeks to extract wealth from the other."[45]

---

43. Brandt et al, *ibid.*, p. 13.

44. Clausewitz, Gen. Karl Von, *On War* (1832), transl. by Col. J. J. Graham, London: Kegan, Paul, Trench, Trubner, 1940, Vol. III, pp. 119, 121-22.

45. Honda Rimei, quoted in Schlossstein, *ibid.*, pp. iv, 60.

In order to emerge genuinely stronger from the challenge that we now inescapably must confront, we must lay out and deploy our best weapons carefully, with a weapon we have long advertised but permitted to rust -- largess -- standing out prominently in our arsenal.

And we, too, can apply a key element of strategy that the Japanese have quite recently been forced by circumstances to learn to use, plainly transforming their world reputation and status. As John Alic of the U.S. Office of Technology Assessment put it: "MITI [Ministry of International Trade and Industry, Japan's official, double-barreled, foreign trade/foreign policy association] doesn't *plan* the Japanese economy, as you know. ...It's more of a vehicle for consciousness raising in the country as a whole -- reaching consensus..."[46] Integrated national cooperation has now become an imperative for our recovery and success as well.

It is an imperative -- once we recognize it -- that is not even beyond the realm of our own longtime, successful experience.

---

46. John Alic, U.S. Office of Technology Assessment, interview quoted in Schlossstein, *ibid.*, p. 227.

Chapter Seven

REGAINING OUR BALANCE

- The Other Road to Serfdom -

Back in 1944, at the high tide of an Allied war effort sparked in large part by an unprecedented degree of national mobilization in the United States, political economist Friedrich Hayek, in his classic *The Road to Serfdom*, voiced the fear that the government-organized effort that was winning the war would be continued in its aftermath, to efficiently organize the peacetime economy of America as well. He warned, that is, that a type of state socialism, even though unintended, could easily result from pursuing the single-minded goal of economic efficiency at the expense of the multitude of other purposes close to the hearts of the multitude of individuals and organizations that together comprise the nation.

Having gotten a whiff of the danger foreshadowed in wartime, Hayek warned this countrymen against "the deliberate organization of the labors of society for a definite social goal." He noted approvingly that "our present society lacks such 'conscious' direction toward a single aim," and he observed something that was rather obvious, namely that "the welfare and happiness of millions cannot be measured on a single scale of less and more. The welfare of a people, like the happiness of a man, depends on a great many things that can be provided in an infinite variety of combinations. It cannot be adequately expressed as a single end..."[1]

The single-criterion approach of the recent administration in shaping domestic spending choices, and the ruinous long-term fixation with the quarterly bottom line by the now politically dominant mega-scale business and financial organizations, has clearly represented just such a single-minded standard in our day. This single standard has increasingly been imposed on American policy, foreign and domestic. Hence, the clear

---

1. Hayek, Friedrich A., *The Road to Serfdom* (1944), Univ. of Chicago Press, 1975, pp. 56-57.

and present threat to the survival of American democracy and democratic life is no longer socialism, as it seemed to be a little over a generation ago when Hayek wrote, but a much further advanced, up to now largely nameless *corporatism*, resulting in the consolidation of a majority of actual political power within a single socioeconomic sector.

When one powerful interest group dominates politically, as the large corporate sector clearly now does through massive consumer advertising and decidedly superior ability to marshal and especially to apply campaign information, disinformation, and financing, it is able to succeed in limiting, channeling, and directing the nation's participation in national affairs to serve the narrow sector's ends. And, thus, the one sector becomes increasingly able to dominate our lives by shaping our laws. Laws and leaders have resulted which, given the precipitate decline of such competing and mitigating interests as organized labor, urban communities, small agriculture, environmental groups, and small business over the past, brief decade and a half, increasingly and systematically exclude from real policy formation all other interests in our society, except the private interests of the commercial houses and their advantaged major institutional backers.

What, then, needs to be done to end this blanket "tyranny" (to use Madison's blunt name for such a condition), in order to restore representative democracy, or genuine "pluralism" in the sense that Madison and other architects of the Constitution avowedly sought to establish? A means, clearly, must be found to deliberately restore to the country's *citizens themselves* the majesty of the principal constituency to whom serious candidates for the highest offices will have to direct their most fervent and candid appeals at all stages of the candidate process. If we want to have a democracy, the dominant role of special interest groups as surrogates for the people of the United States of America in their political system must be bypassed.

In Chapter Three, I discussed the cumulative, ad hoc means by which the electoral process has been preempted and protected from the public at the presidential level. Public television journalist Robert MacNeil has also in the past discussed this growing co-option of the public's power to select the president and thereby determine the direction of national policy. "In the pseudo campaign," MacNeil wrote several years ago, "candidates appear to be chosen by explicitly observable democratic processes of selection taking place before the television cameras on the floors of the conventions, when in actuality all the selective action takes place behind closed doors, where the cameras are barred. The campaign trail looks as if the candidates are addressing themselves to vital issues of the day in every nook and cranny of the land, but in fact, most of those pathways are carefully prearranged and are 'coordinated' to the demands of nighttime television news shows. Additionally, what the candidate says must be carefully tailored to fit the cleverly captioned three minute 'lead story' ..." MacNeil pointed out that Barry Goldwater, when he ran for president more than two decades ago, balked at the wisdom of putting himself in the image-makers' hands, and noted that, in trying to mount a candid campaign, he was virtually eaten alive by the savvy opposition way back then.[2]

The extra-constitutional dependence of our federal political system on investment-minded, inordinately large campaign contributions -- a dependence apparently not slacked to any great extent by legislated attempts at reforming campaign financing -- has subverted the idea of popular representation.

This still-deepening crisis of our system has been decried frequently in the strongest printable terms. Journalist Elizabeth Drew, after extensive investigation of the problem and its lengthening shadow across the terrain of our political landscape, reported her findings in two long articles in *The New Yorker* late in 1982.

"The role that money is currently playing in American politics," Drew concluded, "is different both in scope and in nature from anything that has gone before. The acquisition of campaign funds has become an obsession on the part of nearly every candidate for federal office. The obsession leads the candidates to solicit and accept money from those most able to provide it, and to adjust their behavior in office to the need for money... The only limits on how much money can be directed toward the election of a President are those on *ingenuity*. ...The result is that the basis on which our system of government was supposed to work is slipping away, if it is not already gone. The role of the public representative has been changing dramatically in recent years.

"...The nature of the kind of person who might enter national politics is changing," she went on. "Politicians who seek to enter, and do not have great wealth of their own to spend, are signed up on a systematic basis by interests that wish to enjoy influence over their official conduct."[3] It should be noted that this reporting journalist's conclusions fully accord with those voiced by major Democratic operative Pat

2. MacNeil, Robert, *The People Machine: The Influence of Television in American Politics*, N.Y.: Harper & Row, 1968, pp. xvii, 278-80 ff; Mendelsohn, Harold, and Irving Crespi, *Polls, Television, and the New Politics*, Scranton, PA: Chandler Publishing Company, 1970, pp. 278-82.
3. Drew, Elizabeth, "A Reporter at Large, Politics and Money - I." *The New Yorker*, Dec. 6, 1982, p. 54.

Caddell, which we noted earlier, as well as pointing toward the arcane efforts at electorate management conducted by pollster Richard Wirthlin and like figures in the Reagan and other recently victorious Republican national campaign organizations. *And saying as much is in no way intended to laud or exonerate their less-successful Democratic and Republican rivals.*[4] "We have allowed the basic idea of our democratic process -- representative government -- to slip away," Elizabeth Drew wrote in her summation. "The only question is whether we are serious about trying to retrieve it."[5]

The effect of too much power for sale is, it goes without saying, supremely anti-public in implication, especially as it comes to bear in determining the orientation of the executive branch, the particularly vulnerable focus of national leadership in America's contemporary political economy. The result is that a small, unpresentative, institutional minority of the U.S. electorate is in fact today almost exclusively represented and served by the shape of nation's now hardly-distinguishable internal and foreign policy. The ruled American public is now beginning to discharge a heavy and still-growing burden of interest through the income tax system, payable to the great corporate financial institutions, domestic and foreign, that have eagerly supplied massive emergency funding to the government since taxes were initially lowered in the early 1980s, indeed very much as powerless and uncompensated publics in the debtor Third World have had to do for years.

The basic and growing imbalance of equity in our social and political system that some commentators are now starting to note, favoring the best-heeled and best-placed interests at dual, permanent public expense (both commercially and now through cycled tax money as well), is flagrantly symptomatic of ineffective public representation. Any real solution, therefore, must accordingly address first the procedure by which the direction of predominant national leadership is determined every two and four years. And, again, the outcome simply has to be the institutional re-establishment of the American public in place of the agents and clients who match very large sums of money with effective manipulative techniques as the principal constituency that must be directly and personally courted by the major candidates, in order for the public to win.

---

4. See Chapter Three, supra.
5. Drew, *Ibid.*, II, Dec. 13, 1982, p. 111.

Political power, if it is to consistently serve the interests of the voting public as the legal sovereigns of the United States, must be held strictly to account and selectively conferred by the broad national community, and not by a special-interest minority. Our electoral institutions, thus, need to be refined to favor that intended broad constituency's direct access to candid information and its ability to discharge its mandate, instead of serving the much narrower interests of calculating and understandably evasive candidates and power brokers. If such are to remain viable within our system of choice, individual citizenship rights -- the controllable substance of freedom for the overwhelming majority -- must be accepted and confirmed anew in our procedural institutions.

The alternative, if we do not act to reverse the present powerful, single-interest corporatist trend, must be an increasingly constrictive tyranny in the sense that James Madison, the providential leading author of our Constitution's accommodation of forces, painstakingly and pointedly sought to avoid. The results of failing to act now can only be our society's continued pervasion of alienation, subjection, and mounting ignorance: in a single word, *serfdom*.

- Restoring Balance -

What, then, can be done to right the increasing disbalance in favor of short-term efficiency for the controlling *diastolic* (gross wealth-generating) forces that has served to all but shunt aside our belief in the open, majoritarian public philosophy as the actual basis of our system of governance? Concerns of the kind Elizabeth Drew raised have been inadequately addressed by campaign spending laws that, as she noted, have for the most part not worked. Another, broader attempt at legislation might indeed be in order, this time limiting the role of *all* political action committees in directing the political process with their financial carrots. Yet, this, too, would only address the problem negatively, and in a constitutionally questionable way.

As I have tried to indicate, a far more likely solution lies in the direction of dramatically enhancing the public's role as the real constituency to be courted. This may be done most effectively by Constitutionally mandating a significant increase of public exposure to first-hand information about and directly *from* candidates to *head the administration*, especially including their plans and ideas or dearth thereof concerning the specific issues and issue areas of greatest national public concern.

189

The framers of our Constitution were mindful (see Chapter Two) of Montesquieu's warning that a republican form of government (i.e., a representative democracy) was impractical at any level above that of a small, homogeneous country or community. But Madison, as we saw, did not entirely agree. He argued in *Federalist 10* that a larger extent of territory would, on the contrary, dilute dangerous concentrations of power by multiplying the interests to be represented and accommodated within the system. But the later great accumulation of wealth, leading to and accompanying the expansion of large businesses far outgrowing the environs of individual states charged with governing them, soon eroded his well-reasoned assurance.

Democracy's avowed opponent, Hamilton, expressed a far different view in *Federalist 9*, to the effect that Montesquieu's fears didn't apply because the United States was conceived as a union of sovereign *states*, rather than of *people*.[6] Hamilton, of course, overlooked the significant, opening line of the Constitution's preamble, and, further, his view was effectively rejected by all of the states themselves in gradually adopting universal franchise for their citizens in presidential and congressional elections. Finally, the same, still-lingering difference of opinion on the nature of the Union was decided in favor of Madison's view by arms in the Civil War.

Yet, the American founding fathers did not effectively safeguard Madison's accepted counter-argument to Montesquieu's momentous proviso in framing the Constitution, perhaps above all because no obvious way then existed of doing so. Hence, as I have recounted in Chapters Two and Three, special interests eventually gained control of the electoral system informally, by mediating between the public and the mandated process through ad hoc, extra-Constitutional arrangements. Only in our own day has it finally become possible to supersede special interest control without resort to repressive means, and, hence, to restore the whole public as the essential national constituency.

What I am referring to is this: If advanced media power in the hands of super-moneyed special interests can lead to the scientific manipulation and *neutralization* of rational individual selection on the part of the participating body of citizens (which is clearly the direction in which it is leading), then well-conceived, skillful use of the same media to much

---

6. See Madison, *Federalist 10*; Hamilton, *Federalist 9*; Montesquieu, *Spirit of Laws*, Vol. I, IX:1.

more sharply focus the public's opportunity to choose freely on a reasoned basis, can as surely restore the American public's patented, exclusive right to select its own leadership.

To repeat an analogy I made earlier: it is simply inconceivable that the legally empowered sovereigns of any major corporation in America (normally, the board of directors) would permit a serious candidate for a top-level executive position to determine with complete license his or her own times and means of appearing or not appearing before the selectors for their consideration, even going so far as letting the candidate choose his or her own examiners on the basis of their proven benign predilection and superficiality. Instead, the procedures and mode of examination would be determined and carried out by the delegated sovereigns to best serve the *company's* needs rather than the candidates'.

Yet, the poorly defined public process mandated to fill the most influential leadership position in the United States (and, not at all incidentally, in the world) permits major candidates ample latitude to successfully evade the well-reasoned selectivity of the solely-legitimized voting public. Thus do we at times get presidents whose personal views on *most* basic issues stand opposed to those of the public mainstream, without the differences ever having been clearly brought to light.

No law requires that the candidates for the Presidency must debate or even openly comment on leading concerns for the American public's benefit. Once the leading candidates have agreed to one or more televised face-to-face meetings, finding it in *their* mutual interest to debate a controlled battery of questions from a panel of questioners they themselves have screened, in accordance with a scrupulously innocuous format, the appearance of public benefit is widely projected entirely without the critical representation of the public. The latter is, in more than effect, charged with making a choice between elaborately advertised synthetic products, without any tasting, smelling, thumping, or list of ingredients. The public ought not be expected, on average, to be in-depth policy analysts. And yet, the public *does* have the sole, guaranteed right to representation.

Unfortunately, Congress, composed of the American public's geographically-elected representatives, has not effectively involved itself on the public's behalf in devising a format for presidential candidate debates designed purely to best inform and serve the public interest, as opposed to those of the candidates or their institutional sponsors.

Consequently, as political scientist Sidney Kraus wrote, "The decision of presidential candidates to debate on television has been a political option left to them alone. Politicians make that decision with more concern for political expendiency than regard for the public good. ... [Hence,] politicians and media, not voters, are responsible for the quality of political information in elections."[7] One wonders if this would still be the case if the oft-stated preference for a government of laws and not men were taken more seriously. Kraus points out that a Gallup Poll taken after a recent election revealed that over two-thirds of the public favored mandating televised presidential debates, or "more than has voted for the winning candidate in any presidential election in history." As to format, Kraus avers that "any format which provides enough time to expose candidates' issues and personalities will do. ...The crucial consideration should be the issues to be discussed. ...Why not let the public decide the issues, set the agenda...?"[8] Indeed, why not? Why not require all serious candidates, with due respect for their expressed and intended purpose of *public service*, to undergo the most thorough and revealing public screening devisable, on terms deliberately designed to best serve the public's need for relevant issue-oriented information and candid, direct exposure of communicative abilities and views? Such a bold, new institutionalized source of high-resolution information could well call forth the ablest possible candidates and up-stage the comparatively squalid, obfuscating "pseudo-campaign" by candidate-manipulated media that Robin MacNeil and others have long disparagingly written about. Such a new, open public examination approach could serve to bring the older, anti-public packaging and advertising genre of presidential campaigning into total disrepute, producing a healthy backlash against its mind-blurring media excesses.

But why stop there? The often-suggested innovation of binding regional presidential primaries, covering the whole country, for each major party, could introduce uniform and complete citizen access to the process. The phased contests perhaps could be four in number and follow time zone boundaries, in general, from east to west at two- to three-week intervals, or, better, feature two on each of two weekends, after extensive campaigning in the election year spring and early summer.

The following table, giving the electoral voting strength of each state and generalized time zone region, indicates a way in which regional primaries could be organized without the "regions" being identified with the country's old, bitterly competitive sections, such as the South or the

---

7. Kraus, Sidney, in Kraus, ed., *The Great Debates, Carter vs. Ford, 1976,* Bloomington: Indiana Univ. Press, 1979, pp. 3-4.

8. *Ibid.*, pp. 6-7.

Northeast. It is notable that the combined, population-based voting strength of the Eastern and Mountain regions thus construed are virtually *identical* to those of the combined Central and Pacific regions. The Eastern and Mountain state primaries could perhaps be held on a Tuesday in April or early May, with the Central and Pacific primaries held three weeks later, and the order alternately reversed.

Pacific		Mountain		Central		Eastern	
AK	3	AZ	7	AL	9	CT	8
CA	47	CO	8	AR	6	DC	3
HI	4	ID	4	IL	24	DE	3
NV	4	MT	4	IN	12	FL	21
OR	7	NM	5	IA	8	GA	12
WA	10	UT	5	KS	6	ME	4
		WY	3	KY	9	MD	10
(13.9%)	75	ND	3	LA	10	MA	13
		SD	3	MI	20	NH	4
				MN	10	NJ	16
		(7.8%)	42	MS	7	NY	36
				MO	11	NC	13
				NE	5	OH	23
				OK	8	PA	25
				TN	11	RI	4
				TX	29	SC	8
				WI	11	VT	3
						VA	12
				(36.6%)	197	WV	6
						(41.6%)	224

E + M = 266/(49.44%)
C + P = 272/(50.56%)

Total: 538

In case no *majority* candidate emerged from the state/regional primary process itself, the delegates chosen in the process, favoring the respective candidates in the proportions thus voted for, could select the party's nominee on the second or a later ballot at the party's convention.

By this arrangement, the American people would be enabled, in a far more direct, uniform, and unambiguous way, to choose even the nominees of whichever party they chose to identify with at the national level. Further, the candidates would be obliged to court the public as a single, varied constituency united by a variety of determinable national and nationwide, rather than narrow and sectarian, interests. The opportunity for candidates to tailor their presentations to the pre-tested preferences of separate audiences would still exist, but would be largely displaced by a new-found need to frankly court a broad cross-section of the voters (i.e., of the sovereign national public) simultaneously.

Many informed Europeans -- whose own systems, as we have seen, somehow produce a very markedly higher rate of public participation in elections than ours nowadays -- have expressed surprise at our famous "democratic" system's lack of protection for its public voice. Over a quarter of a century ago, French political scientist Jean Meynaud, in a forward-looking essay entitled *Les Groupes de Pression (Pressure Groups)*, lamented that narrow, interest-oriented groups were on the verge of becoming the real holders of and contenders for power in all the democracies of the West, replacing the people (or what the Greeks called the *demos*) and the popular parties in the role of national direction-setting.[9] Twelve years later, French author Claude Julien referred to the recent Western practice of permitting wealthy organizations, both permanent and ad hoc, virtually free reign in financing and influencing elections as "Le Suicide des Democraties" in a book by that name.[10]

In an interview in 1985, investment banker Baron Guy de Rothschild, who had immigrated to America two years earlier from France to head up a large New York branch of his famed family's bank, interpreted the now-accepted failure of half of the U.S. electorate to vote even in major, crucial elections as "a demonstration of lack of culture in the broadest sense. It means people do not feel themselves sufficiently involved, either intellectually or emotionally, ...[while] in Europe up to 80 percent of the electorate votes in controversial elections."[11]

---

9. Meynaud, Jean, *Les Groupes de Pression*, Paris: Presses Universitaires de France, 1960.

10. See Julien, Claude, *Le Suicide des Democraties*, Paris: Editions Bernard Grasset, 1972, especially Chapter 3 and Conclusion.

11. Rothschild, Baron Guy de, "Tops in American Culture is as Good as Anything in Europe," *U.S. News & World Report*, Aug. 12, 1985, p. 48. In West Germany and Sweden, the measure referred to here has sometimes reached levels as high as 90%.

American political scientist Walter Burnham has, meanwhile, concluded from his research that since 1960, turnout percentages in U.S. presidential elections "show a renewed but very unevenly distributed downward trend. Participation during this period has declined most rapidly ... among those groups of the population (outside the South) which already had come to participate least, [pointing to] functional disfranchisement, especially of the lower classes." The upper and upwardly-mobile classes in America, the politically conservative Professor Burnham thought, participated because they felt the system was responding to their needs, while the masses, contrary to the situation in a number of Western European countries, tended to feel out of touch and politically powerless, and so tuned out of the process.[12]

Reflecting on our long, fateful drift away from the commonly-meaningful participation that once united increasing numbers of us and highlighted our widely-copied national culture, it seems entirely likely that American nationalism -- our shared positive identity and the substance of our reflection in the world -- might yet be rejuvenated and restored. Such a result could follow naturally, at least in large part, a rebirth of truly democratic institutions in the very country that so proudly and with such powerful conviction introduced and first demonstrated them to the modern world.

- Are the Americans Ready for Self-Government? -

Let us return, finally, to the vexing question that occupied the minds of most thoughtful Americans in the late 1790s, at the close of our Revolutionary era. At that time, the dominant faction among the Federalists then in power was working to re-consolidate normal and traditional control over all society by prominent, property-owning interests and operatives (meaning, of course, no one but themselves). They were trying to restore government as a routine instrument to enhance -- and certainly not to interfere with -- their own grip on the country's growing landed wealth and fledgling industry. They were, in fact, as we have seen, working to subjugate the growing and variegating new nation of Americans to their designs for class-centered development, much as they along with everyone else in America had until recently been

---

12. Burnham, *The Great Crisis in American Politics*, pp. 120-21.

uncomfortably subject to British mercantile designs.[13] The burning question hotly debated by both humble and great was whether the American people were capable of periodically choosing and reviewing their leaders sensibly and, thereby, of responsibly mandating policy directions to benefit the majority. In other words: could the American people come to act in concert as genuine citizens under the newly-effective Constitution, or must they once again become more or less tractile subjects, following their few years' experience of weak political and social organization under the discarded Articles of Confederation, leaving the real direction of the system to their "betters"?

The public's clear-cut answer to this leading question of the '90s came in the form of the Jeffersonian "Revolution of 1800" at the ballot box. The outcome of that election, apparently the first anywhere in the world in which an opposition candidate peacefully took over a country's reins of power, was a *clear* repudiation of the Hamiltonian Federalists, who, not too unlike the determined corporatists effectively empowered now, had been busy, in private as well as in the open, consolidating exclusive control over the emerging society for themselves and their dominant caste. The so-called "high" Federalists per se never again recovered the authority they had tried to monopolize and freeze following the stinging 1800 election. The decision to repudiate their narrow, and, as it were, temporary consolidation of power was, highly significantly, Constitutionally made.

In "The Key to Liberty," a yellowed manuscript only lately discovered in an attic in Billerica, Massachusetts, an uneducated farmer, William Manning, who was a supporter of the local "Democraticle" societies that were anathema to the Federalists' oligarchic cause, recorded his impressions of contemporary politics in the mid-1790s. "A free government," he wrote in clear if unvarnished terms, "is one in which all the laws are made & executed according to the will and interest of a majority of the whole people and not by the craft cunning and arts of the few." He noted, insightfully, that "the few ... are interested in having money scarce and the price of labour and produce as low as possible. For instance if the prices of labour and produce should fall one halfe it would be just the same to the few as if their rents fees and salleries were doubled."[14]

---

13. For a more detailed discussion, see Chapter Two.
14. Smith, Page, *The Shaping of America*, pp. 301-302.

Page Smith, who quoted and commented on Manning's treatise, noted that "the critical issue was whether the many could convert their technical majority into genuine power."[15] A great many, of course, felt as Manning did. Manning believed strongly that the new Constitution, produced in convention not long before by those who became the extreme Federalists, together with the likes of Madison, Franklin, etc., provided sufficient means for the people to defend their interests. The results of the 1800 election indicated that he and they had been right when, in their first days, the new leaders quickly scuttled the Federalists' hateful Sedition and Alien laws, which had temporarily (and apparently unconstitutionally) tilted the system's deliberate balance of forces. Even so, the nation remained saddled with the decisively vanquished faction's appointed judiciary, with its new, unexpectedly sweeping powers, for decades. Indeed, we are still feeling the effects of some of that judiciary's arguably anti-public decisions today (e.g., Dartmouth College v. Woodward, cited in Chapter 2).[16]

Historian Joseph Frazier Wall has noted that in the 1840s, when participatory democracy was reputed to operate fairly smoothly in new communities stretching west across the fresh, new interior North American landscape, the typical pioneer citizen "could have stated his hopes and ideals rather simply. He was ready to fight to keep what he had or to get what he wanted but not for any abstract concept that had no immediate bearing upon his life. He demonstrated his patriotism on the Fourth of July, his politics on election day, and perhaps his religious beliefs on Sunday. For the rest of the year he was quite content to live and let live and leave well enough alone."[17] The realization Professor Wall matter-of-factly points up here -- that working democracy doesn't require some sort of mass expertism as its basis, but routinely instead calls for no more than a penchant in favor of one's own perceived interests and values, at least if direct, straightforward information is available -- seems to set aside another of the several classic complaints against the concept of a democratically governed society.

Some critics in recent decades have argued that democracy might work adequately where virtually everyone is either a small farmer or a small townsman -- as its apostle Jefferson early on professed to hope that

---

15. *Ibid.*, pp. 303-304.
16. *Ibid.*
17. Wall, *ibid.*, p. 66.

almost everyone would be -- but that it could not be expected to work so well in the more complex world of today.

Yet the Constitution was specifically designed to accommodate a maximum degree of the stuff of its leading author, Madison's, concept of pluralism, or variety in the social and economic interests of the entire, widely-extended nation. Problems have, to the contrary, arisen instead from effectively *reducing* the nation's great multitude of competing and co-operating interests down to a select few, well-vested special interests. The number of effectively represented interests becomes still smaller when a relative handful of the strongest are able to combine to corner the market on effective power, as Madison expressly feared, at the expense, never admitted by tyrants, of the rest of society.

Such narrowing of the power base is, in fact, the *predictable* product of a largely extra-constitutional political arena in which the elected representatives no longer tend to represent vast numbers of whole persons, but instead, a relative handful of interests lacking in peripheral vision but backed by concentrated political funds.[18] Yet, the solution to this problem again does not lie in politicizing everyone, an impractical chimera endorsed by political junkies. Political scientist Bernard Berelson, in a 1964 article, explodes the common fallacy of supposing that democracies have to depend "solely on the qualifications of the individual voter." Indeed, he asks, "how could a mass democracy work if all the people were deeply involved in politics? Lack of interest by *some* people is not without its benefits... Extreme interest goes with extreme partisanship and might culminate in rigid fanaticism that could destroy democratic processes if generalized throughout the community. Low affect toward the election -- not caring much -- underlies the solution of many political problems."[19]

Hence, the problem is more one of keeping the "fittest" in terms of politicism, expertise, and available funds, from taking over the birthright of everyone in the community through special interest domination of our electoral process. And the most effective solution, as suggested previously, must lie in restoring the voting public itself as the primary

18. In *Federalist 10*, Madison wrote that "among the numerous advantages promised by a well-constructed Union, none deserves to be more accurately developed than its tendency to *break* and *control* the violence of faction." (Italics mine).

19. Berelson, Bernard H., "Democratic Practice and Democratic Theory," in Fein, Leonard J., ed., *American Democracy*, N.Y.: Holt, Rinehart, & Winston, 1964, pp. 190, 193. (Italics mine).

constituency, by building requirements into the system obliging serious candidates to directly address the legal sovereign's broad core of real concerns. Thus could be abruptly ended the quaint and bizarre age of candidate organizations crudely fencing through series of positively- and negatively-appealing, vague allusions and seductive symbols via ultra-expensive, rigidly controlled media air time.

And this objective, indeed, requires accomplishment in the form of a definitive amendment to fill the old, suppurating gap in the Constitution's electoral process. Because only explicit procedural rules can dislodge the seemingly-necessary extra-constitutional arrangements that have proliferated unchecked over the past two centuries and distorted in a hundred ways the Constitution's intent to produce a representative system of national government. Only thus can we reasonably hope to restore the natural balance of interests harnessed otherwise by the Constitution's novel and ingenious accommodation. Only thus can the broad national interest, closely coinciding with the interests of most individual Americans nearly all of the time, again come to be reliably reflected in both foreign and domestic national policy.

Failing such an initiative to correct what amounts to a progressively worsening error of omission, I would expect to see something resembling elite acting schools and agencies, though probably less-open, become clearinghouses for most of our leading politicians, just as certain business schools are now training grounds for most of our leading corporate executives. The talent and know-how to recruit and expensively train promising political aspirants is active in the system now. Subliminal-freighted campaign ads may also enter the electoral equation, staining and completely invalidating it. Such a sinister result, in fact, may be inevitable in this technical age, if we as a culture continue to tolerate avoidance of direct confrontation between the objectives and purposes of the final top leadership candidates and the judgment of the whole dependent electorate. At that ultimate point, the last sparks of institutionalized public control over national government in the United States would be snuffed out, though the show would undoubtedly still go on.[20]

---

20. Recent history does not lack amendments devised and passed to fill recognized procedural gaps in the Constitution. For instance, according to then-Senator Birch Baye, the Senate committee chair most responsible, the Twenty-fifth Amendment, enacted in 1967 to authorize short-term transfers of presidential powers to the vice president in case of a chief executive's temporary incapacity, was an instance of "repairing a gap in the Constitution." Interview on the ABC-TV program "This Week," July 14, 1985.

The disbalance produced by the democratic system's being appropriated by talented media manipulators who owe allegiance to mostly or purely self-interested collective high bidders, contributes tangibly to the attitude of alienation that now regularly surges and recedes in waves through the nearly-defenseless American public at large. More pointedly, having a political system that is so heavily financed and managed by vested interests *in the name of* democracy lends macabre reason to the now all-but-total lack of respect for civil authority that is impossible for even the most casual observer to miss.

Whether we like to acknowledge it or not, repeated American attempts at compulsion backed by the threats and the lack of reasonable democratic inhibitions at home on American corporate activities alienate many potential allies and trading partners abroad, despite democratic rhetoric continuing to pour out of Washington. Likewise, the system of *domestic* rule in this country now increasingly controlled by a sharply narrowed special interest minority is bound to continue to reap serious domestic repercussions, and I would lay odds that Americans will finally turn out not to be the most permissive and tractile people in the world.

The likelihood of mass discontent with imposed, near-irreversible new conditions of rule (specifically, gutted institutional means of governing and allocating necessary infrastructural and community funds) will increase as growing portions of the broad middle class, for instance salaried employees, independent business owners, including small farmers who have owned their own land and have collectively produced too well to sustain the market price, systemically-disadvantaged women, many of the infirm, and still non-productive children, all continue to be progressively compressed into the ranks of a marginalized and increasingly invisible, growing political and hence economic underclass. The blame may continue to be deflected for some time by skilled, top-level administration operatives who know how to *appear* to champion the broader public while remaining actually accountable only to the minute segment of well-served principal owners and managers of international-scale business.

The cost of permitting an institutionally unaccountable elite to determine national policy is widely manifest in the present-day world. For example: Ethiopians perhaps in the millions have starved due to the indifference or hostility of a system of domination unwilling to cooperate in moving and delivering relief supplies, and millions of Cambodians and Russians, and lately, many thousands of Chinese, have been stifled and selectively murdered within recent memory by their so-called "people's regimes". Authoritarian rule by an elite was responsible.

200

Nor are we permanently immuned from the ravages of preoccupied neglect or selective hostility in our own land of relative plenty. According to a respected French historian, M. Ganzin, "the great French famines and food shortages of the Middle Ages occurred during periods when foodstuffs were not lacking; they were indeed produced in great quantity and *exported*. The social system and structure were largely responsible for these deficiencies."[21]

Social economist Susan George comments on this documented assertion: "At the time when the aristocracy was discovering the secrets of exquisite cuisine, people were starving to death in France. No one cared much about the misery of the *menu peuple* -- the little people..."[22] It has, unfortunately, always been so in the undemocratic world at large; and so it must also be increasingly in an emerging monolithically corporatist America. To lose the reality of democracy, to whatever set of circumstances and successors, is a disaster of many dimensions.

Yet, the huge, deferred tax burden from the early and middle 1980s will, without a doubt, further contribute to management problems and instability for the still-consolidating new overall system of rule. Adjusting the electoral system insufficiently spelled out in the Constitution to again achieve the original Madisonian purpose of national self-expression could help bridge the widening and menacing gap separating different levels and prospects in contemporary America. Experiencing the humanizing effects of such a renewal of real political democracy in this country could also help restore our earlier, proper sense of national purpose in a world now literally dying for want of the sort of leadership marked by peaceful technical assistance, understanding, and *mutually* advantageous, interdependent long-term growth.

Perhaps the greatest benefit civilization since its inception has added to humanity is the ability to pull together for mutual protection from the most powerful and dangerous elements inside and outside of society. Yet, the multinational business community's persistent effort to eliminate social controls over its own powerful, often irresponsible activities will no doubt continue to succeed in stages, until such time as informed control through this country's electoral mechanism is literally placed back in the

---

21. Ganzin, M., "Pour Entrer dans une Ere de Justice Alimentaire," *UNESCO, Le Courrier de,* May 1975, quoted, with comments, in George, Susan, *How the Other Half Dies, The Real Reasons for World Hunger,* Montclair, N.J.: Allanheld Osmun, 1977, pp. 113-14 (italics mine).

22. *Ibid.,* p. 114.

hands of the country's citizens. In the interim, increasing tyranny in the process of selecting and sponsoring national leadership will of necessity mean continued erosion of the American public's ability to defend itself politically and forward its interests in competition with other vigorous nations in the larger world. Our genius being democracy, let us *exemplify* it.

We Americans now need to consider certain unaccustomed facts. In the United States, we have a conventionalized democratic governing system two centuries old. And we also have a still-growing entrepreneurial system with which it is, if the latter is permitted to reach its logical destination uninhibited and unchanneled, at odds.

But we need to conserve and continue the basic realities of *both* of the above, for neither can endure satisfactorily without the other. We have proven such to be the case once again. So, we simply must, in effect, now do what Madison and the divided delegates did who together triumphed in the 1787 Constitutional Convention. We must arrive at a mutually-satisfactory accommodation of our interdependent *diastolic* and *systolic* forces in order to re-vitalize and re-integrate our nation. And we must, thereafter, doggedly insist on the integrity and continuance of our adjusted accommodation, as Madison, Jefferson, and a majority of their contemporaries did for theirs.

Their solution stopped on purpose a bit short of *laissez faire*; it involved guarantees and procedures specifically designed for the expression and protection of broadly-shared benefits from the society and its stock of natural wealth.

Their solution could not, of course, have anticipated many of our present difficulties in maintaining it. So, our effort, beyond the two-century mark, at renewing our Constitution's unique and ingenious balance, must start once more with an institutional adjustment; and our effort at rebalance won't solve every problem or last for all time, just as theirs did not.

And yet, that purpose, of self-adjusting rebalance, is precisely what the active system of government that is our common birthright -- the world-renowned "government of the people, by the people, and for the people" -- is for.*

---

* Again, in 1988, we have experienced a presidential election in which the two final choices were posed for, rather than selected by, the great majority of the American public, in which the

terms of competition were set by and for the candidate organizations, with the public at large treated as distantly interested but influential outsiders, and in which labels and negative disinformation, as opposed to serious competition between ideas and programs, played a leading and successful role carefully designed to manage and distort public knowledge and public opinion. The result of this most recent travestly of true democracy was a new administration whose agenda and goals were widely accounted a "mystery". (For instance, see *Miami Herald*, November 10, 1988, p. 5A.) One promising change, however, was in evidence: there was background discussion this time of the fact that the process left completely to candidate and state discretion avoids instead of involving sharpened awareness and rational choice. I have reviewed in this book the stakes and the results to date of tolerating what amounts to a public power vacuum in our nationwide leadership selection system. The turnout for the 1988 election was once more the lowest in many decades. But, then, the old Spaniard Ortega y Gasset was right, too, because a "mass" and a properly-informed public are far from being the same thing. The cost to the American public of becoming manipulated and dependent subjects of collective private and public institutions much more than true citizens is already staggering, as we have seen, even if considered only in economic terms during the past decade. Let us now, finally, formally draft the process in such a way as to restore in full the public profile we once enjoyed as Americans, but have lost.

INDEX

bio-engineering, 170
Blough, Roger, 77 n.
Boak, A.E.R., 111 n.
Bolsheviks, 23 (ref.), 114, 127-129, 141
Bonaparte, Napoleon, 69 n.
Borah, William E., 87 n.
Bracher, Karl Dietrich, 116-117
"brain drain", 174-175
Brandt Commission, 174 ff., 183
Brandt, Willy, 174, 183
Brant, Irving, 42 n., 46 n.
Brazil, 150, 154, 164 n.
Brinton, Crane, 19-20
Britain (United Kingdom), 18, 29, 38, 51, 57-59, 91, 95, 96, 112, 113, 140, 149, 180
British Empire, 109, 180, 196
broadcast industry licensing, 56
Brooke, Christopher, 113 n.
Brown, Stuart Gerry, 50 n.
Brunt, P.A., 110
Bulgaria, 154
Burnham, Forbes, 153-154
Burnham, Walter Dean, 6 n., 70, 195
Bush-Dukakis campaign (1988), 5, 88 (ref.), 202-203
Business Council, 78
Business Roundtable, 78

Caddell, Pat, 80-81, 187-188
Caesar, Julius, 110, 111 n.
Cambodia, 150, 200
"Caribbean Basin Initiative" (Reagan), 166 n.
Carnegie, Andrew, 78
Carneiro, Robert, 11, 60 n.
Carrington, Colonel Edward, 31 n.
Carter, Jimmy, 69, 80, 102 n., 161, 168 (ref.)
caucus system, for nominating (pre-1828), 46-47
Central America, 149-150, 154, 165, 181
Cetron, Martin, 158-160, 175
Chiang Kai-shek, 141 n.
Chile, democracy in, 150
Churchill, Winston, 93 n.
China, 124, 154, 200

Cicero, 110, 180
Civil War, U.S., 34, 52, 55, 60, 190
civil wars, Russian counter-revolutionary, 130, 131, 132 (ref.)
Clausewitz, Karl Von, 183
clientage (Roman Republic), 74 n., 110
Cockburn, Andrew, 132 n., 135 n., 137 n., 140-141
collectivization, Tsarist, 128 n.
Commonwealth v. Hunt (1842), 59
Communist Party Central Committee, 122-123, 127-128, 130, 131, 134-135
Conquest, Robert, 127 n., 128 n.
Constitution of the United States, x, xi, xii, 5, 7, 14-15, 17, 19-20, 24-25,
      27 ff., 35-37, 40, 42, 44-46, 48, 52-53, 57, 105, 117-119, 120 (ref.),
      146, 161, 186, 189-190, 196-199, 201, 202
Constitutional Convention (1787), 28-30, 32, 43-45, 48, 61, 96 (ref.), 104
      (ref.), 119 n., 186 (ref.), 190 (ref.)
"consumer democracy", 181
Containment Doctrine, 169 n.
conventions, party nominating, 46-47, 193
"corporate sovereignty," theory of, 12-14, 21, 75 (ref.), 143 (ref.), 160-162
corporatists, 21, 43, 63, 64 n., 65, 69, 74-77, 84, 88-95, 97, 98 ff., 117-118
      (ref.), 120, 150, 157, 161 (ref.), 165, 172 (ref.), 175, 181 (ref.), 182, 185 (ref.),
      186, 189, 194 (ref.), 200, 201 (ref.), 203 (ref.)
"Council of the Americas", 181
Crankshaw, Edward, 115 n.
Crawford, William H., 47
Crespi, Irving, 187 n.
Crete, ancient, 109
Croce, Benedetto, 18 n.
Cuba, 124, 150, 154
Czudnowski, Moshe, 71-72

Dahrendorf, Ralf, 136 n.
"dangerous classes", 52
Dante Alighieri, 113
Dartmouth College v. Woodward (1819), 54, 146 n., 197
Das Kapital (Marx), 133
Davis, James C., 19 n.
"decapitalization", 164 n.
Declaration of Independence, 28, 35, 154, 156 (ref.)
DeLorean, John Z., 74 n.
democracy, shift in concept of in U.S., ix-x, 1, 4, 16, 24, 67-68, 83-84, 91,
      117-118, 120, 151, 164, 168, 183, 186, 195, 200, 202

"democratic centralism" (Lenin), 123, 124, 127
Democratic Societies (early U.S.), 46, 196
Depression (1930s), 64, 115-116, 170
de-regulation, policy of, 161
Deutscher, Isaac, 132 n., 135 n., 141 n.
Diamond, Ann Stuart, 32 n.
diastolic, definition of, x-xi, 8, 9-10, 18, 22-24, 27, 34, 37, 41, 43, 50, 59, 90, 92, 102, 105-107, 114-115, 123, 130, 138-140, 189, 202
Dickens, Charles, 58
"dirty hands" principle of representation (Soviet), 135-136
Djilas, Milovan, 22, 135 n., 137 n., 138-139
Dobshansky, Theodosius, 133
Domhoff, William, 67 n., 74 n., 88 n., 103, 146 n.
Dominican Republic, 150
Donald, Alexander, 31 n.
Drew, Elizabeth, 187-188, 189
Dunning, William Archiibald, 60 n.

Eastern Bloc, x, 103, 105, 106, 124-125, 138, 142, 148, 175, 177, 181
Egyptians, ancient, 107
Einstein, Albert, 76
Eisenhower, Dwight D., 6, 86
election turnout, U.S. and European, 5, 194, 203
Electoral College, voting strength by state, 46, 193
"Electoral Commission" (1876), 52
Ellis, Richard E., 41 n., 42 n., 48 n.
Ellul, Jacques, 79, 84 n., 88, 94
El Salvador, 150
Engels, Friedrich, 58-59
England, Anglo-Saxon, 11
environmental maintenance, citizen consensus for, 88-89
Environmental Protection Agency (EPA), 14, 102 n.
Ethiopia, 85, 200
Evans, Robert, Jr., 59 n.
Evans, Rowland, 98 n.

"facilitations" for large business (Ellul), 84-85
"family circles," in Soviet elite, 137-138
Farwell, Byron, 180 n.
Federalist Papers, 8, 14-15, 31 n., 40, 43, 44 n., 45-46, 47 n., 49, 53 n., 57 n., 190, 198 n.

Jackson, Andrew, 47, 53 n.
Jacobs, Jane, 140
Jacobsen, T., 112 n.
Jagan, Cheddi, 153
Janeway, Eliot, 48
Japan, 109, 124, 132, 140, 142, 148, 152, 154, 156, 158 ff., 166 n., 168-172, 177, 180, 182
"Japan, Inc.", 161
Jay, John, 36, 49
Jefferson, Thomas, xii, 28, 31-32, 33, 35-36, 37, 39-43, 48-50, 51, 54, 72, 86, 111, 154 n., 196, 197-198, 202
Jensen, Merrill, 30 n.
Johnson, Chalmers, 170
Johnson, Lyndon B., 20
Julien, Claude, 194

Kennedy, John F., 65 (ref.), 77 n.
Khruschev, Nikita, 135
Kidron, Michael, 125 n., 143 n., 176 n.
Kindleberger, C. P., 13 n.
King John (England), 113
Kinzer, Stephen, 149 n.
Kiplinger, Austin, 119 n.
Kleisthenes, 108
Koch, Adrienne, 32 n., 50 n., 51 n.
Kramer, Samuel Noah, 111-112
Kraus, Sidney, 191-192
Kristol, Irving, 78 n., 91

LaFeber, Walter, 149 n.
laissez faire, 202
Latin America, 124, 149-151, 154, 166 n., 173, 181
Lea, James F., 60 n.
League of Women Voters, 46
Lebanon, 153
Lebedoff, David, 66 n., 83
"legal revolution" (Nazi Germany), 117
Lenin, Valdimir I., 122-129, 131, 133-134
Lincoln, Abraham, xii, 43, 53 n., 100, 202 (ref.)
line item veto, presidential, 162 n.
Lippman, Walter, 34, 36 n.

millenarian doctrine, 126
Miller, Arthur Selwyn, 67 n.
Mills, C. Wright, 14
MITI (Ministry of International Trade and Industry, Japan), 169-172
    (ref.), 183
Mithradates IV, 180
Modelski, George, 13 n., 75 n., 94
Mondale, Walter F., 83 n., 99
Montesquieu, Baron de, 38, 96, 190
Morgan, J. Pierpont, 78
Morris, Governeur, 29, 49
Moscati, Sabatino, 112 n.
Mosley, Paul, 176 n.
Moynahan, Daniel Patrick, 99
Mozambique, 151
Muller, Ronald E., 86 n., 163-164, 181
Murphy, Thomas, 77

Nadel, Mark V., 53 n., 55 n.
Nazi Party (Germany), 116-117
Nef, John U., 107 n.
Netherlands, 176
Nettels, Curtis P., 50 n.
"new elite" theorists, 66, 83
New Right, religious, 98
Newfarmer, Richard, 166
New Zealand, 154
Nicaragua, 148-150, 154
Nietzsche, Friedrich, 76
Nixon, Richard, 20, 113 n.
noblesse oblige, 60
Noriega, Manuel, 150
Norman Conquest, 11
"North" (developed countries), 173 ff., 182
"North-South" issues, 173 ff., 182
North, Douglass C., 51 n.
North Korea, 154
Norway, 176
Notes on Virginia (Jefferson), 33 n.
Novak, Michael, 65, 103 n.
Novak, Robert, 98 n.
nuclear ransom, 158

"Old Oligarch" (Athens), 107-108
oligarchy, 32, 119-120
oligopoly, American business, 73, 95 n.
Ollman, Bertell, 133
O'Mahoney, Joseph C., 87 n.
Ortega y Gasset, Jose, 92-93, 111, 119-120, 203
Ostrogorski, M., 45 n., 46 n., 47 n., 53, 60-61, 75 n.

Panama, U.S. policy toward, 150
Parenti, Michael, 30 n.
patent law, Jeffersonian, 50
Paul of Tarsus, 109 n.
Peloponnesian Wars, 179
"people's" regimes, 200
Perry, Roland, 80 n., 82 n., 99 n.
Phoenicians, 107
Pinochet, Augusto, 150
Pipes, Richard, 139 n.
Plamenatz, John, 69 n.
Plummer, William, 54
pluralism, Madisonian concept, 67-68, 104 (ref.), 186, 198
"pluralist" theory, modern, 67-68
Poland, 169
Politburo (Soviet), 122
Polybius, 38, 40, 109
Popper, Karl, 21-22, 91
Portuguese Empire, 151, 165
Pravda (quoted), 134
Presidency, role of, 29-30, 43, 45, 52, 96, 118, 165
primaries, presidential, 47-48, 192-194
"program for developing countries" (Reagan administration), 165-166
property, Lockean concept, 39
"pseudo-campaign" (MacNeil), 186-187
public land policy, early U.S., 40 (ref.), 41-43
"public purpose theory" of incorporation, 53-56, 87, 146 (ref.)

Reagan, Ronald, 5, 81-82, 96 n., 98 n., 102 n., 103 (ref.), 165-166
Reagan administration, ix, 2-4 (ref.), 13-14, 48 (ref.), 88 (ref.), 92, 98 ff., 148, 165-166, 168, 171, 185 (ref.)
realpolitik, 96
Reeves, Richard, 18 n.

Valenta, Jiri, 149 n., 154 n.
Valenta, Virginia, 149 n., 154 n.
Venice, 113
Vernon, Raymond, 172 n.
Victoria, Queen, 180
Vietnam, 178-179
Vietnam War, ix, 20, 145, 150
Von Laue, Theodore H., 129 n.
Voslensky, Michael, 139 n.

Wagner Act (1935), 59 n.
Wall, Joseph Frazier, 50 n., 197
Washington, George, 29, 36, 46, 48
Wealth of Nations (Adam Smith), 36, 71
Weimar Republic (1930s Germany), 76, 115, 116 n., 117
western land policy, 40, 41-43
"white flight", 101
Wilkinson, Frank, 102 n.
Will, George F., 39 n., 50 n., 64 n., 96
Wirthlin, Richard, 81-82, 188
Wise, John, 37-38
"withering away of the state", doctrine, 94, 126
World Bank Atlas, 125 n.

Xenophon, 108

Young, Alfred F., 29 n., 44 n.
Yugoslavia, 22, 138

Dr. Hufferd, a social geographer, has served on the faculty of the University of Minnesota-Duluth, University of Kentucky, and University of Wisconsin, Superior. He has recently been a Visiting Research Scholar at the Federal University of Rio de Janeiro. He is the author of one previous book and a number of articles.